MORE

— THAN A —

THEORY

Revealing a Testable Model *for* Creation

HUGH ROSS

BakerBooks

a division of Baker Publishing Group
Grand Rapids, Michigan

© 2009 by Hugh Ross

Published by Baker Books
a division of Baker Publishing Group
P.O. Box 6287, Grand Rapids, MI 49516-6287
www.bakerbooks.com

Paperback edition published 2012
ISBN 978-0-8010-1442-0

Printed in the United States of America

The Library of Congress has cataloged the original edition as follows:
Ross, Hugh (Hugh Norman), 1945–
      More than a theory : revealing a testable model for creation / Hugh Ross.
          p.   cm.
      Includes bibliographical references.
      ISBN 978-0-8010-1327-0 (cloth)
      1. Creation. I. Title.
    BS651.R766 2009
    231.7′652—dc22   2008046407

To all the students and faculty whose thoughtful questions
and comments at RTB's campus forums
contributed both shape and substance to this book

Contents

LIST OF ILLUSTRATIONS

LIST OF TABLES

ACKNOWLEDGMENTS

For invaluable help in assembling and refining Reasons To Believe's (RTB's) testable creation model, my colleague Fazale Rana deserves huge credit and thanks. My partner in presenting the model on university campuses, Fuz also coauthored *Origins of Life* and *Who Was Adam?* (doing the lion's share of the work). Each of these books sets forth a core component of RTB's model. Recently he added another pivotal part with his book *The Cell's Design*. Fuz's diligence and impeccable scholarship have contributed both scope and balance to the model as well as to this book.

A significant challenge in the writing process was deciding which aspects of the model to include and which would best be left to future books. RTB's editorial team, headed by Patti Townley-Covert, invested countless hours helping me select and craft the content in these pages. They also labored over multiple drafts to make the book readable and useful for readers without science degrees.

Marj Harman, along with Andrew Coleman and Linda Kloth, checked the citations and quotations for accuracy. Jonathan Price assembled the photo images and prepared the figures. And Sandra Dimas handled multiple tasks from copyediting to preparing the index. I could not have gotten the manuscript ready without them.

I owe thanks to Kenneth Samples for his review and recommendations on the theological and philosophical content and to Jeff Zweerink for similar help with regard to the scientific material. My executive assistant, Diana Carrée, played a crucial role by protecting my time and shouldering extra work over the past year. If not for her, my writing deadline would not have been met.

My thanks also to Baker Publishing Group for their enthusiastic support of this project and their commitment to the purposes for which Reasons To Believe exists. I especially appreciate the hard work of Bob Hosack, Kristin Kornoelje, and Wendy Wetzel, plus the entire Baker team for their efforts on this book.

Most of all I thank my wife, Kathy, for her wisdom, grace, time, and patience over the past thirty years in helping me, step-by-step, to improve the manner in which I communicate our creation model. She has served as my sounding board during all the years of the model's development and refinement, processes that continue to this day. During the past year she also took on many of my executive responsibilities at Reasons To Believe so I could focus on writing.

Hugh Ross

1

IS IT SCIENCE?

My family insists that I'm a compulsive scientist. Experiments I performed before I could talk convinced my father and mother. And scientific tests involving my sons flabbergasted my wife. To me, testing just seemed like the natural thing to do.

One experiment took place when my two sons were infants. I wanted to find out whether babies could tell the difference between a particular toy and a full-size two-dimensional look-alike.

Why did I do such a thing? During my wife's first pregnancy, an idea occurred to me, and performing tests was the only way to determine if my hypothesis was correct. Could it be that human beings are born thinking two-dimensionally and that it takes time, experience, and education for them to transition to three-dimensional thinking?

For each of my sons, I observed the same results. Between two and four months of age, neither Joel nor David appeared able to distinguish the difference between the real toy and its two-dimensional representation. At five to seven months old, often they could; sometimes they could not. However, from seven months on, the pictures could not fool them.

The ideas of creation and evolution also involve discerning realities from pseudo representations. The universe, life, and humanity were either designed with purpose and meaning, or they were not. The entire cosmos either explains itself, or it does not. Creation either happened, or it's a figment of someone's imagination.

What a person believes about his origin colors every other part of his view on life. Strictly natural outcomes reflect no care, no reason, no hope. Yet these characteristics belong inherently to the concept of biblical creation. Because individuals behave as they believe, perspectives on evolution and creation embody a critical determinant for how people choose to live and plan their lives.

Personal Faith versus Real Religion

Religion (defined as a belief system about the cause, nature, and purpose of the universe and humanity[1]) has always been an emotionally charged subject. People of many belief systems often use emotion to further their own agendas. One might think of extremists who incite hate against infidels. But sometimes unthinking Christians do the same kind of playing on "righteous anger" as they forward emails designed to heighten fears about a particular political candidate or cause.

Outspoken atheist and Oxford biologist Richard Dawkins evokes similar emotions by claiming that the Creator described in the Bible is nothing but "a pernicious delusion,"[2] and that "faith can be very very dangerous, and deliberately to implant it into the vulnerable mind of an innocent child is a grievous wrong."[3]

Dawkins made a valid point, however, in explaining why religious beliefs are inherently scientific and why it is absurd to consider creation-evolution debates as nonreligious. He says that "a universe with a supernaturally intelligent creator is a very different kind of universe from one without." Therefore, "the presence or absence of a creative super-intelligence is unequivocally a scientific question."[4]

So the Creator's role, or lack thereof, is either real or imagined. One's interpretation of the origin and history of the universe and life could be judged as real religion or pseudo religion but certainly not nonreligion.

Unfortunately, leaders on all sides of the creation-evolution controversy resort to political and legal efforts to force their particular interpretation of the issue upon others. Such attempts typically create more confusion and suspicion for people who want to discern what's true and what's not.

Personal Assessments versus Real Science

Several years ago Patrick Henry College, a small but prestigious Christian institution, was denied accreditation. The American Academy for Liberal

Education (AALE) acknowledged the high test scores and outstanding achievements of Patrick Henry's students but rejected an accreditation bid because of the college's stance on a young-earth creation.[5] In defending the rejection, AALE president Jeffrey Wallin explained, "They teach creation as a science which it is not."[6] He justified this conclusion by pointing out "there is nothing in a [sic] scientific literature that would ever cough up to you the creationist view."[7]

Wallin's defense was reasonable. To qualify as science, a particular explanation of nature's record must cite at least some physical evidence in support of its claims.

At the same time, Wallin clarified that the complete lack of supporting scientific evidence applied to only one specific interpretation of creation—young-earth creationism. This position asserts that the universe and Earth are less than 10,000 years old.[8] However, many creation and evolution proponents overlook this nuance, just as they have in interpreting the United States District Court and United States Supreme Court rulings on teaching creationism (see chapter 15, pp. 219–29).

A presumption that the courts and accrediting institutions ruled against all creation positions gave rise to the intelligent design movement (IDM; see p. 31). In an attempt to remain religiously neutral, leaders within the IDM proposed that an undefined intelligent designer played an undefined role in bringing about an undefined history of life on Earth. However, this lack of specificity prevents the IDM from using the testable approach essential to science.

The Importance of Testing

To adhere to objective principles, scientists must present their positions in the form of models that can be tested. In science, the term "model" refers to the schematic description of a system (or set of phenomena) that accounts for its observed and inferred features. A model is much more than a mere idea, inference, method, hypothesis, or rudimentary theory. It's a scenario that offers reasonable explanations for the entire origin and history of a particular system in nature, as well as for its relationship to other phenomena.

Using a model approach supplies researchers with enough detail to determine whether they are on the right track. A model offers explanations of how, when, where, in what order, and why a phenomenon takes place. The best models yield specific suggestions for how near-future research may improve understanding of the systems or phenomena that a particular model intends to explain. This approach anticipates the discoveries that can either verify or falsify the model's explanations.

The lack of detail and scope in the IDM's positions makes them difficult to fully falsify or confirm through observations or experiments. This lack of definitive means to put the IDM ideas to the test propels the widespread charge that ID is not science.[9]

Creation Can Be Science

Not all creationist explanations for the origin and history of the universe, Earth, and life are nonscientific. An explanation cast in the form of a comprehensive and detailed model (with citable scientific research findings in support of its primary premises and suggesting specific scientific tests or observations to either confirm or falsify its premises) qualifies as science—regardless of what that model depicts, even if it is creation. Such a model earns legitimacy as a scientific enterprise.

When a model suggests research projects that will improve scientific understanding of the record of nature and when that model makes specific predictions of what scientists will discover in the near future, it is not only science, it is also science at its best. If a model offers more comprehensive and detailed explanations of nature's record than competing models and if its predictions prove more accurate than those of competing models, then that model sheds valuable scientific light on the origins and history of the universe and life.

The purpose of this book is to present a creation explanation for the record of nature in an acceptable scientific form. For the creation model developed at Reasons To Believe (RTB) to have a fair evaluation, however, certain censorship efforts must be overcome, while others are encouraged.

Truth Discriminates

The greatest resistance to a creation explanation of nature's record I've encountered over the past thirty years is the fear that bad science will creep into scientific research and education. Technological advance provides definitive data on the age of the universe and Earth. There's simply no scientific basis for thinking that the universe and Earth are not billions of years old. As a result, scientists have pleaded with me to use whatever influence I have in the Christian community to bring about a strong and unequivocal repudiation of young-earth teaching and advocacy.

Scientists' greatest concern about the intelligent design movement (even more than its ambiguity and lack of a model) is the failure of the movement's leaders to publicly declare young-earth creationism a failed hypothesis.

Christians should be equally concerned. To force a creation timescale of only a few thousand years on an interpretation of Genesis 1 would make other biblical passages on the origin of the universe and Earth (see chapter 5, p. 61) contradict each other.[10] According to the appropriate interpretive methodology (see chapter 4, pp. 50–51, and Appendix B), it is not sufficient to interpret the Bible literally. Rather, the Bible must be interpreted both literally (unless the context indicates otherwise) and consistently.

The Bible explicitly declares that the physical world is not an illusion and that nature's record reliably reveals truth (see for example Numbers 23:19; Psalm 12:6; 19:1–4, 7–8; 119:160; Romans 1:18–20; Hebrews 6:18). Scientific evidence for an ancient universe and Earth[11] cannot be swept under the proverbial rug.

The bottom line is that no model (or portion thereof) should be insulated from testing. For both science and theology to remain objective, appropriate discrimination must be exercised. In a free market economy, savvy consumers evaluate and choose, eventually eliminating inferior or overpriced products. In the past, Christians and non-Christians alike rejected both belief in a flat Earth and the doctrine of an Earth-centered solar system. Pursuers of truth have nothing to fear in a discriminating search for reality.

Abandoning a Bottom-Up Approach

Some young-earth creationists and intelligent design proponents are committed to a bottom-up approach in attempts to change the course of science. This strategy may be symptomatic of laypeople's frustrations with what is often perceived to be a strong anti-God, anti-creation bias on the part of many top-level research scientists. Ben Stein sensationalized this perceived bias in the movie *Expelled: No Intelligence Allowed.*

A bottom-up approach can do serious damage to the scientific enterprise. This was the case with the Lysenko affair in the Soviet Union, which stalled both genetics research and agricultural development. When less-credible positions threaten to gain a foothold among educators and students at the high school and undergraduate level, researchers at the highest levels of scientific and academic endeavor become increasingly protective of their freedom to conduct research as they see fit. In a backlash against this political approach, some influential evolutionists understandably attempt to stonewall all creation advocates in a similarly problematic manner.

Redefining Science

Since the birth of the scientific method (see pp. 50–51), science has been defined as the pursuit of systematized knowledge and understanding about the way the universe, with its governing laws and all it contains, operates.[12] Such a definition leaves the investigation open to consideration of the causal agent(s) that may be responsible for these operations.

However, in an attempt to shut down perceived abuses of science perpetrated by young-earth creationists and some intelligent design proponents, certain prominent leaders within the scientific community have tried to narrow the definition of science. Eugenie Scott, executive director of the National Center for Science Education, redefines science as "an attempt to explain the natural world in terms of *natural* processes, not supernatural ones" (italics in the original).[13]

Lawrence Krauss, director of the Center for Education and Research in Cosmology and Astrophysics at Case Western Reserve University, echoes this restrictive definition: "Science assumes that natural phenomena have natural causes."[14] In an official response to creationism and intelligent design, the board of directors of the American Association for the Advancement of Science wrote, "Science is a process of seeking natural explanations for natural phenomena."[15]

By attempting to exclude supernatural explanations from scientific consideration, these naturalists demonstrate a bias equal to that of young-earth and IDM proponents. They insist the natural realm has no Creator. They assume a priori that an atheistic perspective is the only possible basis for doing scientific research and education.

Acknowledging the blatant censorship inherent in such redefinitions of science, Scott has tried to soften her stance by saying it's not that science denies God's existence or his possible role as a Creator. It's just that science is incapable of ever detecting it. Because it is not possible to "hold constant the actions of supernatural forces" under laboratory conditions, Scott concludes that the possibility of a supernatural cause is "outside of what science can tell us."[16] She claims that science and scientific testing must be limited to direct observations of events occurring in nature or under controlled laboratory conditions.

However, many scientists realize that Scott's definition guts much, if not most, of the scientific endeavor. It eliminates historical and theoretical science disciplines including theoretical physics, astronomy, paleontology, geophysics, theoretical chemistry, and physical anthropology, as well as mathematics.

Top-Down Approach

Shifts in science almost always occur when the most talented and well-trained researchers become persuaded of the need for change. As ongoing testing confirms the validity of a more plausible theory, that finding trickles down to lower-level researchers, where more testing occurs, then to the broader community of science professors and graduate students. Eventually public school teachers and journalists begin to inform younger students and the general public.

Some may complain that the scientific community would never grant evolution critique, much less grant creation proponents top-level access. Yet *Proceedings of the National Academy of Sciences, USA* recently published an article critical of the evolutionary paradigm (see chapter 10, pp. 169–70).[17] And RTB scientists have had opportunities to present their testable creation model before faculty and researchers at several leading universities.[18] These opportunities have yielded much valuable critique for improving and extending RTB's model. Our book *Origins of Life* garnered a commendable review in the journal *Origins of Life and Evolution of Biospheres*,[19] and some components of the RTB creation model have been published in reputable science journals.[20] RTB resources even prompted a Nobel laureate in chemistry to change his worldview perspective from stridently anti-Christian to ardently Christian.[21]

A Viable Creation Model

RTB respects the standards for good science. Our creation model is comprehensive as well as flexible and self-correcting. In its ongoing development, there's an openness to understanding how new discoveries either strengthen or falsify various aspects of it.

Comprehensive

Many people treat creation/evolution issues as involving only the life sciences—the disciplines of biology, paleontology, and anthropology. They typically ignore how the disciplines of mathematics, astronomy, physics, geology, and chemistry come to bear on the preparation of a suitable home for life. Most intelligent design proponents, in attempts to maintain religious neutrality and to avoid offending either young- or old-earth creationists, often limit their arguments to biochemistry. Drawing from other disciplines would force them into a position they are unwilling to take.

The creation model outlined in this book demonstrates how a more comprehensive and integrated explanation for the origins and history of the universe and life can be developed by incorporating multiple scientific disciplines. This approach engenders greater robustness—more tests of the model and more predictions of the discoveries that can be anticipated if the model indeed is correct.

Flexible and Self-Correcting

One serious critique of young-earth creationist attempts to explain the natural realm is that their explanations, typically rooted in religious dogma, have no flexibility to adapt and self-correct as knowledge increases. Nor has a young-earth explanation proven very effective in guiding research endeavors.

RTB suggests that the application of appropriate biblical interpretative techniques actually supports a scientifically plausible model. The Bible, unlike any other holy book I've encountered, provides at least two dozen creation accounts (see chapter 5, p. 61), and a careful integration of these descriptions yields a well-defined outline for the origin and history of the universe, Earth, and life. These explanations, however, are by no means exhaustive. For example, while stipulating the means by which God created birds, mammals, and humans, the Bible leaves open a wide range of possibilities for God bringing forth plants and lower animals. Yet the major elements of nature's record are accounted for.

According to the familiar Reformation creedal statement, the Belgic Confession, God's second revelation, the book of nature, supplies additional information.[22] The International Council on Biblical Inerrancy states that "in some cases extrabiblical data have value for clarifying what Scripture teaches, and for prompting correction of faulty interpretations."[23]

Ongoing

The RTB creation model is dynamic. It has been under development for more than thirty years. While the basics of the model remain unchanged, the model's extent and depth have grown significantly. Many details in the original model have been refined. (The model's growth and development can be clearly seen over the four editions—1973, 1979, 1983, and 2006—of my booklet presenting a scientific perspective on Genesis 1.[24])

Even after so many years of development, the RTB model remains a work in progress. My fellow scholars at RTB and I continue to invite researchers with appropriate training and expertise to offer critique and constructive advice that will further improve and extend the model.

A driving force behind the development of RTB's model is the desire to go beyond the *what* and *how* of an issue and ask the *why*. The RTB model demonstrates how asking the right kinds of *why* questions can lead to deeper scientific insights and clearer answers to some of the most polarizing issues.

Putting a Variety of Models to the Test

After more than two centuries of vigorous debate on the topic of creation/ evolution, proponents of various positions have developed surprisingly few serious tests of their own (or other) models. Nor have they produced many model-based predictions of future scientific discoveries. The RTB creation model illustrates how to build tests and develop predictions that can either falsify or confirm the components of any model.

Recognizing that such tests and predictions are most effective when contrasted with comparable ones from competing models, I've spent considerable time over the past two decades interviewing advocates of other models. My goal was to learn what they would consider to be significant tests of and predictions from their models. In Appendix C, these tests and predictions are contrasted with those that arise from RTB's creation model. (Though it may seem presumptuous, perhaps even arrogant to speak on behalf of competing models, my goal is only to stimulate their proponents to either correct this list or produce their own.)

All these ideas and more unfold in the chapters ahead. They show how to test competing models for validity and vitality. Through vigorous development of competing models, researchers can produce distinctive tests and predictions to help determine which models produce the best and most comprehensive explanation of the record of nature and which best anticipate future scientific advances.

Please keep in mind, though, that this book contains merely a descriptive outline of the RTB creation model. No single volume could possibly include extensive explanations, tests, and predictions for the origin and complete history of the universe, Earth, life, and humanity. Fortunately, several RTB books already present some of that detailed material: *The Creator and the Cosmos, Origins of Life, Who Was Adam?, A Matter of Days, The Cell's Design, A World of Difference, Why the Universe Is the Way It Is*, and *Lights in the Sky and Little Green Men* are some of them.[25] Others are in the research and writing stage.

One Step at a Time

The first step in any model-building process is to gain greater understanding of the array of explanations. Chapter 2 examines the major positions. Chapter 3 looks at the strategies used by proponents of competing positions in attempts to gain an advantage. The birth and development of the scientific method and ways to apply that method in the construction of creation/evolution models are discussed in chapter 4. Chapter 5 explains RTB's model-building principles and organizes those elements of data from both the record of nature and the Bible that are most critical for any comprehensive creation model. Then chapter 6 sets forth the biblical foundations of RTB's testable creation model.

Chapters 7–12 describe how well the RTB model explains observed natural phenomena and experiments in the most relevant scientific disciplines, progressing from the simple sciences to the more complex. For simpler natural phenomena (stars, for example, are much simpler systems than humans), more definitive and comprehensive descriptions and interpretations can be discerned. Rather than avoid the simple sciences, these chapters use that which is simple and more comprehensively examined to frame and interpret more complex and less completely researched disciplines.

Challenging *why* questions for RTB's model are posed in chapter 13, questions such as "Why would a Creator make carnivores and parasites?" and "Why are there so many apparently bad designs in nature?" Some possible answers also show how such *why* questions provide some of the most penetrating tests for all creation/evolution models. Chapter 14 tests the validity of the most recent attempts by atheists to explain away the most compelling astronomical evidences for a cosmic Creator. Chapter 15 examines recent creation/evolution court cases for legal constraints on science education and research. A few examples of how predictions of future discoveries can be used to test the various creation/evolution models are offered in chapter 16.

Chapter 17 comments on how well the RTB model has fared in its past predictions of scientific discoveries. The book concludes in chapter 18 by introducing new avenues of testing—beyond explanatory power and predictive success—that may make the RTB model more than a theory.

Scientists love testing. I did as a child and still do. I want to find out the what, when, and how. I also want to know why. Such research adds to scientific understanding. My hope is that by developing RTB's creation model and testing it against other explanations, we may see scientific progress on the origins and history of the universe, Earth, and life. The first step for developing and testing any model is to understand the competing positions. Chapter 2 sets them forth.

2

MULTIPLE CHOICE

For the first four years of my life I lived with my parents and two sisters in a small apartment near McGill University in Montreal. Then, after a business setback, my father went to look for work in Vancouver, while the rest of us stayed with my grandmother in Calgary.

Grandmother Ross had a large wood-burning stove in the middle of her home for heating and cooking. One day I watched her start a fire inside that stove. The next morning I decided to test whether it was possible to start one outside the stove. I picked a place in the middle of the kitchen, gathered some kindling from the wood storage box, crumpled an old newspaper, found a book of matches, and in no time had a nice fire burning.

My grandmother woke to the smell of smoke. She quickly put out the fire and gave me the worst licking of my life. That day I learned a couple of lessons about testing. First, what I consider an acceptable experiment may not always be considered acceptable by others. And that people tend to be very protective of their turf.

Danger, Danger!

Some people consider my willingness to challenge cherished beliefs about the origins of the universe, Earth, and life as unacceptable and dangerous as that fire. Almost every position across the creation/evolution spectrum appears as protective of their turf as my grandmother was of her home. This battle is not one of ideas alone. It's a war over the very soul of humanity. Each participant issues dire warnings about the consequences of the other positions.

In 1984 biochemistry professor Isaac Asimov wrote "The 'Threat' of Creationism," an article which has since appeared in several books, magazines, and Web postings. It warns fellow scientists and the public that creationists are "a strong and frightening force, impervious to, and immunized against, the feeble lance of mere reason."[1] Although creationists are a relatively small group, Asimov sees them as a threat since "smaller groups have used intense pressure and forceful campaigning—as the creationists do—and have succeeded in disrupting and taking over whole societies."[2] Asimov concludes by warning that "with creationists in the saddle, American science will wither. We will raise a generation of ignoramuses. . . . We will inevitably recede into the backwater of civilization."[3]

These fears continue on a larger scale today. Parliamentarians from the forty-seven nation Council of Europe issued a resolution on October 4, 2007, in which they alerted both their member states and the world that "creationism could become a threat to human rights."[4] The council members saw this threat emerging from the creationists' "total rejection of science."[5] They wrote,

> We are witnessing a growth of modes of thought which challenge established knowledge about nature, evolution, our origins and our place in the universe. . . . The "intelligent design" idea, which is the latest, more refined version of creationism, does not deny a certain degree of evolution. However, intelligent design, presented in a more subtle way, seeks to portray its approach as scientific, and therein lies the danger.[6]

On the other hand, Henry Morris, past president of the Institute for Creation Research (ICR) and for several decades the leading young-earth creationist spokesman, declared in 1988 that the theory of biological evolution must be strenuously opposed by all Christians. He said that "the bitter fruits of widespread amorality, materialism, the drug culture, abortionism, pornography, social diseases and a host of other ills—not to mention communism and fascism" spring from the roots of evolutionary humanism.[7] Henry Morris also accuses evolutionists of stultifying the progress of science. He wrote that evolution has produced "not one good fruit in the form of real scientific advance in either living standards or altruistic behavior."[8]

Even more recently, the movie *Expelled: No Intelligence Allowed* intimated that public universities, museums, and research institutes terminate any academic who dares to disagree with the hypothesis that life on Earth originated and evolved by strictly natural means. Jewish narrator and interviewer Ben Stein also blames the Holocaust and the evils of both communism and Nazism on Darwinian beliefs.[9]

Meanwhile, young-earth creationists loudly denounce any attempt to integrate creation and evolution, popularly referred to as theistic evolution. In an article "10 Dangers of Theistic Evolution," ChristianAnswers. net charges that "the doctrine of theistic evolution undermines this basic way of reading the Bible. . . . Events reported in the Bible are reduced to mythical imagery."[10] Answers in Genesis (AiG) doesn't like old-earth creationism any better. AiG spokesmen say my old-earth perspective "(1) contradicts the clear teaching of Scripture, (2) assaults the character of God, (3) severely damages and distorts the Bible's teaching on death, and (4) undermines the gospel."[11]

To sum up, many young-earth creationist leaders consider anyone who disagrees with their particular doctrine as a dangerous enemy that must be strenuously opposed until their credibility is destroyed. On the other end of the creation/evolution spectrum, British biologist Richard Dawkins in his book *The God Delusion* asserts that faith is fundamentally evil.[12] He describes belief in God as a mental virus.[13] The back cover of his book claims that "faith is not just irrational but potentially deadly."[14]

Is It A, B, C, D, E, F, G, or H?

Each of the major participants in the controversy wants exclusive rights to the story of the cosmos and life. It's a powerful story, one that carries enormous significance for every person on Earth.

All sides seem to agree that the origins scenario holds the key to answering the great questions of life: Where did the universe and Earth come from? How did humanity get here and why? Where is life headed? Did humans invent God (or gods) out of insecurity or wishful thinking? Or is there really a God who endowed individuals with his creative and imaginative powers? Ultimately, what's at stake is who or what determines the meaning of life.

Wielding authority over the story of life's origin and history appears to have eclipsed all other objectives. However, understanding the variety of choices for origins' scenarios supplies a context for testing which positions are indeed the most viable. Any hope of understanding creation/evolution issues requires a comprehension of the various positions.

A. Evolutionists

Scientists initially used the term "evolution" with reference to nature's change over time—change brought about by whatever means. By this broad definition, even the Bible describes evolution, and creationists are evolutionists.

In recent decades, however, the word "evolutionist" has generally been applied to someone who asserts that all the changes observed in the record of nature (including the origin and history of the universe, Earth, and all life) can be attributed to natural causes alone. Some evolutionists argue that the natural causes are not random. For example, quantum evolutionists posit that quantum mechanics gives cells and organisms the ability to initiate tiny, undetectable "directed" actions that are advantageous to their survival and well-being.[15] For our discussion, unless otherwise qualified, the terms "evolutionist," "evolutionism," and "evolution science" refer to the belief that the entirety of the natural realm can be attributed to strictly natural causes.

B. Young-Earth Creationists

Historically, "creationist" referred to anyone who acknowledges that a Creator is responsible for bringing the universe and life into existence. According to that definition, nearly half of all practicing scientists are creationists (see chapter 3, pp. 36–37).[16] Over the past several decades, however, the term has taken on a much narrower meaning. Today "creationist" typically is used to refer to someone who believes:

- the Genesis creation days must be six consecutive 24-hour periods; that is, God created all things within 144 hours;
- the Genesis genealogies contain few if any gaps. Thus, the creation week occurred between 6,000 and 10,000 years ago;

- Neanderthals, archaic *Homo sapiens*, and *Homo erectus* are the human descendents of Adam and Eve. All other supposed bipedal primate species are either fraudulent or misidentified as such;
- the flood of Noah's time (Genesis 6–9) was a global event that submerged all the continents and destroyed all land-dwelling, air-breathing animals (except those aboard the ark). This flood, lasting about a year, accounts for virtually all of Earth's geological features, fossils, and biodeposits (coal, oil, natural gas, limestone, marble, top soil, etc.);
- all land animals alive today naturally descended from pairs of creatures on Noah's ship.

Several parachurch organizations have advanced these teachings, commonly referred to as "creationism" and "creation science," so effectively and so exclusively that many evangelical pastors, congregations, schools, broadcasters, ministry leaders, and missionaries adhere to them by default and remain largely unaware or distrustful of any alternate biblical view. Most reporters and secular scientists see these teachings as part of the evangelical belief system.

C. Intelligent Design Movement

For thousands of years, scholars from various cultural and religious backgrounds have proposed intelligent design as an explanation for many of the special properties of the universe, Earth, life, and humanity. For over a century, every student at Britain's Cambridge University was required to study William Paley's famous text, *Natural Theology*. In it Paley draws the inference from his detailed study of nature that the properties of living organisms demand a divine Designer.[17]

Even apart from questions about how the universe and life began, intelligent design has long been acknowledged as a legitimate scientific conclusion. In such disciplines as archaeology, anthropology, and forensics, researchers evaluate, differentiate, and interpret evidence or artifacts based on various indicators of intentionality or purposeful design.

About a decade ago, however, a diverse group of creation advocates formed an alliance widely known as the intelligent design movement (IDM). Their goal is to advance public instruction about the intelligent design concept, the inference that an intelligent designer is responsible for the origin and history of life. By refraining from making a specific identification of the designer or of any specific history of the universe or life, the movement has sought to remove any religious bias and, therefore, any apparent legal basis for disallowing the teaching of intelligent design in classrooms.

D. Old-Earth Creationists

Coupled with the old-earth adjective, this "creationist" refers to someone who, in contrast to a young-earth view, believes not only the biblical account of creation but also the findings of mainstream science. These individuals typically embrace both the truthfulness of Scripture and the scientific evidence for a multibillion-year history of the universe, Earth, and life on Earth.[18]

Old-earth creationists, however, hold a variety of positions on the correct interpretation of the Genesis creation days and genealogies, on the bipedal primates that preceded human beings, and on the nature and extent of Noah's flood.

E. Theistic Evolutionists

During the latter part of the nineteenth century and early part of the twentieth, the term "theistic evolutionist" typically referred to anyone who believed that God's creation work took place over a long period of time—millions or billions of years rather than thousands. Many theistic evolutionists of that era held that God's creative involvement went beyond merely working through natural processes and laws and included countless miraculous interventions, particularly when new species appeared on Earth.

Though a few still suggest that God may have miraculously intervened at the origin of the universe, the origin of the first life-form, the Cambrian explosion (when a broad diversity of complex life-forms suddenly appeared 543 million years ago; see chapter 10, pp. 162–63), and/or at the origin of humanity, by the end of the twentieth century the term theistic evolutionist had changed. The vast majority now take the view that the Creator intervened only on extremely rare occasions. And, most theistic evolutionists claim that he transcended the natural order only once, at the origin of the universe.

Fully gifted creationists assert that God personally intervened in the natural order on just one occasion, the origin of the universe. According to this view, God so gifted the laws of physics and the universe at that cosmic beginning that thereafter, strictly natural processes brought about God's desired outcomes specifically as he had planned. This particular subset of theistic evolution is scientifically indistinguishable from deism, the belief that God is responsible only for the initial creation of the universe.

While some fully gifted creationists allow for the possibility of divine interventions beyond the cosmic creation event, they claim scientists can never detect such interventions. For example, the interventions of God are hidden underneath the umbrella of the Heisenberg uncertainty principle of quantum mechanics. (One implication of the Heisenberg uncertainty principle is that causality at the quantum level remains concealed.)

Evolutionary creationists claim that God created the universe and all life through an evolutionary process. They see this process as planned and directed by God with every aspect and entity in the natural realm serving a specified purpose. Many (though not most) evolutionary creationists are more willing than most theistic evolutionists to entertain the possibility that God intervened in more dramatic and frequent ways. Unless otherwise qualified, in this book the terms "theistic evolution" and "theistic evolutionist" refer to the fully-gifted creationist position.

F. Framework Theorists

The framework view upholds the accuracy of events described in the biblical creation accounts. Framework theorists, however, see little or no chronological ordering of the biblical creation events. Furthermore, they consider these events primarily as pictures or metaphors for God's creative activity in the kingdom of heaven.

For framework theorists, there is no creation-evolution debate. With the Bible silent on the chronology and timescale of creation events and ambiguous on the physical details of creation, they see few, if any, points of contact between the findings of mainstream science and the message of Scripture.

G. Progressive Creationists

Like many of the previous descriptors, progressive creationism has changed over the past several decades. About sixty years ago, the label applied to those who believe the universe and Earth are billions of years old and that God created life several billion years ago, miraculously intervening numerous times throughout biological history to produce new life-forms. In this type of progressive creationism, microevolution occurs within a species or a genus but new genera and, with few exceptions, new species do not descend from a common ancestor.

Today some scientists who call themselves progressive creationists believe that all life-forms are linked by common ancestry in a natural way. Thus their position is virtually indistinguishable from a number of the theistic evolutionary views. While some progressive creationists agree with the mainstream science that shows the universe and solar system as billions of years old, they also concur with young-earth creationists that life has been present on Earth for only thousands of years.

H. Concordists

Concordism is the view that the scientific record and the biblical message of creation extensively overlap. In that overlap concordists see complete harmony and consistency between the biblical account and nature's record. Any conflict or discordance between the two sets of data arises from incomplete understanding or faulty interpretation. Concordists express confidence that ongoing scientific and theological research will always resolve any perceived contradictions.

Distinct from framework theorists and most theistic evolutionists, concordists draw considerable scientific detail from the biblical creation texts. They believe the descriptions offer a dependable depiction of the origin and history of the universe, Earth, and Earth's life. Moreover, they believe the Bible presents those events in a specified chronological sequence and frequently designates the manner in which God brings them about. Concordists accept the historic Christian creed that the record of nature serves as a second "book" of God's revelation to humanity.

A Not-So-Simple Choice

To say that people must choose between atheistic naturalism and young-earth creationism—between science and the Bible—oversimplifies an extremely complex issue. Not only are there many more options, but the different positions also employ a wide diversity of strategies to advance their own particular perspectives. The next chapter takes a brief look at these tactics in an effort to establish an accurate context for testing the viability of various views.

3

DIFFERENT STRATEGIES

I don't possess much body fat. In fact, I have so little that if I don't take and hold a deep breath when I jump into a freshwater pool or lake, I sink straight to the bottom. This sinking ability once led me to propose a test: how far could I walk completely and continuously submerged on the bottom of a pool? To make things interesting, my brother-in-law, Wade, bet I couldn't go more than thirty feet.

Wanting to win the bet, I worked hard to develop the best possible strategy. If I moved too fast, my oxygen would dissipate too quickly. Going too slow might still cause the oxygen to run out too fast. Taking a deep breath meant I wouldn't quickly sink to the bottom. Achieving the maximum distance underwater meant that the just-right amount of air must be in my lungs and that I must walk at a just-right pace.

To Wade's dismay, I won the bet by going forty-five feet.

Many leading participants in the creation-evolution debates also hope to figure out what it takes to win. For some, winning matters more than anything, and consequently they go to great lengths to find the just-right tactic, regardless of whether it advances the search for truth.

One method is simply to declare victory and hope the general public concurs. In *The Triumph of Evolution: And the Failure of Creationism*, renowned evolutionist Niles Eldredge pronounced evolution's complete victory.[1] However, despite its prominence in media and public education, the study of evolution has far from vanquished belief in creation.

Public Opinion

In 1914 psychologist James Leuba surveyed a thousand randomly selected scientists from *American Men of Science* (AMS) to assess their religious beliefs. He found that 40 percent believed in a personal God and an afterlife, 40 percent disbelieved, and 20 percent were unsure.[2] Comparing these statistics with the American population as a whole (90 percent believed in God), Leuba concluded that scientific literacy accounted for the difference.

Fewer than 40 percent of American adults born around the turn of the century finished high school, and not even 10 percent completed college.[3] Based on this data, Leuba predicted that with the growing breadth and depth of science education, belief in God would decline. He also claimed that as scientific discovery advanced, the percentage of scientists believing in God would dramatically dwindle.

Today, 84 percent of American adults over twenty-five have finished high school, and 27 percent have a college degree.[4] Science classes are required subjects. Data has multiplied enormously, and so has media coverage. People of the twenty-first century know far more science than their predecessors. Yet statistics confirm that roughly 73 percent of Americans still believe in God.[5] And, 80 percent believe that a Creator played the primary role in initiating and shaping life.[6]

A Harris Poll of 1,000 American adults shows how belief in the evolutionary explanation actually waned between 1994 and 2005 (see table 3.1, p. 37).

Even professional scientists reflect little change in their views over the past century. A 1996 survey mailed to a thousand scientists randomly selected from the latest edition of *American Men and Women of Science* proved Leuba's prediction incorrect. Of those who responded, about 40 percent indicated their belief in a personal God and an afterlife, 45 percent said they disbelieve, and 15 percent identified themselves as agnostic.[7] Scientific advance and education's emphasis on evolution appear to have had no dramatic influence on the beliefs of either laypeople or scientists. (However, see "Do 'Greater' Scientists Reject God?," p. 38, for an attempted rebuttal.)

Table 3.1: Harris Poll Results[8]

Question	Answer	March 1994	June 2005
Do you think human beings developed from earlier species or not?	Yes	44%	38%
	No	46%	54%
	Not sure/ Decline to answer	11%	8%
Do you believe apes and man have a common ancestry or not?	Yes	51%	46%
	No	43%	47%
	Not sure/ Decline to answer	5%	7%

Which of the following do you believe about how human beings came to be?

Human beings evolved from earlier species.	22%
Human beings were created directly by God.	64%
Human beings are so complex that they required a powerful force or intelligent being to help create them.	10%
Not sure/Decline to answer	4%

So What's the Problem?

The mainstream statistics baffle everyone. Evolutionary biologist Edward O. Wilson remarks in his anthology of Charles Darwin's writings that the general public's disbelief in evolution is "surpassingly strange."[9]

Evolutionists must ask why—given evolution's strong and steady influence in public education—naturalistic teachings fail to impact people's beliefs. Young-earth creationists must ask why—given the persistence and prevalence of belief in creation and the pervasiveness of their teaching—their views have failed to impact what's taught in public schools and colleges,[10] and even in many (or most) Christian colleges and seminaries.[11] The reasons seem obvious on both accounts.

Insistence on strict naturalism thwarts the evolutionist cause. If nature (the physical universe with all its contents) is the only reality, then all

Do "Greater" Scientists Reject God?

During the early twentieth century, the editors of *American Men of Science* designated "great" scientists among their entries. In his 1914 study, Leuba conducted a separate survey of these top scientists and found that only 21 percent of those who responded believed in a personal God. In 1933 he repeated the survey (though in a different form) of AMS greats. This time only 14 percent believed in a personal God. Leuba attributed the apparent declining belief in God among these scientists to their "superior knowledge, understanding, and experience."[12]

The publisher of *American Men and Women of Science* no longer labels certain scientists as great. No objective criteria could be developed for that designation. So the 1996 survey team conducted a different kind of follow-up study in 1998. It surveyed all 517 members of the United States National Academy of Sciences (NAS) listed in the same discipline categories of Leuba's great scientists. A mere 7 percent of those who responded indicated belief in a personal God.[13]

However, variables of these three surveys render them less than definitive. The survey results seem to show the chosen scientists as less likely to express belief in God than scientists as a whole group. But the reasons for the difference remain unclear. The surveys were worded differently, for one. And given that only members of the NAS can elect new members, the biases of current members influence who is elected. More importantly, many of America's most distinguished scientists do not belong to this organization.

theories, thoughts, and feelings are merely the result of physical interactions. No event contains meaning beyond mere sequential timing or that which is arbitrarily assigned.

With naturalism, the answers to the big questions of life become insignificant. *Where did we humans come from?* Random physical phenomena. *Where are we going?* Most likely to extinction. Such answers rarely captivate a student's curiosity or ignite the general public's imagination. Nor do they satisfy the soul's hunger for meaning, purpose, or hope.

On the other hand, insistence on one particular interpretation of the Genesis creation accounts has thwarted the young-earth creationist enterprise. Overlooking many other relevant biblical creation passages, young-earth creationists conclude that science is either wrong or illusory. Scientists are either deluded or conspirators. Thus these creationists have placed their ideas above evaluation by the scientific community. In doing so, they lost the capacity to influence the scholars who most control public education's science curricula.

Political Routes

Finding no success with academia, young-earth creationists in America sought to convince people through grassroots political action. They lobbied local school boards and state legislatures for "equal access" (equal time for young-earth views) whenever and wherever evolution is taught.

Though occasionally equal access laws were passed, none has yet gone into effect. Various organizations and citizens groups have consistently challenged these rulings in court, where state and federal judges have overturned them.

Leading young-earth creationist proponents typically claim these judges were motivated by anti-Christian bias and misguided application of the United States Constitution. Yet case documents easily reveal the basis for those rulings: the courts could not find any scientific merit in the young-earth creationist cases (see chapter 15, pp. 220–26).

In particular, the United States Supreme Court justices pointed out that "requiring the teaching of creation science with evolution does not give schoolteachers a flexibility that they did not already possess to supplant the present science curriculum with the presentation of theories, besides evolution, about the origin of life."[14]

The Supreme Court affirmed that if creationism is valid as science, its right to a place in the public school science curriculum is assured, no matter what its connection to religion.[15] Based on testimony and documentation from both Christian and non-Christian experts, however, the courts found a complete lack of scientific credibility with the young-earth position. So the young-earth hypothesis was ruled out— not because it is religious but because it lacks scientific integrity. The appeal to protect equal access for public school science curriculum was appropriately denied.

Scientific credibility has been the issue at stake in all the major American cases over the past fifty years. The courts have repeatedly acknowledged that neither perfection nor completeness is expected, but a reasonable level of plausibility must set the standard. In the courts' assessments, young-earth creationism failed to meet that requirement.

These judgments were not bold judicial maneuvers. They were, in fact, historically consistent decisions. For example, until the 1920s a sizeable group of Americans believed (according to their "literal" reading of the Bible) that the Earth was flat rather than spherical.[16] Though Christian proponents of this view were serious and devout, their beliefs did not justify inclusion of flat-Earth lessons in school curriculum. The same standard holds true for geocentrism (belief that Earth rather than the Sun is the center of the solar system). Though that idea has been part of the religious landscape for the past 250 years, it is still not taught in school.[17]

Religious Neutrality

The need for an alternative approach became obvious. Most recently the intelligent design movement (IDM) has been working to enter public education under the banner of religious neutrality. Based on the incorrect assumption that courts ruled against creationism primarily due to its religious agenda, intelligent design (ID) leaders assembled a diverse coalition of nonnaturalist scholars and organizations to strip all visible signs of religious affiliation from its platform.

ID spokesman Phillip Johnson laid out his plan for restoring the damaged image and influence of creation advocates in a series of four books.[18] His expertise and experience as a legal scholar led to the building of a coalition, a "big tent," that would hopefully drive a "wedge of truth" into the controversy. This big tent includes deists, agnostics, Mormons, Muslims, Jews, Roman Catholics, Eastern Orthodox, Protestants, evangelicals, and even some atheists who believe aliens deposited life on Earth. ID leaders presumed such a polyglot of perspectives would prevent any challenge based on the First Amendment of the United States Constitution: "Congress shall make no law respecting an establishment of religion, or prohibiting the free exercise thereof."

Johnson argued that only a broad-based coalition offered any hope of mobilizing the necessary talent and financial resources to challenge and overthrow materialistic naturalism and the evolution establishment. He argues for a "unite-and-win strategy"[19] and strongly urged all anti-materialists to put aside their different perspectives and disputes with one another.

Many ID theorists suggest that the easiest creation truth to establish in secular circles is the existence of some type of intelligent design (as opposed to Darwinism) to explain nature's record. Once that truth becomes firmly established, Johnson and his colleagues believe other basic creation ideas can be added, including discussion about the kind of divine Being responsible for the design.

Instead, scientists' reaction to the IDM has been hostile and dismissive. Evolutionary biologist Jerry Coyne refers to the research and writing from one ID scholar as "stealth creationism."[20] Physicist Mark Perakh accuses an ID leader of "disdainful dismissal of all and every criticism."[21]

Lawrence Krauss, director of the Center for Education and Research in Cosmology and Astrophysics at Case Western Reserve University, claims ID is definitely not science.[22] Jennifer Palonus, director of the online forum *Creation/Evolution: The Eternal Debate,* says intelligent design proponents "have not been able to articulate a positive scientific case for 'intelligent design.' ID is still just a collection of negative claims about evolution" (see "Evolution Bashing," below).[23]

This reaction toward ID proponents may seem harsh, but it makes sense. Scientists tend to associate ID with young-earth creationism. They note that significant financial backing for the IDM's scholars and spokespersons comes from young-earth creationists, who also buy the majority of ID materials.[24] Evolutionary science researchers are suspicious of the

Evolution Bashing

ID proponents typically argue for creation by focusing on all the negatives of evolution. Hence, they have earned the label "evolution bashers." While conceding that problems and shortcomings exist in Darwinian theory, Darwinists note the lack of any credible comprehensive explanation for life's history from the ID camp.

Many evolutionists claim that if ID (and young-earth) proponents really had the courage of their convictions, they would set forth their models in enough detail to invite meaningful critique. Philip Kitcher, a philosophy of science professor at Columbia University, asked, "What's the nonevolutionary explanation? Johnson doesn't tell us. . . . Johnson's attempt to dispute the 'fact of evolution' is an exercise in evasion."[25]

This point is well taken. It's easy to criticize a position's problems and shortcomings. But it's tough (as well as a mark of valor and integrity) to expose one's own beliefs and interpretations to public scrutiny and criticism.

IDM's reluctance to offend young-earth creationists or to debate unscientific or antiscientific beliefs.

Missing Model

Scientists repeatedly ask ID leaders to clarify their stance on young-earth creationism. A persistent unwillingness to do so reinforces the notion that ID may simply represent young-earth creationism in disguise. Astrophysicist Adrian Melott's headline in *Physics Today* claimed "Intelligent Design Is Creationism in a Cheap Tuxedo."[26]

Carl Wieland, himself a young-earth creationist, pinpoints another major reason for this negative response. He notes that ID theorists "refuse to be drawn on the sequence of events, or the exact history of life on Earth, or its duration."[27] Therefore, "they can never offer a 'story of the past.'"[28] He asks, "If the origins debate is not about a 'story of the past,' what is it about?"[29]

When it comes to the origins of the universe, life, and humanity, scientists want history's story. They insist that this story be presented in the form of a testable model (see chapter 1, pp. 15–16).

Without a model, the ID paradigm cannot present specific explanations for natural history that can be tested or falsified, nor does it generate significant predictions of scientific discoveries. This lack of substantive testability gives rise to the repeated charge that ID is "not science."

The insufficiency of a detailed model for the origin and history of the universe, Earth, life, and humanity keeps the IDM from gaining access to public education. Efforts to persuade the Kansas School Board, Ohio State Board of Education, and Dover (Pennsylvania) School Board to allow the teaching of ID concepts and to limit promotion of naturalistic biological evolution all failed. In Kansas, the attempt to make instruction about radiometric dating and astronomical objects beyond the solar system "optional" (in defense of young-earth creationism) not only failed but also generated a serious backlash.

In Ohio, Patricia Princehouse of Ohio Citizens for Science exulted, "We won big time here. The creationists have lost. There is more evolution in the standards now than there would have been had they kept their mouths shut."[30]

In Dover, Pennsylvania, United States District Judge John E. Jones III ruled, "the overwhelming evidence at trial established that ID is a religious view, a mere relabeling of creationism, and not a scientific theory."[31] Only a more coherent and comprehensive explanation of natural history, the fossil record, and other data than that covered by evolutionary theory will entice scientists to consider another view. Still, some researchers try to avoid the issue altogether.

Separate Magisteria

In one of his most famous essays, the late paleontologist Stephen Jay Gould proposed another way to settle the creation-evolution controversy. He claimed no solution is even necessary because science and religion are mutually exclusive "magisteria" (realms of knowledge and authority).[32] Science reigns supreme and alone in the realm of nature and facts, while theology reigns above all in the realm of spirit and faith. According to Gould, these two domains *do not* and *need not* overlap. Keeping them isolated means disputes or conflicts over creation and evolution would never arise—*if only* people don't overstep the boundaries of each magisterium.

Gould's appeal resonates throughout the scientific community and even with some theologians. John A. Moore, evolutionary biologist and cofounder of the Biological Sciences Curriculum Study, describes science as belonging to the domain of the "rational, demanding data and logic," while religion belongs to the realm of the "more romantic, involving emotion, faith, and personal preference."[33] Moore labeled the evolution/creation disputes as "political disagreements, not scientific ones," because "only one side deals with science." He adds, "The theories of science have nothing to say about gods."[34]

America's National Academy of Sciences (NAS) concurs. In *Teaching about Evolution and the Nature of Science*, NAS editors wrote, "Usually 'faith' refers to beliefs that are accepted without empirical evidence. . . . Science can say nothing about the supernatural."[35]

In an attempt to erect an impenetrable wall that banishes references to the supernatural from discussions of cosmic and life history, some scientists opt to redefine science. They claim that science is the realm of inquiry that engages in repeatable, controlled experiments producing results with determined values (and numeric error bars).

Science cannot hope to explain nature's record, however, without considering observations of and inferences about what happened in the past. Likewise to ignore relevant theoretical disciplines seriously impedes scientific advance. While scientists, philosophers, and theologians may not always fully agree on a definition of science, most concur that science proceeds most productively when observations and theories are used along with experiments to test competing explanations of nature's record.

The implications by Gould, Moore, and the NAS that science is all about facts, reason, and logic while religion and theology are merely romantic delusions strikes some scholars as too extreme. Consequently, less patronizing and marginalizing forms of separate magisteria have been proposed.

Almost-Separate Magisteria

Some scientists and theologians divide science into two domains: origins science, where theological considerations are permissible, and operations (or ongoing-process) science, where they are not.[36] As with Gould's supposed solution, this approach creates artificial boundaries between science and theology that limit the extent and effectiveness of education, research, and the testing of various creation/evolution models.

This division of truth into objective (fact-based) and subjective (feeling-based) domains, with science on the objective side and religious notions on the subjective side, may seem an easy way out. However, philosophical reality makes such separation untenable. Naturalism, which acknowledges no transcendent absolutes, has no necessary ground or foundation for logic, reason, or even mathematics. The very concept of truth comes from the spiritual domain.

Christianity (based on the two books of revelation: the Bible and the record of nature) allows for a complete or nearly complete overlap of theology and science. From a scientific perspective, biblical material has earned the right to consideration based on its record of accuracy in forecasting scientific discoveries. The Bible states that God's presence fills the entirety of the universe (see Jer. 23:24) and that the whole universe declares his glory (Ps. 19:1–4; 50:6; 97:6). Scripture also declares that God has established fixed laws to govern the heavens and earth (Jer. 33:25).

Thus the Bible allows for a variety of natural and supernatural causes in varying combinations within both origins and operations science. Christianity upholds the values and ethics crucial to the scientific endeavor, including support for the laws of logic.[37] That's how Christian theology gave birth to the scientific revolution (see chapter 4).

Fallacies of the Gaps

In an attempt to sidestep testing and critiques of their models, both atheistic and theistic evolutionists charge that believers in creation commit the "God of the gaps" fallacy. Supposedly whenever gaps in the knowledge or understanding of natural phenomena are encountered, that's where creation proponents claim God supernaturally intervened.

Later discoveries sometimes reveal that these "blanks" have natural explanations. As a result, scientists are typically reluctant to identify any perceived gap with the work of a supernatural agent. Some insist that whether or not God exists, the record of nature doesn't include real gaps. So, they argue, while appeals to the supernatural are permissible during religious services, such appeals must remain off-limits for scientific research and education. The conclusion: no creation explanation for any phenomenon within the record of nature should ever be entertained.

Ironically, a reasonable case could be made that scientists sometimes engage in similarly flawed logic. They commit what could be called the "nature of the gaps" fallacy. Some researchers presume that an unknown force or phenomenon of nature must fill *all* the gaps in human knowledge and understanding.

Many theoreticians have appealed to the existence of unknown laws, principles, constants, dimensions, or hypothetical variations in the constants and laws of physics to explain a gap and dissolve supposed evidence for supernatural intervention. Stuart Kauffman and other scientists at the Santa Fe Institute, for example, without any observational support or physical evidence, appeal to a hypothesized "fourth law of thermodynamics." They say that this imaginative law spontaneously produced a high degree of order, complexity, and information content where none existed. That's how they explain the "natural," sudden, and very early appearance of life on Earth despite the lack of both a primordial soup and a supply of prebiotics (building blocks of life molecules—see chapter 9, pp. 139–41).[38]

Similarly, some nontheistic cosmologists have made ad hoc appeals to hypothesized new laws or constants of physics as ways to avoid concluding that the universe arose from a singularity or that the universe manifests extreme fine-tuning to allow for life's possible existence.[39]

The most productive approach is to test what happens as scientists gain more knowledge and understanding. If a certain gap becomes narrower and less problematic from a naturalistic perspective as data accumulate, then that natural explanation for the gap appears appropriate. However, if the gap becomes wider and more problematic as scientists learn more, then a supernatural explanation may make better sense.

The entire ensemble of gaps can be exploited to evaluate and contrast competing creation/evolution models. Such testing calls for answers to questions such as:

Which interpretation or model contains the fewest gaps?

Which model(s) most accurately predict(s) where as-yet-undiscovered gaps will be observed?

Which model(s) most accurately forecast(s) what scientists will discover as they use new data and technology to explore the gaps?

Which model is the least contrived and most straightforward in explaining both the known and the unknown?

Researchers must make the case for their models based on factual evidence—what is known, not what's unknown. The measure of a model's success should be how well it explains existing data and predicts what will be discovered as researchers continue to explore current gaps in knowledge and understanding. Astronomers, biochemists, paleontologists, and anthropologists, among others, can take advantage of such apparent chasms in scientific understanding to direct their efforts in trying to determine which explanations best account for certain phenomena relevant to the origin and history of the universe, life, and human beings.

Integrative Approach

Almost every significant description of the natural realm reveals at least some element of design. Even things as mundane as electron orbits about atomic nuclei or the nuclear ground state energy levels of various elements fall within remarkably narrow limits for life's possible existence. Such apparent fine-tuning suggests at least the possibility of prior planning and purpose.

The magisteria of science and religion find harmony in Christian doctrine. Biblical faith is fact-based. Such faith includes confidence, based on testable evidence, in the reality of that faith's object. Every major Christian doctrine is either founded upon or linked to thousands of wide-ranging scientific details on the origins, structure, and history of the universe, Earth, life, and humanity (see chapter 5, p. 61).

The psalmist declared that God has revealed himself to humanity in two books, the written record and nature's record (see Ps. 19). Both are said to be completely reliable, having as their source the One who embodies Truth, the One who does not lie (Num. 23:19; Ps. 12:6; 19:7–8; 119:160; Prov. 30:5; Heb. 6:18). According to the Bible (e.g., Ps. 19:1–4; 97:6; Rom. 1:18–23), these two books are more than merely compatible—they overlap.

The scientific method originated in Scripture and in the development of Reformation theology (see Appendix A, pp. 257–60). Few scientists seem to realize how the Bible and science work together to define this historic methodology for observing, testing, and interpreting nature's phenomena.

On the other hand, most Christians don't recognize that the benefits of the scientific age come from applying the testing process as set forth in Scripture. Paul, in his letter to the Thessalonians, exhorts readers to put all teachings to the test and to "hold on to the good" (1 Thess. 5:21). Such a practice benefits everyone.

Making the Grade

Virtually every theory known to science has been established through the scientific method. By it, hypotheses are refined, revised, or rejected. As all available evidence is considered, explanations draw closer and closer to reality.

When a concept shows no consistency with physical reality, then that idea can and should be eliminated. The most valid model will grow in explanatory power and accuracy through ongoing scientific testing. Chapter 4 explains this testable approach and shows how it reveals more and more of the truth that corresponds to the universe and the life it contains.

4

AN OBJECTIVE
TESTING METHOD

In the British Columbia public schools I attended, my teachers drummed into me the importance of taking deliberate steps before forming any interpretation and rigorously and thoroughly testing it. This training in the scientific method paid off at age seventeen when I started my first serious read of the Bible.

As soon as I opened my Bible to Genesis 1, I recognized the first two steps of the scientific method. The description of the six creation days that followed and the creation account in Genesis 2 revealed the remaining steps.

With the Spirit of God hovering over the waters (see Gen. 1:2), the point of view was Earth's surface. Additional details in the verse showed me how Earth started empty of life and unfit for it. Water covered the entire surface, and it was dark. Given this frame of reference and initial conditions, I realized after only a couple more hours that the events of the creation days were all correctly described and sequenced with respect to the scientifically established record of Earth's history. Discovering many more creation accounts throughout the Bible gave me the opportunity to test whether my interpretation of Genesis 1 was reasonable.

Scientific evidence for the big bang model of the universe had already persuaded me that a Creator must exist. Seeing Scripture's opening words reflect that cosmic event, then go on to describe the point of view and initial conditions of primordial Earth, as well as accurately predict scientific discoveries of Earth's and life's history thousands of years ahead of time, persuaded me that the God of the universe must have inspired the Bible's words.

A decade later I found out why the Bible so perfectly and consistently followed the scientific method. A study of the rest of the creation accounts and of the history of the Reformation revealed that Scripture was the source of this process. During the Reformation, people outside the priesthood, including scientists, began to read and study the Bible for themselves. When European Reformation scientists began to apply the biblical interpretation method to the record of nature, their efforts gave birth to the scientific method (see Appendix A, pp. 257–58). That process also initiated the scientific revolution.

Time-Tested

The best biblical interpretations and the best scientific interpretations come from consistent application of the scientific method. This step-by-step process encourages the necessary meticulousness, restraint, and humility warranted by any truth quest. Use of the scientific method also guards against the human tendency to form conclusions too quickly or firmly. Certain basic steps must be completed before an initial hypothesis is developed. Emotional commitment to that hypothesis should be avoided.

Use of this process presumes that the natural realm is well-ordered, consistent, and contradiction-free. Repeated and varied experiments and observations throughout the past five hundred years overwhelmingly validate this assumption.

The number and wording of steps outlining the scientific method may vary slightly depending on the type of investigation. But the method's basic components—as used for explaining the origins and history of the universe, life, and humanity—include these sequential tasks:

1. Identify the phenomenon to be investigated and explained.
2. Identify the frame(s) of reference or point(s) of view being used to study and describe the phenomenon.

3. Determine the initial conditions before the observation or experiment begins.
4. Perform an experiment or observe the phenomenon, noting what takes place when, where, and in what order.
5. Note the final conditions yielded by the experiment or observation of the phenomenon.
6. Form a tentative explanation, or hypothesis, for how and why things transpired as they did.
7. Test the hypothesis with further experiments or observations.
8. Revise the hypothesis accordingly.
9. Determine how well the explanation of the phenomenon integrates with explanations of related phenomena.

(Note: These steps apply equally to interpretations of biblical exposition and to natural events.)

While the scientific method doesn't guarantee objectivity and accuracy, it does minimize the effects of oversight, personal bias, and presuppositions. Even the most careful interpreter possesses only limited knowledge, understanding, and objectivity. Every interpretation, no matter how well-developed or thoroughly tested, falls short of perfection. So, the need for ongoing adjustment and refinement never ends.

This investigative method works best when practiced in an ongoing cycle. Each stage moves researchers closer to a more complete grasp of the truth. Repeated passes through the steps uncover new information and insights. Along with them, new questions and challenges arise.

The process never ends. It's exhilarating for anyone who loves truth.

The scientific method has built-in quality controls, and appropriate application of them preserves good science. The need for major revisions exposes faulty or grossly incomplete interpretations that should be discarded. Good interpretations yield progressively smaller revisions with each cycle through the steps. The explanatory power and predictive success of a good hypothesis continue to increase until that hypothesis becomes a theory. With greater substantiation, that theory expands into a detailed and comprehensive model. Ongoing application of the scientific method continues to refine, improve, and extend the model.

The scientific method makes open, equitable dialogue about creation and evolution possible. Anyone wanting to participate can present an interpretive scenario—developed and refined by observations and testing—for comparison with other scenarios. Those models that demonstrate the greatest explanatory power and predictive success warrant further study. Models requiring larger and larger revisions after failing predictive tests deserve to be eliminated.

Over time, the field narrows. Researchers focus on the models that most closely correspond with reality. As the more successful models mature, they multiply into more detailed variants.

No doubt this process often involves emotion. Researchers, like other people, can become attached to their ideas, but when they bring their personal biases out into the open, science advances with increasing freedom and productivity.

Within the realm of scientific research, a model's failure carries no stigma. So-called "failed" models often illuminate and foster the growth of more successful ones. Determining what does *not* work often helps elucidate what *does*.

When all participants remain committed to following the findings wherever they lead, researchers can work in partnership through failures, successes, and disagreements. Scientists become free to resolve disputes and solve mysteries. Recent progress in cosmology shows how truth ultimately can prevail on creation/evolution questions when researchers are willing to put their ideological, philosophical, and theological commitments to the test.[1]

Developing a Better Model

At the beginning of the twentieth century, scientists were convinced that Newton's laws of motion explained all the dynamics of the universe. Thus, they viewed the universe to be roughly static throughout infinite space and time. This infinitely old, infinitely large universe model (also known as the Newtonian cosmological model) reigned supreme because it:

- led to the discovery of Uranus and Neptune by successfully predicting their orbits and locations (based on an analysis of the orbits and locations of the six planets visible to the naked eye);
- explained the motions and positions of all stars then visible to astronomers;

- allowed for the necessary time, quantity of material, and static conditions required by the emerging theory of Darwinian evolution;
- had no competition. No other cosmic model came close to explaining so much of what scientists observed.

Though the Newtonian model was the only credible cosmological model, unexpected measurements revealed two significant irregularities. In 1859, French astronomer Urbain-Jean-Joseph Le Verrier published calculations showing a tiny but regular advance in the point at which Mercury's orbit comes closest to the Sun (Mercury's perihelion). This advance remained after astronomers took into account all the gravitational influences of the other planets on Mercury's orbit.[2]

Then, in 1887, physicists began noticing that the velocity of light was not dependent upon the velocity of either the light's emitter or the observer's frame of reference. Contrary to what the Newtonian model predicted, the speed of light was constant.[3]

Published in 1905, Albert Einstein's special theory of relativity was founded on the principle of the constancy of light's velocity. This principle implied a number of observable effects that all proved correct. In 1916, Einstein's general theory of relativity explained the mystery of Mercury's orbit in addition to predicting several never-before-seen phenomena.[4] Both these theories led to a radically different cosmic model—one that specified a continuously expanding universe. This new approach revealed that the universe had a beginning and was finite with respect to time.

The expanding universe model quickly attracted scientific attention. Not only did it explain the two anomalies, but even more importantly it predicted phenomena not yet seen. For example, Einstein's first paper on general relativity predicted gravity would bend space by specified amounts, which observations could either verify or refute.[5]

As appropriate instruments and techniques developed, astronomers put these new ideas to the test. The success of Einstein's predictions, along with the additional measurements and observations made possible by advanced technology, so convincingly affirmed the universe's continuous expansion that astronomers reluctantly began to abandon the Newtonian model.

Britain's famous mathematical physicist Sir Arthur Stanley Eddington nevertheless described the concept of a cosmic beginning as "philosophically repugnant"[6] because it did not "allow evolution an infinite time to get started."[7] Unhappy with the theistic implications of a creation event, Eddington (like most scientists) tried to salvage as much of the old science as possible. He and many other astrophysicists attempted to modify Einstein's model in a way that would still allow enough time. They proposed three classes of cosmic models:

1. The hesitation model—the universe expands, but a hypothesized physical constant and a careful choice of the constant's sign and value slows its expansion rate to zero. Nearly an infinite time later, the universe starts to expand again.

2. The steady state model—the universe continuously expands, but with a hypothesized "creation force" always bringing new matter into existence so the universe maintains the same conditions for infinite time.

3. The oscillating model—the universe alternates between expansion and contraction for infinite time due to hypothesized new physical mechanisms and constants of physics.[8]

None of these sets of cosmic models was supported by physical evidence. Normally, models based solely on assumption make the scientific community skeptical. However, many nontheistic scientists judged the avoidance of the implications of a single cosmic beginning sufficient reason to research each scenario.

More importantly, these models offered predictions about what astronomers might find as they looked deeply and precisely into the cosmic past. But when put to the test, none of the observations matched the predictions. Eventually these models were abandoned, and astronomers focused on a narrower cluster of cosmic scenarios. A new set of three incorporated Einstein's single cosmic beginning in finite time:

1. Cold big bang models (the universe expands from an infinitesimally small but cold volume)

2. Hot big bang models (the universe expands from an infinitesimally small and nearly infinitely hot volume) dominated by ordinary matter—protons, neutrons, and electrons—that strongly interacts with radiation

3. Hot big bang models dominated by exotic matter—particles such as neutrinos, axions, and neutralinos—that weakly interacts with radiation

These models did fit the observations, at least initially.

As researchers continued to make observations and conduct tests, they eventually ruled out the first two sets. Meanwhile, new research reinforced the plausibility of the third. Furthermore, astrophysicists established an array of amazingly detailed models fitting within that category.

Today, a proliferation of viable models remains within an even narrower range. These inflationary hot big bang models propose that dark energy (the self-stretching property of the cosmic space fabric) dominates exotic dark matter (particles that do not strongly interact with photons), which in turn dominates ordinary dark matter (aggregates of protons, neutrons, and electrons that do not emit appreciable light),[9] as table 4.1 shows. By using the scientific method, researchers continue making remarkable progress despite philosophical and/or religious preferences.

Table 4.1: Cosmic Inventory

Cosmic Component	Percentage of Total Cosmic Density
Dark energy (self-stretching property of the cosmic space surface)	72.1
Exotic dark matter (particles that weakly interact with light)	23.3
Ordinary dark matter (protons and neutrons)	4.34
Ordinary bright matter (stars and star remnants)	0.27
Planets	0.0001

Note: This inventory, from an exhaustive compilation by Princeton cosmologists Masataka Fukugita and James Peebles, is based on the best measurements made prior to 2005.[10] It includes updates made possible by the 2008 third release of the Wilkinson Microwave Anisotropy Probe (WMAP).[11]

Testing Worldviews

Because philosophical and theological worldviews inevitably make assertions about the nature of the physical realm, cosmologists now realize their research provides a powerful crucible for testing different belief systems. The Hubble Ultra Deep Field (see figure 4.1) is a good example of such a test. This discovery shows that galaxies far away are much closer together than galaxies up close. The spreading apart of galaxies through time provides direct evidence of the continuous expansion of the universe from an infinitesimal volume.

No religion or philosophy, or lack thereof, remains insulated from astronomical observational tests. China's famous astrophysicist Fang Li Zhi said, "A question that has always been considered a topic of metaphys-

Figure 4.1. Hubble Ultra Deep Field

The Hubble Space Telescope revealed the first galaxies ever to form, showing the deepest view of the visible universe yet achieved. Field width is about a tenth the angular diameter of the Moon. Exposure time was one million seconds. From the number of galaxies visible in the image, astronomers estimate that the universe contains 200 billion medium- and large-sized galaxies. (Image courtesy of NASA, ESA, S. Beckwith [STScI] and the HUDF Team)

ics or theology, the creation of the universe, has now become an idea of active research in physics."[12]

What is true for cosmologists will eventually become true for scientists in other disciplines. As the pace of scientific research continues to accelerate, scientists will increasingly see their discoveries challenging cherished philosophical and religious beliefs.

Implementing Change

The shift in cosmology over the past century demonstrates how scientific advances and the scientific method can replace vague or inaccurate concepts of nature with more precise and comprehensive explanations. Typically, researchers hold fast to an existing model, defects and all, until they see how an alternate model works better in five ways. The new model must:

1. give a wider and more detailed view of what's going on;
2. make better sense of established data;
3. provide more reasonable and consistent explanations for the phenomena under investigation;
4. result in fewer unexplained anomalies and gaps;
5. prove more successful in anticipating or predicting future findings.

Every model to some extent is inadequate and imperfect. However, knowledge can and does advance when a new approach yields better explanations and predictions than its predecessors. Eventually these advances filter into education—from the graduate level down to the elementary. By the time a scientific theory reaches children, the new model has usually been accepted by the general public.

Though still slow moving, this trickle-down effect proceeds more rapidly today than in the past because of better communication. But that same technology also spreads misinformation, giving educators good reason to be more cautious than researchers. Teachers and curriculum providers don't generally "boldly go where no man has gone before" until they see considerable consensus among research scholars and until new models become well established.

Paradigm shifts in cosmology, as in other disciplines, arise from new data or from evidence not previously considered. For several decades now, progress on resolving the creation-evolution debates has been stymied by the limitations of the databases. Expanding on the information being considered is key to building a better model for the origin and history of the universe, Earth, life, and humanity. The next chapter describes how that expansion can take place.

5

RESOURCES AND STANDARDS FOR RTB'S MODEL

The first time I read Genesis 2, the location of the Garden of Eden really puzzled me. There seemed no way the Pishon, Gihon, Tigris, and Euphrates rivers could come together in one place. The Pishon was thought to flow out of Havilah (south central Arabia), the Gihon from Cush (Ethiopia and Yemen), and the Tigris and Euphrates from Asshur (Mesopotamia).

Not until thirty years later, while writing a book on the first eleven chapters of Genesis, did I discover new research on the history of the Bering and Hecate Straits, which made it possible to calibrate the Genesis 5 and 11 genealogies. That calibration yielded a date for the creation of Adam and Eve in the neighborhood of 50,000 years ago.

At that time Earth was experiencing its last ice age. Ocean levels were much lower, and the pressure of ice on the north latitude landmasses caused several seafloors to rise. That meant it was possible that at the time of Adam and Eve, the present Persian Gulf was dry ground. With Eden located in the southeastern part of the gulf, all four rivers could have easily come together.

As with Eden's location, many conundrums within creation/evolution discussions remain unresolved for lack of data. But a considerable body of data does exist, and it's growing all the time. Assembling as complete a database as possible for the origin and history of the universe, Earth, and life is a crucial first step in the development of new and better models.

Some scientists cling to evolutionism and naturalism because they've not yet seen a more comprehensive scientific model. Likewise, some Christians hold onto either young-earth creationism or some form of theistic evolution because they've not understood a more comprehensive interpretation.

More than twenty years ago, Reasons To Believe (RTB) scientists began to look beyond the usual disciplines of biology, biochemistry, paleontology, and anthropology to build a more extensive database for comprehending creation/evolution issues. Likewise, RTB scholars began examining additional biblical texts, beyond Genesis 1–2, to build a more expansive creation theology.

This increasing awareness of additional scientific and biblical information provided RTB scholars with the tools to reconcile dozens of anomalous features. Consequently, many scientists and theologians frustrated by the lack of progress made by other creation/evolution models became attracted to this cause. Those researchers, in turn, have helped assemble even more extensive databases.

The facts relevant to the construction of the RTB creation model are far more extensive than this book can contain. But the most important resources for extending the explanatory power and predictive success of RTB's model can be set forth. Doing so lays out the most significant principles used for analyzing the origins and history of the cosmos and life.

Biblical Material

RTB's creation model arises from a theistic hypothesis (see step 6 in the scientific method, p. 51) set forth in one specific source—the Bible. This model attempts to integrate all the content found within all sixty-six books included in Scripture.

While acknowledging that a considerable portion of the Bible's creation descriptions contain metaphors and figurative language, RTB maintains that scriptural explanations of natural phenomena are predominantly literal. These creation accounts are considered reliably factual in their declarations about the origin, history, chronology, and current state of the physical universe and life. RTB's model also remains consistent with the creation tenets of the Reformation confessional statements.[1]

Any biblical model's validity depends substantially upon the soundness of human attempts to interpret Scripture. Such a model also rests heavily on the soundness of efforts to integrate those theological understandings with human interpretations of natural data (science). So any weaknesses in RTB's model are assumed to come from human error, *not from the source material itself.*

The RTB model attempts to take into account every biblical passage with recognized relevance to creation and evolution. A list of these references appears on RTB's website.[2] The major biblical creation accounts and their themes are listed in table 5.2.

Table 5.2: The Major Biblical Creation Accounts

Reference	Theme
Genesis 1	Creation chronology: physical perspective
Genesis 2	Creation chronology: spiritual perspective
Genesis 3–5	Human sin and its damage
Genesis 6–9	God's damage control
Genesis 10–11	Global dispersion of humanity
Job 9	Creator's transcendent creation power
Job 34–38	Physical creation's intricacy and complexity
Job 39–42	Soulish creation's intricacy and complexity
Psalm 8	Creation's appeal to humility
Psalm 19	Creation's "speech"
Psalm 33	God's control and sovereignty over nature
Psalm 65	Creator's authority and optimal provision
Psalm 104	Elaboration of physical creation events
Psalm 139	Creation of individual humans
Psalms 147–148	Testimony of the Creator's power, wisdom, and care in nature
Proverbs 8	Creator's existence before creation
Ecclesiastes 1–3	Constancy of physical laws
Ecclesiastes 8–12	Limits to human control of nature
Isaiah 40–51	Origin and development of the universe
Romans 1–8	Purposes of the creation
1 Corinthians 15	Life after life
2 Corinthians 4	Creator's glory in and beyond creation
Colossians 1	Creation's extent
Hebrews 1	Cosmic creation's temporality; role of angels in creation
Hebrews 4	Role of God's rest in creation
2 Peter 3	Creation's end
Revelation 20–22	The new creation

Nature's Material

Since Darwin first attempted to explain life's history, the body of relevant research findings has multiplied many times. In some scientific disciplines, the knowledge base doubles every five years or less. This accumulation of new facts fuels optimism for the rapid emergence of better models for the origins and history of the universe, Earth, life, and humanity.

The sheer abundance of information can pose a problem, however. It forces researchers to focus on increasingly specialized subjects. The task of integrating all the scientific data, even of selecting the most important details, is daunting. As a result, RTB's model-building process requires an enormous team effort. Many scientists besides those on staff have contributed to the assembly and analysis of the science database for RTB's model.

Most of the input comes from the physical and life sciences. Some comes from the humanities. As with any viable model, RTB's must either demonstrate how it anticipates and explains each item in the following list or show valid testable reasons why that item is irrelevant or false. (This list of data has been highly abbreviated. Endnotes indicate where more extensive explanations of specific aspects of RTB's creation model can be found.) Relevant scientific data includes the:

1. beginning of the universe about 13.73 billion years ago[3]
2. beginning of cosmic space-time configuration[4]
3. transcendence of the cause for the beginning of space, time, matter, and energy
4. adequate dimensionality, in addition to length, width, height, and time, to account for the pervasive coexistence of gravity and quantum mechanics (a total of ten dimensions)
5. distribution of matter and energy across the cosmic space-time surface
6. precise values of the physical laws and constants necessary to make physical life possible[5]
7. constancy of the physical laws and constants[6]
8. exquisitely fine-tuned continuous cosmic expansion essential to life[7]
9. continuous cooling of cosmic background radiation from near infinite temperature

10. degree of cosmic uniformity and homogeneity
11. relative abundances of the elements before the advent of stars
12. buildup and relative abundances of nonradiometric elements heavier than helium
13. history of the relative abundances of radiometric isotopes
14. size of the universe[8]
15. cosmic dominance of darkness rather than light
16. location and abundance of exotic matter relative to ordinary matter
17. anthropic principle[9]
18. anthropic principle inequality[10]
19. optimized location for viewing the cosmos[11]
20. optimized time window for viewing the cosmos[12]
21. Milky Way Galaxy's past merging, collision, and close flybys with other galaxies
22. cosmic timing of the peak abundances for uranium and thorium
23. timing and locations of supernovae occurrences at Earth's solar system origin site[13]
24. timing and all other details of an early collision between a Mars-sized body and Earth[14]
25. effects and timing of the Late Heavy Bombardment[15]
26. lack of evidence for possible extraterrestrial intelligence (ETI)[16]
27. lack of any known possible location for the existence of ETI[17]
28. uniqueness of Earth's solar system among all observed planetary systems for the possible support of advanced life
29. absence of detected life on other solar system bodies
30. extraordinary life-essential properties of the Earth-Moon system
31. transfer of the Sun's orbit from its birthing position
32. position of the Sun's orbit relative to the Milky Way Galaxy's co-rotation distance
33. timing of the solar system's last crossing of a spiral arm
34. decline (by a factor of six) in Earth's rotation rate
35. decline (by a factor of five) in Earth's heat from radioactive decay
36. long-term stability and strength of Earth's terrestrial magnetic field and internal dynamo
37. Earth's plate-tectonic history

38. absence of terrestrial prebiotics
39. absence of any known extraterrestrial source of concentrated prebiotics
40. absence of any known amino acids, nucleotides, or 5-carbon sugars in interstellar molecular clouds
41. lack of any abiotic terrestrial source for homochiral building blocks of biomolecules
42. lack of any known extraterrestrial source for homochiral building blocks of biomolecules
43. early timing of life's origin[18]
44. suddenness of life's origin[19]
45. complexity and diversity of Earth's first life
46. lack of a primordial soup[20]
47. predominance of bacterial life for the first 3 billion years of life's history
48. ubiquity and complexity of biochemical design[21]
49. ubiquity and complexity of biochemical organization[22]
50. history and diversity of Earth's sulfate-reducing bacteria[23]
51. history and location of cryptogamic colonies[24]
52. Earth's oxygenation history[25]
53. stellar mass loss during early and late periods of stellar burning
54. stellar brightening during the middle and late periods of stellar burning
55. Sun's dimming (by 15 percent) during its first 1.5 billion years[26]
56. Sun's brightening (by 15 percent) during the past 3 billion years
57. current extreme, short-lived stability of the Sun's luminosity
58. capacity of the past history of life to adjust Earth's atmosphere so as to perfectly compensate for changes in the Sun's luminosity
59. pattern of advances in life's complexity
60. history and abundances of water-soluble elemental (but life-essential) poisons
61. Avalon explosion
62. Cambrian explosion[27]
63. frequency and magnitude of mass speciation events[28]
64. frequency and magnitude of mass extinction events[29]
65. rapidity and diversity of life's recovery from mass extinction events
66. rate of progression from simple to complex life-forms

67. rate of appearance of new species of large body-sized organisms
68. rapid appearance of higher-metabolism, larger-bodied species after each oxygenation event
69. Lazarus taxa phenomena[30]
70. occurrence of biological and biomolecular convergence events (repeated evolutionary outcomes)[31]
71. DNA similarities among diverse species[32]
72. sudden recent cessation of speciation[33]
73. timing of Earth's petroleum production peak[34]
74. timing of Earth's petroleum storage peak[35]
75. history and frequency of multiple-species symbiosis[36]
76. emergence of a self-preservation drive in life
77. emergence of the uniquely human drive for meaning (a sense of hope, purpose, and destiny)
78. emergence of "soulish" behavior as expressed in higher animals
79. diversity of "soulish" behavior in higher animals
80. motivation of higher animals to serve or please humans in diverse ways
81. emergence of "spiritual" behavior as expressed in humans
82. human capacity for altruism
83. human capacity for evil[37]
84. quantity and diversity of expressions of altruism in nature
85. social structure and division of labor among certain insect species
86. timing of vascular plants' origin, diversity, and proliferation
87. ubiquity and diversity of carnivores and parasites[38]
88. ubiquitous optimization of ecological relationships throughout life's history on Earth
89. longevity and stability of various species in the fossil record
90. abundance of transitional forms among large-bodied, low-population species[39]
91. scarcity of transitional forms among small-bodied, large-population species
92. rapid development of optimized ecologies[40]
93. apparent "bad designs" in complex organisms[41]
94. absence of "bad designs" in simple organisms and inorganic structures
95. life spans of various species

96. DNA similarities and differences among humans, Neanderthals, and chimpanzees[42]
97. low population levels of hominid species
98. absence of any evidence for evolution within hominid species
99. timing and other characteristics of humanity's origin[43]
100. cultural "big bangs" in the arrival of jewelry, art, technology, clothing, communication
101. changes in the human life span[44]
102. uniqueness of human characteristics and capabilities[45]
103. over-endowment for humanity's basic survival[46]
104. location of humanity's origin
105. timing of the Neolithic revolution in human culture
106. descent of modern humans from one man[47] (or a few men and from one woman or a few women)
107. narrow physical limits on the time window for human civilization[48]
108. broad physical limits on the time window for simple life-forms
109. optimization of the physical laws and constants for restraining evil

RTB's goal is to explain these data sets in a manner that upholds both biblical and scientific integrity. As with all models, RTB's model can only benefit from competition—the more models that fully account for the preceding data (for either evolution or creation), the better. The best models will continually undergo revision and refinement as test results accumulate and research advances. As long as participants remain committed to following the facts wherever they lead, they can work in partnership through failures, successes, and disagreements toward solving the remaining mysteries.

Model-Building Principles

Several commitments infuse RTB's model with the potential for growing explanatory power and scope. To the best of our ability, RTB is committed to keeping or maintaining:

- simplicity first—the incomplete or poorly understood, inadequately tested, and highly complex will be interpreted in light of that which is simple, better understood, and more thoroughly tested (see "Why Simple Sciences First?" p. 68).

* the big picture first—explanations for the overall phenomenon precede attempts to interpret and understand details.

* biblical integrity—hermeneutical principles will be wholly applied to interpret and integrate all biblical data.

* scientific integrity—the scientific method will be wholly applied to well-established, observationally tested data.

* humility—nature and students of nature, Scripture and students of Scripture, and human limitations will be respected.

* continual improvement—because there is always more to learn and understand about any phenomenon, the model will be constantly updated and revised.

* diligence and creativity in generating predictions—so RTB's model can be tested by discoveries generated as scientific and theological research advance.

An additional RTB commitment is the most important—a commitment to follow, regardless of personal cost, wherever the evidence leads.

RTB's commitments should reassure skeptics on all sides—those who say the metaphysical realm doesn't exist, those who complain that they won't be allowed to ask hard questions, those who worry that the Bible's message may be given too much or too little consideration, and those who worry that the achievements of science and scientists may be belittled. The high regard for objectivity means that dogmatism of any kind will not trump the truth. Upholding these commitments is necessary to help dispel doubts and concerns about the model-building process—that's why RTB sets them forth.

Another RTB goal is for its model to help restore the partnership once enjoyed by scientific and biblical researchers as they considered some of life's greatest questions. This effort attempts to integrate the achievements of science, philosophy, and theology.

Sometimes the presuppositions and research principles undergirding other creation/evolution models are either hidden or incompletely spelled out. RTB's creation model differs in that regard. The biblical, theological, philosophical, and scientific presuppositions on which the model rests

Why Simple Sciences First?

Simple sciences are not "simple" because they are easy to understand. In contrast to complex sciences, simple sciences are disciplines in which the phenomena being studied can be well-defined by mathematical equations. These equations of state effectively describe the past, present, and future behavior of particular phenomena. As a result of this simplicity, determinations about possible causal agents contain less ambiguity and thus permit rigorous testing. In this regard, philosophical and theological conclusions may be more easily drawn from the simple sciences than from the complex.

Specifically, RTB's scientific case for the God of the Bible as the Designer and Creator of all nature goes from mathematics to astronomy and physics, to planetary science and geophysics, to geology and chemistry, to biochemistry and microbiology, to botany, zoology, anthropology, and sociology. Building the model in these incremental steps aids stability and the integration process.

It also allows for progressive evaluation of the evidence—to test whether the indications of a supernatural, caring, intelligent Designer grow progressively stronger or weaker. If compelling evidence for the Bible's God becomes discernible in the simple sciences, then it should reveal itself in the complex sciences as well—with two important prerequisites: (1) the database must be sufficiently complete, and (2) testing must be thorough and persistent enough to expose evidence of design within the complexity.

are clearly stated for everyone to see. Ongoing investigation can either falsify or confirm these assumptions.

While some creation/evolution models attempt to explain only the biological, geophysical, or cosmic realms, the RTB creation model attempts to integrate and address all these disciplines. Rather than focus strictly on nature's what, where, and when, this model also tackles the how and why. RTB acknowledges that such a comprehensive approach requires a willingness to continually expand and improve its model.

While attempting to provide the best answers to questions about the origin and history of the universe, Earth, life, and humanity—answers corresponding to both physical and spiritual reality—the RTB creation model invites a response. Its builders hope to stimulate the development of equally comprehensive competing creation/evolution models. Such competition will generate refinements at a faster pace than when one model stands alone.

Understanding RTB's Model

The next eight chapters present only the highlights of RTB's creation model (details are available in other RTB books) and demonstrate how this model fares in light of emerging research findings.

• Chapter 6 describes the core biblical, theological, and philosophical foundations of the RTB creation model.

• Chapters 7 through 13 test the scientific validity of these foundations and show how scientific advances during the past few decades have actually enhanced the model's explanatory power. This material progresses from the simpler science disciplines (mathematics, astronomy, and physics) to the more complex (geology and chemistry, anthropology, and sociology). These chapters move from the large scale to the small—from the universe as a whole to the Milky Way Galaxy, the solar system, Earth, Earth's surface and life-forms, then on to the cities, farms, mines, and resorts where humans live, work, and play. Not only do these chapters consider questions of causation, but they also discuss some intriguing how and why questions.

• Chapter 14 addresses what some skeptics describe as the most difficult and complex challenges to RTB's creation model.

• The final three chapters (16–18) suggest ways the RTB model can be tested further through the success or failure of research predictions and through development of new testing standards, tools, and practices.

The standards for building RTB's model were carefully set and are constantly kept in mind. Its resources are continually being collected and compiled into databases. The next chapter unfolds the model's biblical and theological aspects.

6

THE BIBLICAL STRUCTURE OF RTB's CREATION MODEL

For a kid in Canada, snow meant snowball fights. After watching several of these battles from a safe distance, I figured out the key to winning—the design and sturdiness of one's snow fort. Therefore, while other kids in our neighborhood tried to make the best snowballs, I experimented with my fort's design.

Using various kinds of snow, I built walls then tested them to see how intense a snowball fusillade they could withstand. I soon found out that snow fort strength depends on three factors: the average size of falling snowflakes (the bigger the better), the atmosphere's humidity (around 90 percent was ideal), and the ambient temperature (about two or three degrees below freezing was best).

When conditions weren't optimal, I stayed inside and read. However, when nature cooperated, I went outside to build a sturdy structure, provoke an attack, and then "retreat" to my fort and stash of ammunition.

Constructing a good model to explain the origin and history of the universe and life also requires a well-built structure that can withstand attacks. Over fifty years ago British cosmologist Sir Fred Hoyle, though much opposed to the Christian faith, conceded that the Bible offered a worthy cosmological foundation. He wrote, "There is a good deal of cosmology in the Bible. . . . It is a remarkable conception."[1]

While the Bible is not a scientific textbook, it contains a great quantity of information about the origin, structure, and history of the universe and life—more than any other religious text (see table 5.2, p. 61). These descriptions also uniquely predict scientific discoveries thousands of years ahead of time. Furthermore, the Bible frequently exhorts readers to discover the Creator's handiwork in nature, referring to it as a second and complementary revelation from him.

This surpassingly abundant commentary on the natural realm makes the Bible the best possible choice on which to erect a theistic model—one that is scientifically testable. Far from being just another ancient Near Eastern creation myth, the account of the six creation days in Genesis 1, Job 38–39, Psalm 104, and Proverbs 8 offers a sweeping, plausible creation narrative. Its structure reflects the classic scientific method. Each feature of RTB's model emerged as this method was applied. (See chapter 4, pp. 49–58, and Appendix A, "The Scientific Method's Biblical Origins," pp. 257–58.)

Four Key Points

RTB's creation model rests upon four cornerstone inferences from Scripture:

1. **Dual revelation:** the Creator's attributes (truth, love, wisdom, power, etc.) ensure the harmony of his creative works (nature) with his verbally inspired Word (the Bible).
2. **Creation purposes:** nature fulfills the Creator's stated and implied reasons for creating.
3. **Creation chronology:** the Creator transcends creation; the realm of nature has a beginning and an end, a before and an after.
4. **Detectability of the divine:** close and careful study of nature's record can reveal evidence of the Creator's miraculous interventions.

These four inferences lay the foundation for every component of RTB's creation model. Given their structural significance, the four cornerstones provide the context for understanding some of the most intriguing characteristics of creation.

Dual Revelation

The Bible repeatedly declares that God is truthful and does not lie in word or in deed (see Num. 23:19; Ps. 119:160; Isa. 45:18–19; John 8:31–32;

10:35; Titus 1:2; Heb. 6:18; 1 John 5:6). He is unchanging (Ps. 33:11; Lam. 3:22–24; Mal. 3:6; Heb. 6:17; James 1:17). He is almighty (Gen. 17:1; 35:11; Job 40:2; Isa. 44:6; Rev. 4:8; 11:17; 21:22). He is the personification of wisdom and love (Prov. 1–9; 1 John 4:7–12). Therefore, God's dual revelation through the record of nature and through the words of the Bible must be trustworthy, free of contradiction and error.

One of the great Reformation creeds, the Belgic Confession, describes this crucial cornerstone:

> Article 2: The Means by Which We Know God
>
> We know him by two means: First, by the creation, preservation, and government of the universe, since that universe is before our eyes like a beautiful book in which all creatures, great and small, are as letters to make us ponder the invisible things of God: his eternal power and his divinity, as the apostle Paul says in Romans 1:20. All these things are enough to convict men and to leave them without excuse. Second, he makes himself known to us more openly by his holy and divine Word, as much as we need in this life, for his glory and for the salvation of his own.[2]

The RTB creation model thus implies that the record of nature and the words of the Bible will always be in harmony with no possibility of contradiction. However, science is not the same as the record of nature. The disciplines of science involve human interpretation. In some instances these interpretations can be faulty and/or incomplete.

Similarly, Christian theology is not the same as the words of Scripture. Like science, theology involves human interpretation, which may be inaccurate. So conflicts between science and theology don't necessarily falsify or damage RTB's creation model. Rather, such discord provides opportunities for exposing incomplete understanding and faulty interpretations and for discovering a deeper, more complete knowledge of creation's story and history.

Creation Purposes

The Bible says no finite mind can fully grasp all of God's reasons for creating the universe, Earth, and all life—and for creating them in his chosen manner (see Isa. 55:8–9; Rom. 11:34; 1 Cor. 2:16). The apostle Peter comments that even angels lack full understanding of God's plans and purposes (1 Pet. 1:12). Nevertheless, the Bible explicitly states several reasons God created as he did and implies others, including his intention to:

- express his attributes, specifically his glory, righteousness, majesty, power, wisdom, and love;
- provide a suitable habitat for all physical life and for humanity in particular until the stage is set for his entirely new creation;
- relate to human beings, revealing not only his glory but also the wonders and weaknesses of their nature;
- supply physical resources for the rapid development of civilization and technology and the achievement of global human occupation;
- provide the necessary array of life-forms in the appropriate abundances and geographies to serve and please humanity and support civilization;
- supply the best possible viewing conditions for humans to discover, through a careful examination of the cosmos, his existence and attributes;
- set up the optimal physical conditions, including an optimal human life span, for conquering sin and evil in the quickest and most efficient manner;
- provide the physical theatre for carrying out his plan of redemption through Jesus Christ;
- provide a means for the instruction of the angels;
- demonstrate his attributes—specifically his glory, righteousness, power, wisdom, and love—in the incarnation of Jesus Christ;
- offer all people a way to live forever in his presence in a new creation, apart from sin and death and every consequence of rebellion against him;
- equip all who accept the offer of immortality to fulfill their roles in both the present and new creations and to enjoy their rewards as a result.

This limited list of God's purposes for creating may help answer some troubling *why* questions—questions such as "Why would a good and all-powerful God create a universe that yields so much human suffering?"[3]

Creation Chronology

A critical distinctive of RTB's creation model is its perspective on the cosmos as part of a larger reality. The Bible offers a wide-angle view of creation's story that shows what happens before, during, and after.

Before the beginning of the universe and space and time God existed (see Isa. 40:28; 41:4; 43:10–11; 44:6; 45:14–25; 48:12–17; John 1:1–4; 3:34–35; 8:58; 10:15, 30–38; 14:9–14; 17:1–26; Col. 1:15–20; 2 Thess. 2:13–16; Heb. 1:1–13; Rev. 4:8; 21:6; 22:13). The three members of the Godhead related to one another in ways that expressed their love, beauty, goodness, and wisdom, among other characteristics (Gen. 1:1; John 1:1–3; Col. 1:15–17; Heb. 11:3). God planned, prior to the creation of time, to give the hope of eternal life to future human beings (Titus 1:2) and grant them his grace (2 Tim. 1:9). Angels and the angelic realm may or may not have been created before the universe began, but Job 38:4–7 says that they witnessed God laying the foundations of the earth.

This present creation is intended to prepare individuals for the new creation. God uses this current, familiar realm to reveal himself and draw those people who are willing (whom he has called) into a relationship with himself. According to Scripture, everything in and about this creation contributes to the larger creation purposes described in the preceding list.

The new creation to come is an entirely new realm (see Isa. 65:16–17; 66:22; Rev. 21–22). The most significant feature is that God and his people will live there together face-to-face, by choice, without the effects of decay, pain, suffering, evil, and darkness (physical and spiritual). Yet individuals will still be fully capable of personal, purposeful loving action and interaction.

This new creation is not merely paradise restored. It is radically different from the Garden of Eden (see Genesis 2)—framed by different dimensions and governed by different laws.[4] A critical distinctive of the biblical worldview, this promise separates the Bible's creation story from all others. The new creation sets RTB's model apart from other models describing the origin and history of the universe and life.

A sequential outline of RTB's model summarizes the creation chronology from the beginning of this creation to the appearance of the new one:

1. God (who exists apart from space and time) caused the universe of matter, energy, space, and time to come into existence.

2. God guided the expansion and cooling of the universe toward the formation of a suitable planetary home for humanity.

3. God successively transformed Earth and the solar system through six major creative stages in preparation for human habitation. During this time he successively layered increasingly advanced plant and animal life to maximize support for humanity's global expansion and civilization.

4. God personally and directly created Adam, the first human, then placed him in Eden. The Creator taught Adam to care for this magnificent garden, then created Eve to be his mate and helper.

5. God allowed Lucifer, the most beautiful and powerful of his angelic creatures and the perpetrator of a rebellion against God in the supernatural realm, to enter Eden. There, Lucifer was permitted to entice Adam and Eve toward autonomy and self-exaltation.

6. Adam and Eve defied God's authority, thereby introducing sin (and the evil it produces) into the earthly environment.

7. God banished Adam and Eve from Eden, removed their access to physical immortality (the Tree of Life), and later shortened the life span of their descendents. These actions restrained the expression of evil and made way for redemption.

8. God chose to communicate—through Abraham and his progeny—specific instructions for his plan to redeem humanity from their hopeless plight. This plan, along with God's promise to fulfill it, gave humankind hope.

9. God came to Earth, taking on a human nature (Jesus Christ), resisted temptation to sin, and paid sin's death penalty on humanity's behalf. Motivated by love, Jesus endured death on a cross so that anyone, through faith, may receive justification before God, fellowship with him, and the capacity to grow in godliness. This provision includes the promise of eternal life with God.

10. Jesus Christ conquered death, proved his resurrection by appearing physically to hundreds of eyewitnesses, and then ascended into the transcendent realm (heaven), where he is preparing the new creation for all who accept his provision.

11. Jesus Christ commissioned his followers to spread the good news about his offer—with gentleness, respect, and a clear conscience—to every person on the planet.

12. Jesus Christ will remove from his presence all who refuse his gift and reject God's authority. He will escort his people into the new creation, where they will live forever face-to-face with him. Once there, his people will fulfill new leadership roles in his service.

This chronology, as related to the fulfillment of God's purposes for creation, delineates the time frame for RTB's model. It is the key to understanding the model's features.

Detectability of the Divine

The entire chronology of God's plan for humanity rests on the *reality* of a supernatural realm. Belief in that reality is not merely subjective—nature provides observable, measurable verification. Science provides the means (e.g., cosmology and biochemistry).

The Bible claims that creation began in a miracle and that it unfolds in a miraculous way for the benefit of humanity, sustained moment by moment under the Creator's constant care (see chapters 7–13). Scripture describes three different kinds of creation miracles:

Transcendent miracles involve acts God performed outside or beyond the limitations imposed by the laws of physics and the space-time dimensions of the universe. Obvious examples from the Bible include the creation of cosmic space-time dimensions and the physical laws as well as humanity's spiritual nature.

Transformation miracles involve God's direct actions to refashion a particular aspect of his created realm to produce something of much higher complexity and functionality. These miracles took place within the laws of physics and space-time dimensions of the universe.

God worked with what already exists in a manner that yields results far beyond what natural processes alone could, given space and time constraints. Two examples are the origin of purely physical life (see chapter 9, pp. 135–46) and the fashioning of Earth, its continents, and oceans with the exact features necessary to sustain advanced life on an abundant, diverse, and global scale (see chapter 10, pp. 149–64).

Sustaining miracles involve God's continuous work throughout cosmic history to ensure that everything in the universe maintains the just-right delicately balanced conditions necessary to support human life. According to Colossians 1:16–17, "For by him [Christ] all things were created: things in heaven and on earth, visible and invisible . . . and in him all things hold together." If that's true, scientists can expect to discover that the laws and constants of physics—as well as all discoverable characteristics of the universe, Earth, and life—manifest exquisite, continual fine-tuning for fulfilling the purposes God set for them (see pp. 93–132).

Extensive study of Scripture also indicates that God performed relatively few miracles of the transformational or transcendent types. He did as few creation miracles in those categories as necessary to achieve his purposes. The Bible further indicates such miracles were episodic—short periods when several or many transformational and/or transcendent miracles may have occurred separated by long time spans during which none took place. According to the biblical pattern, transformational miracles far outnumbered transcendent.

This rarity of transcendent and transformational creation miracles helps explain why many scientists, especially those focused on narrowly specialized disciplines, fail to detect God's involvement in the natural realm. The historical context of such miracles is part of their explanation. From a biblical perspective, creation miracles occurred "in the beginning," or during the six creation epochs. The sixth creation epoch ended with the creation of humanity.[5] Then, on the seventh day, God ceased from his work of creating, and his "day of rest" continues even now.[6] So only research probing the era before human history would yield evidence of these miracles.

Characteristics of Creation

No book could possibly narrate and describe everything that has happened in the universe to date. The Bible cannot possibly contain every detail of natural history. So the fact that the planet Neptune isn't mentioned does not mean it doesn't exist.

Likewise, no team of researchers, however global, learned, transgenerational, and well-funded, can ever discover and record every fact of nature. So a perfect and complete creation model will stay beyond reach, and some mysteries will always remain. Yet the existing biblical content does account for many of the most significant characteristics of this present creation.

God's biblically stated purposes for the natural realm provide essential insight into many issues pertaining to creation and evolution. In particular, the Bible addresses either explicitly or implicitly what scientists should discover about the:

- physical laws and constants
- seemingly "imperfect" designs
- origin, dimensions, and structure of the universe
- cosmic time scale
- progression from simple to complex life
- interruptions to life (mass extinction events), including the flood of Noah
- re-creations of life (mass speciation events)
- existence of common designs among creatures

Examining and discussing these characteristics from the perspective of the Bible's story supplies further insight into the foundations of RTB's testable model.

Physical Laws and Constants

Through the prophet Jeremiah, God says the laws governing the heavens and Earth are "fixed" (Jer. 33:25). He determined them from the beginning, and their values align precisely with his unfolding plans. RTB's biblical creation model expects scientific research and exploration of the cosmos to show that physical laws do not vary to any significant degree throughout space and time.

Some young-earth creationists argue that Adam and Eve's rebellion against God's authority brought about major changes in physics—either the first appearance of decay, a dramatic rise in the level and/or rate of decay, or a huge decline in a hypothetical divine counterbalancing action. Neither the biblical text nor the scientific data seem to warrant such assertions.

From the beginning, the second law of thermodynamics has been in continuous operation to allow many physical realities to exist. Genesis (along with other Bible passages) affirms that sunlight, starlight, metabolism of food, and Adam's human work all predate human sin.[7] This physical evidence validates Paul's writing in Romans, where he explains that "creation was subjected to frustration, not by its own choice, but by the will of the one who subjected it, in hope that the creation itself will be liberated from its bondage to decay" (8:20–21). The slightest variation in any of the physical laws would have rendered many life-sustaining functions impossible.[8]

Seemingly "Imperfect" Designs

Throughout the account of the six creation days in Genesis 1, the narrator quotes God's evaluation of his creation as "good." This assessment appears six times (see Gen. 1:4, 10, 12, 18, 21, 25). Finally, as God surveys the whole sweep of his creative work, he calls it "very good" (Gen. 1:31).

Some evolutionists and young-earth creationists interpret these words to mean "perfect." Evolutionists point out apparent imperfections in nature as evidence against biblical creation, while young-earth creationists frequently blame sin for any apparent imperfection. But the scriptural context does not necessitate either interpretation.

"Very good" more reasonably implies that nature manifests appropriate design for fulfillment of its purposes. The ideal design for a particular purpose must not be confused with ultimate perfection. This current realm is optimal in that it perfectly suits God's plans—the triumph of life over death, good over evil, love over apathy, light over darkness, and freedom over bondage.[9]

Achievement of these victories requires the operation of thermodynamic laws, including the pervasive law of decay. The Bible explains why.

Creation's "bondage to decay" plays a crucial part in God's plan to bring his followers to "glorious freedom" (see Rom. 8:20–23). The decay process (including the second law of thermodynamics) implies that God's very good designs degrade over time. Researchers may expect optimally designed creations to gradually accumulate imperfections, perhaps at least partly for the purpose of heightening human yearning for and anticipation of the perfect creation to come.

Origin, Dimensions, and Structure of the Universe

Strict naturalists explain the dimensions and structure of the universe essentially as happenstance. They can observe and measure "what is," but meaning is assigned only by humans.

Creation myths attempt to do more. While many refer to "the beginning," they typically pick up *after* something already exists. Their stories don't begin at the beginning. Only the Bible gives an abundance of specific, testable detail about the cosmic beginning and ending—data that proves accurate—written prior to the second century AD. The following details (with the exception of 9 and 10) have already been confirmed by twentieth-century cosmologists.

1. The universe has a beginning in finite time (see Gen. 1:1; 2:3–4; Ps. 148:5; Isa. 40:26; 42:5; 45:18; John 1:3; Col. 1:15–17; Heb. 11:3).

2. The beginning of space and time coincides with the beginning of the physical universe (Gen. 1:1; Col. 1:15–17; 2 Tim. 1:9; Titus 1:2; Heb. 11:3).

3. The material universe was not made from that which is material, visible, or detectable (Heb. 11:3).

4. The universe has been continuously expanding from the beginning of space and time (Job 9:8; Ps. 104:2; Isa. 40:22; 42:5; 44:24; 45:12; 48:13; 51:13; Jer. 10:12; 51:15; Zech. 12:1).

5. The expansion of the universe appears precisely guided for the benefit of life (Job 9:8; Isa. 44:24; 45:12; 48:13).

6. The expansion of the universe resembles the spreading out and setting up of a tent (Ps. 104:2; Isa. 40:22).

7. The universe functions according to fixed physical laws (Jer. 33:25).

8. The entire universe is subject to those physical laws (Rom. 8:20–22).

9. The universe has an ending in finite time (Job 14:12; Eccles. 12:2; Isa. 34:4; 51:6; 65:17; 66:22; Matt. 24:35; Heb. 1:10–12; 12:27–28; 2 Peter 3:7,10–13; Rev. 21:1–5).

10. At its end, the universe will roll up like a scroll and vanish in a burst of extreme heat (Isa. 34:4; 2 Peter 3:7, 10; Rev. 6:14).

Statements 4, 7, and 8 imply the universe must get colder as it grows older. Statement 6 suggests that just as a tent is a surface with no physical center, so too the universe has no physical center or anything either interior or exterior to its surface. Thousands of years prior to any scientific speculation or research into big bang cosmology, the Bible predicted all of the fundamental attributes of a big bang universe. In its account of the demise of the cosmos, Scripture may even imply what kind of big bang universe this is (see "Time Limits" below).

Creation Time Scales

Sometimes evolutionists see an ancient cosmos as evidence against creation. They wonder why God would waste billions of years if all he wanted was a home for humans.[10]

On this issue, young-earth creationists agree. They claim God didn't need all that time, so six twenty-four-hour creation days a few thousand years ago make more sense.

Scripture's time markers for the creation-week events address both interpretations. Numerous metaphors (interpreted relative to one another) imply great age—eons as opposed to a few millennia of cosmic and geologic history. God's eternal existence is compared to the duration of the mountains, oceans, rivers, hills, soil, and fields (see Ps. 90:2; Prov. 8:24–26; Eccles. 1:4–10). Micah 6:2 refers directly to the antiquity of Earth's foundations. Habakkuk 3:6 declares the mountains "ancient" and the hills "age-old." Peter says the heavens and earth existed "long ago" (2 Peter 3:5).

Time Limits

The Bible explicitly states that this universe will not last forever. The apostle Peter declared, "The heavens will disappear with a roar; the elements will be destroyed by fire. . . . That day will bring about the destruction of the heavens by fire, and the elements will melt in the heat" (2 Peter 3:10, 12). Isaiah wrote, "All the stars of the heavens will be dissolved and the sky rolled up like a scroll" (Isa. 34:4).

These Bible passages are metaphorical, and some scholars debate how literally they should be interpreted. However, one class of big bang models predicts a cosmic end remarkably consistent with their heat imagery.[11]

The ekpyrotic big bang models propose that instead of the universe being laid out as a ten-dimensional flat sheet, the sheet is folded to form a gigantic "U." That means one ten-dimensional flat surface parallels another. If the two surfaces are close enough together (about a millimeter apart) for a long enough time (billions of years), a quantum fluctuation in the space-time fabric of one of the two surfaces could peel (bump up or down) and make contact with a quantum fluctuation in the space-time fabric of the other. If that contact were to happen, the space-time fabric of the entire universe would curl up and disappear, taking the whole universe with it in a fiery implosion.

Biblical metaphors about the size of the cosmos—the expanse of stars is described as being as numerous as Earth's grains of sand—also indicate great age (see Gen. 13:16; 15:5; 22:17; Jer. 33:22; Heb. 11:12). Given star formation rates, average distances between stars, and the fixed velocity of light, the age must be more than several hundred million years.[12]

According to the Bible, God's unlimited power meant he could have chosen any time scale, short or long, to perform his creative work (see Isa. 40–48). Concerning the six "days" of creation, the Hebrew allows for more than one literal interpretation. In Genesis 1, the word translated "day," *yôm*, could have any of four different definitions: (1) a portion of the daylight hours, (2) the entire daylight segment of a twenty-four-hour day, (3) a twenty-four-hour day, and (4) a long but finite time period.[13] (Unlike English or Modern Hebrew, biblical Hebrew had no other word for a finite era or epoch.)

RTB's model posits that the fourth definition shows the greatest consistency with all the biblical creation accounts (see chapter 5, p. 61).[14] Chapters 10–12 (pp. 149–93) discuss why God would have taken so long for the creation process.

Progression from Simple to Complex Life

Long before anyone possessed tools to study life's history, biblical writers described the simplest meaning for *evolution*—"change with respect to time." Genesis 1 and 2, Job 38–42, and Psalm 104 all depict a series of purposeful and progressive creation events—from the origin of simpler life-forms (e.g., bacteria) to the more complex (e.g., human beings)—a pattern no ancient person could have known. Nor would natural processes necessarily yield that particular order.

Genesis 1:2–5 implies that the first life created on Earth was simple marine life,[15] and it appeared while Earth was still emerging from extremely hostile-to-life conditions.[16] With supporting material from Job 38–42 and Psalm 104, Genesis 1 outlines the progression brought about by divine intervention—primitive marine life to plant life on Earth's newly forming continents, then swarms of small sea animals, birds, and sea mammals, followed by three kinds of advanced land mammals, and finally, human beings.[17]

This progression in complexity takes place on more than one level. The biblical creation accounts claim the first life-forms were purely physical in nature. Relatively late in creation history, the first "soulish" animals appeared. These unique new creatures, predominantly birds and mammals, showed some capacity for emotion, volition, and intellect. They could relate to and nurture not only other members of their species but later human beings as well. (Soulish animals can interpret tone of voice and respond to training.)[18]

Scripture indicates that all life on Earth was designed to serve humanity. Soulish life-forms please humans in two different ways: first through their physical bodies and second through their "souls." For example, a dog will use his body to protect the person to whom he feels great loyalty and affection.

According to the Bible, a creature's soulish characteristics may not at all be related to its physical features. For example, Job 39 explains that soulish animals whose physical designs are similar to one another, like the donkey and the horse, nonetheless can manifest very different soulish designs. The difference becomes especially noticeable when these animals begin relating to people.

The last species to appear on Earth, human beings (*Homo sapiens sapiens*), manifests not only far greater soulish capacities but also a unique characteristic the Bible identifies as "spirit."[19] No other species, past or present, expresses spirituality as defined by an innate:

- awareness of right and wrong, or conscience;
- awareness of mortality and concerns about what lies beyond death;
- hunger for hope, purpose, and destiny;
- compulsion to discover and create;
- capacity for analysis, mathematics, and meditation;
- capacity to recognize beauty, truth, logic, and absolutes;
- propensity to worship and communicate with a deity.

With respect to soulish and spiritual animals, the Hebrew verbs in the relevant texts—*āśâ, bārā', and yāṣar*—indicate the direct miraculous intervention of God in the introduction of each particular type of creature. Such verbs seem to preclude the possibility that God worked through natural-process evolution to produce these special characteristics. Any viable creation and/or evolution model must account for the emergence not only of Earth's first life but also of soulish and then spiritual life.

Interruptions and Re-creations of Life

The Bible suggests that life on Earth was seriously disrupted on more than one occasion. Perhaps it was even extinguished on some large scale (see Ps. 104:29–30). But always life returned, each time with just-right characteristics suited to the changing environment.

Meanwhile, the planet was gaining the optimal biomass and biodiversity to support humans. Earth gradually built up sufficient biodeposits for the launch and rapid development of global human civilization and technology. The Creator appears to have used massive creation, extinction, and re-creation (or speciation) events to store up certain resources—including the layers of organic material, deposits of fossil fuels, and deposits of ores and minerals—all ideal for human civilization and technology. Psalm 104:27–30 depicts this cycle:

> These [creatures] all look to you
> to give them food at the proper time.
> When you give it to them,
> they gather it up;
> when you open your hand,
> they are satisfied with good things.
> When you hide your face,
> they are terrified;
> when you take away their breath,
> they die and return to the dust.
> When you send your Spirit,
> they are created,
> and you renew the face of the earth.

The story of life, death, and new life is part of RTB's biblical model. It does not contradict New Testament statements about the kind of death that originated with Adam.[20] Romans 5:12 clarifies this position: "Sin entered the world through one man, and death through sin, and in this way death came to all men, because all sinned."

This death, introduced by Adam's sin, applies strictly to humans.[21] The whole of Scripture confirms that only humans, among all life created on Earth, can (and do) sin. Therefore, this "death through sin" applies to humans alone, not to plants and animals. In addition, the passage states specifically that this "death came to all men." It does not say "to all creation" or "to all creatures." The verses make no apparent reference to plant or animal life, nor do other parallel passages (see 1 Cor. 15:20–23).

Scripture specifically describes one particular interruption to life—the flood in Noah's day. It occurred at a time when humanity was still localized and, according to Genesis 6:5, had become dangerously and catastrophically corrupt. For the sake of humanity's long-term survivability, God sent a flood to cleanse the earth of all but one family of humans. The soulish animals associated with the reprobate humans were also destroyed.

This flood was more catastrophic to humans than any other calamity before or since. It nearly extinguished humanity. However, the biblical text does not lump all Earth's geological cataclysms into this one event as some young-earth creationists insist. Careful analysis of relevant biblical texts shows that Noah's flood, though "universal" with respect to humanity, was geographically limited.[22]

Common Designs among Creatures

Unlike standard evolutionary models, RTB's biblical creation model predicts common designs even among diverse species. Many Bible passages, particularly Job 38–41 and Psalms 104 and 139, suggest that when God created, he used optimal designs. It makes sense that what worked well for one species likely worked well for other creatures too. Therefore, RTB's model anticipates scientific discoveries of many shared designs—or common morphology. For example, the lung has an unsurpassed, even unsurpassable,[23] respiratory efficiency for large-bodied, air-breathing animals. Therefore, a biblical perspective anticipates that all large air-breathing animal species would have lungs for respiration.

Pervasive common morphological designs demand pervasive common biochemical designs. Because morphological features are specified and programmed by DNA, DNA similarities should be widespread.

These similarities would be most pronounced in a biblical creation model's structure. One God—the Bible's wise and loving Creator—would likely use the same DNA blueprints for optimized designs again and again. Naturalistic models for life, based on chance or random outcomes, would predict a wide range of DNA diversity (see chapter 10, pp. 164–69).

Latitude of Biblical Language

In some cases, biblical authors used nonspecific language to describe God's creative activity. For example, the Hebrew verb *hāyâ* expresses how light first appeared on Earth's surface (see Gen. 1:3). It asserts establishment of the water cycle (Gen. 1:6), emergence of continental landmasses (Gen. 1:9), and the first appearance of the Sun, Moon, and stars on Earth's surface (Gen. 1:14). The Hebrew verb *dāshā'* depicts the production of plants on the continents (Gen. 1:11).

Both *hāyâ* and *dāshā'* allow some flexibility in the interpretation of how these phenomena came about. Their range of use encompasses the possibility of either a transformational miracle or a set of well-timed sustaining miracles or some combination of the two.[24] In other words, the plants and swarms of small sea creatures could have been the result of:

1. God's direct momentary miraculous intervention,
2. God's guidance and timing of natural processes, or
3. both, in any combination.

Therefore, the biblical data alone cannot settle the debate over exactly how plants and small sea life originated. In this instance, the record of nature holds greater detail and specificity.

For other events, the text gives a clear indication of causality. The use of a more specific verb, *bārā'*, indicates that the universe came about through a transcendent miracle. The use of two Hebrew verbs, *bārā'* and *'āśâ*, for soulish animal and human life, implies that these creatures came about through a combination of transcendent and transformational miracles. Genesis and other biblical texts also seem to place some boundaries around speciation, saying certain creatures reproduce "according to their kinds" (see Gen. 1:11–12, 21, 24–25; Lev. 19:19).

God's Creative Options

The Bible ascribes both *immanence* and *transcendence* to the Creator. It says God fills the entirety of his creation; his presence permeates the whole of it. Yet the universe does not and cannot contain him.

God's transcendence means he exists in complete independence from matter and energy, the laws and constants of physics, and the space-time dimensions of the cosmos. His freedom to operate and create knows no boundaries.

A very different world could have been created. The New Testament's closing chapters show how different God's future creation will be. Reve-

lation 21 and 22, along with other passages in Scripture, describe how the
new creation will operate by radically different physics and dimensionality.
Some of these characteristics apparently include:[25]

- a much more expansive habitat for humanity than is possible in
  this universe
- radically different creation laws and constants (no thermodynamics,
  no gravity, no electromagnetism)
- no decay, no death, no pain, no evil, no regrets, no grief
- no darkness, no shadows
- no sun, no stars, and yet light everywhere
- different dimensionality
- unimaginable splendor, joy, beauty, peace, and love
- greatly expanded access to knowledge
- multiple simultaneously intimate relationships that eclipse the need
  or desire for marriage (or sex) and families
- unlimited relational delight
- unlimited capacity for pleasure
- wholly meaningful and satisfying work
- opportunity to lead and instruct angels

The apostle Paul claims that in this lifetime no one can possibly imagine
how glorious and rewarding life in the new creation will be (see 1 Cor.
2:9).

The characteristics of the universe, Earth, and life reflect God's choice
and design. RTB's model, therefore, expects that his purposes infuse
meaning into every observed property of the universe and life. Connections between revealed purposes and discernible features, including
those for physical life and the laws of physics, should become clearer as
understanding increases.

Anticipation of Discovery

The connections between the biblical and scientific data set forth in these
pages may seem obvious. In other words, they may appear as "hindsight"
links—as if the interpreter worked backward from current knowledge to

find biblical texts that fit. Or perhaps biblical manuscripts were altered over the years to fit emerging discoveries. Yet three considerations are worth keeping in mind:

1. Greek manuscripts that contain the entire New Testament date from the fourth century AD. Portions date back more than 1,900 years.
2. The most recent Old Testament creation account, Isaiah 40–51, dates back more than 2,700 years. One of the Dead Sea Scrolls dates to second century BC. It contains the entire book of Isaiah, with content essentially identical to that found in much later manuscripts. Such an early date reasonably eliminates any possibility for significant tampering with the text.
3. People have become aware only in the past few centuries that (a) the history of life on Earth progresses from simple to complex; (b) the laws of physics are fixed and apply to the entire universe; (c) the universe is continuously expanding; (d) Earth once had no continents; and (e) conditions on early Earth were extremely hostile to life, and so on.

The list for modern discoveries forecast in Scripture could go on to include many more facts about stars, cosmic darkness, animal husbandry, farming, medicine, sanitation, meteorology, and tectonics, for example. In second century BC (or even in the New Testament era), the most learned scholars had little or no knowledge of these facts about the natural realm—outside of those recorded in the Hebrew Scriptures.

From the biblical texts, a structure emerges for RTB's creation model that explains the features of the natural realm in logical and scientifically testable terms. This biblical material on the origins and natural history of the universe, Earth, life, and humanity includes details for:

The universe, which

- began (once) in finite time;
- has a beginning that coincides with the beginning of space and time;
- was not made from that which is material, visible, or detectable;
- continuously expands from the beginning;
- is governed by constant laws of physics;

- manifests precise fine-tuning for humanity's benefit;
- has enormous volume, encompassing an "uncountable" (to ancient peoples) number of stars;
- contains stars that differ from one another and eventually stop shining;
- will someday cease to exist.

Earth, which

- emerged from the cosmos at a specific time;
- was enshrouded by an opaque cloud layer in the beginning;
- began with an ocean that covered its whole surface;
- was precisely fine-tuned for humanity's benefit;
- contains resources essential for launching and sustaining human civilization;
- has a Sun and Moon and other astronomical companions specially designed to benefit life and humanity;
- carries finite resources and time-limiting conditions for sustaining human civilization.

Life, which

- began early in Earth's history;
- began under hostile conditions;
- began by divine intervention;
- began with optimal ecological relationships;
- began with optimal design for environmental conditions;
- appeared in abundance, in diversity, and for long eras for the specific benefit of humanity;
- started as physical only (most life-forms); then soulish creatures (many species) appeared; and finally, one spiritual species was introduced—an original pair of humans and all their descendents;
- progresses from simple to complex through a series of extinction and replacement (speciation) events;
- reflects shared common designs;
- in its soulish characteristics, appears designed to serve and/or please humanity.

Humanity, which

- arrived late in Earth's history;
- resulted from divine intervention;
- represents the culmination of God's creation work on Earth;
- remains the only earthly creature with a spiritual nature;
- descended from one man and one woman who lived in a God-designed garden near the juncture of Africa, Asia, and Europe;
- migrated rapidly from area of origin shortly after the flood of Noah's time;
- experienced a significant drop in the potential life span after the time of the flood;
- genetically bottlenecked at a later date for males than for females (because male flood survivors were all biologically related to Noah, whereas females were not related to one another);
- was gifted from the outset with attributes needed for functioning in a high-tech civilization.

The Science Challenge

The RTB biblical creation model based on this framework invites side-by-side comparison with competing models on the scientific findings already established and still accumulating. As mentioned in chapter 1 (see p. 22), specific details of significant portions of RTB's testable/falsifiable, predictive model have already been set forth in other books.[26] The following chapters briefly highlight some ways this creation model-in-progress is faring in light of established evidence. They also show how the most recent scientific discoveries test the credibility of the Bible's creation story.

7

PUTTING RTB'S MODEL FOR THE COSMOS TO THE TEST

At age sixteen, I gave my first public lecture on astronomy. Afterward, someone asked a question that stumped me: "Is it possible to see planets with the naked eye during the middle of the day?" Because I didn't know, the next time Venus and Jupiter were close to maximum brightness, I decided to test their visibility.

During the night I leveled my equatorial-mount telescope and fixed its polar axis to within a quarter of a degree of the true North Pole for the celestial sky. That permitted me to track the positions of Jupiter and Venus with accuracy, even if they couldn't be seen with the naked eye.

All through the morning twilight, Jupiter and Venus were easily visible without the telescope. Once the Sun came up, Venus could still be seen, but Jupiter could be viewed only by first using the telescope to determine its precise position. An hour later, I couldn't see Jupiter at all. But Venus continued to remain visible to the naked eye throughout the entire day.

Astronomers face a similar challenge when trying to detect the first galaxies and stars that formed after the cosmic creation event. Looking far enough back in cosmic history to measure what the universe was like at the beginning is not easy.

In the 1940s, Princeton physicist Robert Dicke used Einstein's general relativity theory to calculate that the temperature of the radiation left over from the cosmic creation event was only about five degrees above absolute zero. He and other scientists presumed such a cool temperature would be undetectable. Yet today the technology exists to measure what was once deemed impossible.

Probably no discipline of science has seen such remarkable recent advances in both observation and theory as cosmology. At the beginning of the twentieth century, astronomers could see only a tiny fraction—barely more than a billionth—of the potentially observable universe. They couldn't see the Milky Way Galaxy or its spiral structure. They had not yet established that other galaxies exist. Nor did they have any idea how much cosmic history they were viewing.

Now astronomers can see to the very limits imposed by the laws of physics—all the way back to the beginning of time. Today's astronomers have mapped out virtually all of the Milky Way's visible matter and most of its dark matter. They know the observable universe contains between 200 and 300 billion galaxies. They've determined how many of each type of galaxy (e.g., spirals, ellipticals, irregulars, quasars, and Seyferts) the universe contains. Astronomers can now witness all of cosmic history back to the cosmic creation event (see figure 7.1, p. 95).

To see across the entire electromagnetic spectrum from the beginning of the universe to the present moment, astronomers use both Earth-based and space-based telescopes. By focusing progressively on more distant objects, they directly observe the past.

Because light takes time to travel, scientists can directly map the state of the universe at any epoch simply by observing an object at the appropriate distance. The constancy of the velocity of light permits this observational time travel. It's like leafing through a detailed photo album of a middle-aged person whose life has been documented from the moment he was formed in his mother's womb until his most recent picture. In other disciplines scientists infer the past. In astronomy they directly see and measure it.

Armed with telescopic time machines, astronomers today can put scientific models for the origin, structure, and history of the universe to ever more rigorous tests. RTB's creation model is no exception.

As previously mentioned, this book can't possibly supply the extensive evaluation on this specific portion of RTB's model already detailed in other works, especially *The Creator and the Cosmos*.[1] However, a brief

Figure 7.1. Looking Back in Time

Through their telescopes, astronomers can see only the past. They observe the Andromeda Galaxy as it was 2.52 million years ago. That's because it takes 2.52 million years for light to travel from the galaxy to Earth. Light from the Sun takes 8.3 minutes. The most distantly imaged galaxies present in the Hubble Ultra Deep Field reveal the state of the universe 13 billion years ago, an epoch when the cosmos was less than a billion years old. (Panel 1: Image courtesy of iStock Photo; Panel 2: Image courtesy of SOHO [ESA & NASA]; Panel 3: Image courtesy of NASA, ESA, R. Windhorst [Arizona State University] and H. Yan [Spitzer Science Center, Caltech]) list of these cosmic characteristics permits a glimpse of how this creation model can be evaluated scientifically.

Some Testable Features

RTB's cosmic creation model is based on the following biblical premises. The universe:

- has a beginning—a single beginning as opposed to many. This start of matter, energy, space, and time points to a causal Agent.
- has a Beginner, who exists beyond the laws of physics and the space-time dimensions of the universe.
- experiences continual expansion.
- is a physical surface with no center.
- is enormous, containing more stars than ancient peoples could count.
- was extraordinarily designed to make life possible, especially human life.
- operates under fixed physical laws.
- manifests the most significant features of the big bang model as predicted in the Bible thousands of years ago.
- supplies humanity with the best cosmic location at the best cosmic time to observe the characteristics (such as beauty, power, wisdom, and love) of the Creator, who created and shaped the cosmos for humanity's benefit.

Because these premises are specific, scientific tests can be performed to determine if they are accurate.

In the Beginning

Prior to 1970, astronomers knew the universe had a beginning but understood little about exactly how the universe got its start. Then two physicists, Stephen Hawking and Roger Penrose, produced the first space-time theorems of general relativity.[2] Their theorem proved, within the framework of classical general relativity, that if the universe contains mass and if the equations of general relativity reliably describe the universe's dynamics, then its space and time dimensions must have had a beginning that coincides with the universe's origin.

The proof that time was created has enormous philosophical implications. Within the universe, time is the dimension in which cause-and-effect relationships occur. Effects follow their causes. So the beginning of cosmic time implies that an Agent (cause) outside the universe's space-time dimensions is responsible for bringing into existence the space, time, matter, and energy (effects) astronomers observe.[3]

Now a whole family of space-time theorems exists.[4] These theorems apply to *any* expanding universe model wherein physical life could possibly exist. Specifically, they are applicable for all life-permitting inflationary hot big bang cosmic models as well as all life-suitable quantum gravity models. (In inflationary hot big bang models, the effect of general relativity is augmented by a "scalar field" that stretched the universe at many times the velocity of light during a brief period when the universe was younger than a quadrillionth of a quadrillionth of a second.)

Cosmologists don't doubt that the universe contains mass. Neither do most people. However, at the time the first space-time theorem of general relativity was published, astronomers had performed only three independent tests of its reliability. And they had determined to only 1 percent precision that general relativity reliably describes the dynamics of the universe.

Today, astronomers have performed more than a dozen independent tests of general relativity and have confirmed the reliability of general relativity to describe the dynamics of the universe to better than 0.000000000001 percent precision. British mathematical physicist Sir Roger Penrose, coauthor of the first space-time theorem, said, "This makes Einstein's general relativity, in this particular sense, the most accurately tested theory known to science."[5] The thoroughness of testing and the precision of results combined with the breadth of the space-time theorems leave no reasonable basis for doubting that a causal Agent outside space and time brought the universe of space, time, matter, and energy into existence.[6]

In 1970 astronomers possessed only three methods for determining the universe's origin date. None of them yielded a date any more accurate than ±35 percent. Today, many independent lines of measurement now validate, with better than 1 percent precision, that the universe began 13.73 billion years ago.[7]

This progress in cosmology contradicts the fundamental belief of philosophical naturalism—the claim that all causes and effects are contained within nature. No longer can scientists operate under the assumption that miracles never occur in the natural realm. The beginning of the universe exposes the greatest miracle imaginable, one that can't be rationally denied. Given that the cosmic causal Agent beyond space and time intervened (performed a miracle) on one occasion, the possibility must also exist that he could intervene on other occasions. Science can and should test for such possibilities.

Scientific progress in cosmology also refutes Kantian philosophy and a fundamental doctrine of world religions based on nonbiblical content. Such beliefs claim that space and time are absolute and eternal and that a god or gods created within them.

Theoretical and observational evidences for a transcendent cosmic origin, on the other hand, coincide with biblical descriptions in at least two ways: One, the Bible claims a cosmic beginning—the origin not only of matter and energy but also of space and time. Two, the biblical God transcends the universe. This means God can relate, operate, and create without limitation, independent of or outside of space and time.

RTB's biblical creation model anticipates continued accumulation of evidence for a single cosmic beginning that coincides with the origin of space and time. It also expects evidence to become even more compelling for the transcendent causal Agent implied by the space-time theorems of general relativity.

Extra Dimensions

When the Bible describes God's triune intra-relationship (the Father, Son, and Holy Spirit relating to one another) and causal activity (for example, his putting "grace" into effect) as occurring before time started (see Gen. 1:1; 2 Tim. 1:9; Titus 1:2), it suggests the possibility of some kind of dimensionality and/or temporality or the equivalent beyond the universe. The declaration in Hebrews that the detectable universe was not made from that which is visible may imply the same possibility (Heb.

11:3). These ideas, along with the more likely biblical implication that God created the universe "out of nothing," remain consistent with the singularity feature of most (though not all) big bang models.

By adding one extra dimension of space, mathematicians can prove theoretically that a three-dimensional basketball can be turned inside out without making a cut or a hole in its surface. But limitations on human imagination prevent people from being able to visualize how such a phenomenon occurs. People simply cannot imagine phenomena in more dimensions than they experience. This limitation has significant theological and scientific implications.

Religions that are mere human inventions (without inspiration from a Being beyond the dimensions of length, width, height, and time) will lack any transcendent teachings. They won't include information that demands the existence of dimensions beyond the familiar four. (Though such religions might appeal to magic or seemingly transdimensional entities, their attributes, activities, or behaviors can be comprehended fully within the dimensions of length, width, height, and time.)

By contrast, the Bible describes many extra- or transdimensional doctrines that reflect a reality beyond length, width, height, and time. Some examples include the triune nature of God (three persons yet only one essence), God's simultaneous transcendence and immanence, and the simultaneity of human free choice and divine predetermination. Scripture also contains accounts of transdimensional or extradimensional events, such as Jesus's transfiguration (see Matt. 17:1–13; Mark 9:2–13; Luke 9:28–36) and his physical body's ability to enter a locked room *after* the resurrection (John 20:19–31). A God with the capacity to operate both within and beyond extra dimensions could make such "impossibilities" possible.[8]

The scientific application of the dimensional differences implies that if a transcendent Creator brought this universe into existence, he could structure it with more dimensions than people can imagine. Because the Bible declares that the Creator intends his creation to reveal both his existence and nature to humans (see Rom. 1:18–20), a universe structured with more than four dimensions *could* be discoverable.

Recently, scientists dramatically verified that indeed more space dimensions than length, width, and height frame the universe. These breakthroughs resulted when physicists and astronomers tackled two seemingly intractable problems plaguing big bang creation models.

Problem #1: Particles Can't Be Points

Treating fundamental particles as point entities (the traditional view) made unification of any of the four fundamental forces of physics (gravity, electromagnetism, and the strong and weak nuclear forces) impossible. Complete theoretical and experimental proof that this unification existed for the weak nuclear force (the force governing radioactivity) and the electromagnetic force[9] demanded a new approach. Lines or loops of energy called "strings" provided that explanation.

When theoreticians treated fundamental particles as highly stretched, vibrating, rotating "elastic bands," or strings, in the extreme heat of the first split second after creation (the era of force unification), the dilemma resolved itself. These strings, however, needed more room to operate. They required the existence of more than three spatial dimensions.

Problem #2: Gravity and Quantum Mechanics Can't Coexist

In the easily recognizable four space-time dimensions of the universe, all gravitational theories contradict the possibility of quantum mechanics, and all quantum mechanical theories contradict the possibility of gravity. There simply isn't enough room within the dimensions of length, width, height, and time for all the symmetries quantum mechanics and gravity demand. The dilemma is that without both, physical life isn't possible.

Theoretical physicist Andrew Strominger hypothesized a brilliant solution in the form of "extremal" (very small) black holes that become massless at critical moments.[10] At first, however, he seemed merely to have traded one dilemma for another.

Black holes are massive objects so highly collapsed that their gravity attracts anything nearby. How could a black hole be massless without violating the definition of a black hole or without violating the principles of gravity? Simply put, how can gravity exist without mass?

Extradimensionality supplied the answer. Strominger discovered that in six spatial dimensions, an extremal black hole's mass is proportional to its surface area. As the black hole's surface area shrinks, the mass eventually drops to zero. The possibility of zero-mass black holes permits both gravity and quantum mechanics to fully coexist.

Solution: Nine Space Dimensions

One theory solved two great dilemmas: The universe was created with nine rapidly expanding space dimensions. When the universe was just 10^{-43} seconds old (a ten-trillionth of a quadrillionth of a quadrillionth of a second), gravity separated from the strong-electroweak force, and at that moment six of the nine dimensions quit expanding. Today, those six dimensions still exist as components of the universe, but remain as tightly curled (with cross sections measuring less than a millionth of a trillionth the diameter of an electron) as when the cosmos was only 10^{-43} seconds old.

Six sets of evidence indicate this theory is correct.[11] One of the more remarkable is that string theory, on its own, produces all the equations of special and general relativity. If scientists knew nothing at all about relativity, this ten-dimensional (one time dimension plus nine space dimensions) string theory would have revealed it in complete form. Therefore, experimental confirmation of special and general relativity (independent of any string theory) implies that ten space-time dimensions frame the physical universe. (Scientists have yet to determine exactly what form these ten dimensions take or whether an eleventh dimension somehow interacts with them.)

Scientific evidence establishing the existence of nine space dimensions for the universe along with the space-time theorems implying that the cosmic Creator operates in or beyond at least the equivalent of one additional time dimension provide important confirmations of RTB's biblical creation model.[12]

Stretching Out the Heavens

The continual expansion of the universe from the creation event onward is the most frequently described cosmic feature cited in the Bible (see Job 9:8; Ps. 104:2; Isa. 40:22; 42:5; 44:24; 45:12; 48:13; 51:13; Jer. 10:12; 51:15; Zech. 12:1).[13] This biblical claim is based on the Hebrew verb *natah*, which means to expand or stretch out. With respect to the universe this verb appears in seven different Bible verses in the Qal active participle form, implying that the universe has experienced, is experiencing, and will continue to experience ongoing uninterrupted expansion (Job 9:8, Ps. 104:2, Isa. 40:22; 42:5; 44:24; 51:13; Zech. 12:1).

The biblical declaration of the universe's continual expansion predates the scientific discoveries that verify this cosmic feature by more than three thousand years. It also predates any other known written scientific or philosophical discussion of cosmic expansion by that same amount of time. Thus, the Bible's repeated declaration of continual cosmic expansion ranks as one of Scripture's boldest predictions of future scientific discoveries. Testing its veracity, therefore, has huge implications for the creation/evolution debates. The importance of this prediction looms even larger considering that different biblical models predict different outcomes for this characteristic.

Today astronomers possess many distinct tests for the nature of the ongoing cosmic expansion. Six of the most dramatic and explicit include the:

1. law of redshifts (galaxy velocity–galaxy distance relationship);
2. spreading apart of galaxies and galaxy clusters;
3. Tolman test for the surface brightness of identical objects;
4. lifetimes of supernova eruptions and gamma-ray bursts;
5. population statistics of stars and planets;
6. cooling of cosmic background radiation.

Brief descriptions show how these tests validate the biblical premise of a continuously expanding cosmos and how current creation/evolution models score on these tests. (See the WMAP in figure 7.2, p. 103, for additional evidence from cosmic background radiation.)

Law of Redshifts

The first observational evidence for cosmic expansion came from measurements establishing the "law of redshifts." This law states that velocities at which galaxies move away from Earth are directly proportional to their distances. The faster a galaxy moves, the more its spectral lines shift toward the red end of the spectrum. Astronomers consistently observe that the more distant the galaxy, the greater its redshift.

Imagine the way dots painted on the surface of a balloon being blown up separate from one another at rates directly proportional to the distances between them (see figure 7.3, p. 103). Any matter and energy on

Figure 7.2. Detailed Map of the Cosmic Background Radiation

The WMAP delivered the most detailed all-sky map ever produced of radiation left over from the cosmic origin event. Variations in shading show temperature differences from region to region in the early universe. The Sloan Digital Sky Survey of hundreds of thousands of galaxies established that the warmer regions were the "seeds" that grew into galaxies and galaxy clusters.

This map is based on five years of continuous observation. Astronomers can directly observe the instant when light from the cosmic creation event first separated from darkness, 13.73 billion years ago. The infant universe was only 380,000 years old at that time. The WMAP also supplies evidence for the stretching out of the universe (see pp. 104–107). (Image courtesy of NASA/WMAP Science Team)

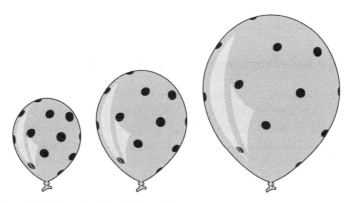

Figure 7.3. Analogy for Cosmic Expansion

As the dots on an expanding balloon move farther and faster away from each other, galaxies on the cosmic space surface also move farther and faster apart as the universe expands. However, the galaxies themselves (represented by the balloon dots) do not grow bigger with the expansion, because local gravity from the mass within each galaxy prevents them from expanding significantly. (Illustration by Jonathan Price) the surface of the universe—stars, planets, galaxies, dust, gas, photons, and exotic matter—do the same as the cosmos expands.

Galaxies Spreading Apart

Because light takes time to get from distant sources to a telescope, the farther away astronomers look, the farther back in time they see. Images showing extremely distant galaxies (revealing the state of the universe when it was younger) jammed much more tightly together than nearby galaxies (revealing the state of the universe closer to its current age) supply visual evidence of continual cosmic expansion (see figure 7.4, p. 105).[14]

Tolman Test

In 1930 Caltech physicist Richard Tolman proposed an elegant test to determine whether observed redshifts indeed result from the universe's general expansion.[15] He demonstrated that the surface brightness of certain objects would be dramatically diminished (from being stretched out over a larger area) if the universe is expanding. In a nonexpanding universe, the surface brightness of identical objects would be the same everywhere, with no dimming. Surface brightness measurements of numerous astronomical bodies made possible by the Hubble Space Telescope revealed the exact degree of dimming predicted by the ongoing expansion of the cosmos.[16]

Supernova Eruptions and Gamma-ray Bursts

Yet another test for cosmic expansion is relativistic time dilation. If the universe has been rapidly expanding for billions of years, the most distant objects will move away at extremely high velocities (speeds close to the velocity of light). Einstein's special relativity theory predicts that distant "clocks" in such a universe will run about 10 to 60 percent slower (due to velocity effects) than equivalent clocks in the vicinity of the Milky Way Galaxy.

In the Milky Way, an exploding star (a supernova) takes about seven months to transition from maximum to minimum brightness, while a typical gamma-ray burst near our galaxy takes an average of about 15 seconds to undergo this same transition. Observations show these transitions take longer, by the exact amounts consistent with their distances, for a universe that has rapidly expanded for the past 13.73 billion years.[17]

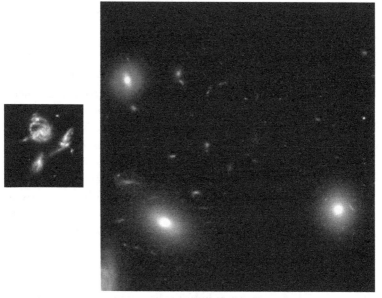

Figure 7.4. Cosmic Expansion Evidence: Spreading Apart of Galaxies

When astronomers look back in cosmic time, they observe galaxies jammed much more tightly together than in the present universe. The image on the left shows galaxies about twelve billion light-years away (almost twelve billion years ago). These galaxies are so close together that their mutual gravity causes them to rip away each other's spiral arms. The image on the right shows galaxies almost two billion light-years away (about two billion years ago). By that time the galaxies are far enough apart that they don't typically rip one another apart. (Image courtesy of NASA, N. Benitez [JHU], T. Broadhurst [Racah Institute of Physics/The Hebrew University], H. Ford [JHU], M. Clampin [STScI], G. Hartig [STScI], G. Illingworth [UCO/Lick Observatory], the ACS Science Team and ESA)

This particular expansion test not only rules out nonexpanding universe models but also rules out the most popular young-earth creationist models. Those young-earth models predict very distant supernovae will take only 18 to 25 seconds to transition from maximum to minimum brightness, not the eight to ten months astronomers actually observe.[18]

Star and Planet Population

The presence of stars and planets, which permit the existence of life, serves as the basis for the fifth test. (See pp. 116–17 for a description of the sixth test.) Planets like Earth and stars like the Sun are possible only in a universe that continuously expands at a just-right rate for a just-right duration.

A cosmos expanding too slowly produces only neutron stars and black holes.[19] A universe expanding too rapidly produces no stars at all and, therefore, no planets.[20] Astronomers and physicists note that the two factors governing the expansion rate (cosmic mass density and cosmic dark energy density) reflect the most exquisite fine-tuning anywhere in the sciences.

According to recent studies, the universe can produce the kinds of galaxies, stars, planets, and chemical elements essential for the existence of physical life only if the cosmic mass density is fine-tuned to at least one part in 10^{60}. That's the result if there were no dark energy factor (the self-stretching property of the cosmic surface) contributing to cosmic expansion. If dark energy does exist, the fine-tuning of the cosmic mass density is reduced, but does not go away. For example, independent of dark energy, the universe would fail to produce life-essential heavy elements in the required abundances and in the necessary locations unless the mass densities of both ordinary and exotic matter are fine-tuned. However, while dark energy reduces the fine-tuning of the cosmic mass density, it in no way weakens the case for design. Instead it implies the most spectacular fine-tuning known to humanity.[21]

For life to be possible, the cosmic dark energy density that governs the degree to which the cosmic space surface stretches must be fine-tuned to at least one part in 10^{120}. This quantity, 10^{120}, exceeds the number of protons and neutrons in the observable universe by 100 billion quadrillion quadrillion times.[22] Fine-tuning to within one part in 10^{120} exceeds by a factor of more than a million quadrillion quadrillion quadrillion quadrillion quadrillion quadrillion times the best engineering achievements of the human race.[23]

In the face of such a staggeringly high degree of fine-tuning, even nontheistic scientists have made bold concessions. Given the existence of dark energy, one research team said, "Arranging the universe as we think it is arranged would have required a miracle. . . . It seems an external agent intervened in cosmic history for reasons of its own."[24]

On the Cosmic Surface

Three thousand years ago, a psalmist depicted God's stretching out of the universe metaphorically as the unfolding of a tent (see Ps. 104:2).

Isaiah used the same imagery 2,700 years ago, saying God stretches out the heavens as one would stretch out a tent to live in (Isa. 40:22). This biblical word picture implies that like a tent, the physical cosmos is a surface. Such a concept for the universe stood radically apart from the cosmologies of other religions, philosophies, and sciences prior to the twentieth century.

Today the biblical concept of a cosmic surface can be put to the test. The expanding balloon analogy (see figure 7.3) not only illustrates the continual expansion of the universe but also helps us visualize its geometry. The balloon's physical material is its two-dimensional surface. No balloon stuff resides either interior to or exterior to that surface. Consequently, no item located on the balloon can be said to reside at the balloon's center.

Similarly, from the positions and dynamics of the universe's galaxies, astronomers observe that all the matter and energy of the cosmos reside on the cosmic surface. According to general relativity, all the space-time dimensions are likewise contained there. So too (as with the balloon) no star or galaxy can be said to reside at the cosmic center. It is literally impossible for any physical entity to exist at the "center" of the space-time surface.

With its shape and number of dimensions, the balloon analogy obviously breaks down. The surface of the universe is three-dimensional, not two like the balloon. Instead of a spherically shaped surface, the cosmic surface is nearly flat in its geometry.

Immense Realm

In his book *God: The Failed Hypothesis*, physicist Victor Stenger argues that there can't be a God who designed the universe for humanity's specific benefit. He reasons that "if the universe were congenial to human life, then you would expect it to be easy for humanlike life to develop and survive throughout the universe."[25] Instead, "the strong conclusion is that humans are not constructed to live anywhere but on this tiny blue speck in a vast universe."[26]

To Stenger "it seems inconceivable that a creator exists who has a special love for humanity and then just relegated it to a tiny point in space and time."[27] Even though this point may seem valid, recent discoveries provide at least two reasons why such a vast cosmos is necessary.

First, the density of the protons and neutrons in the universe (cosmic baryon density) must have been fine-tuned to support the nuclear fusion that produced life's required elements. With a slightly lower baryon density (producing fewer than about 10 billion trillion observable stars), little or no helium would have formed during the first few minutes after the cosmic creation event. That would make subsequent nuclear fusion less productive. The cosmos could not have generated elements heavier than helium.

A slightly higher baryon density (producing more than about 10 billion trillion observable stars) would have formed too much deuterium (heavy hydrogen), making nuclear fusion too productive. All elements would have quickly become as heavy as, or heavier than, iron. Either way, life-essential elements such as carbon, nitrogen, oxygen, and phosphorous would not exist.

Second, the total cosmic mass density (density of baryons plus density of exotic mass particles) plays a key role in determining the cosmic expansion rate. If the mass density were slightly lower, gravity could not apply sufficient braking to the expansion. The universe would stretch too rapidly for galaxies, stars, and planets to form. Life would lack a home.

With a cosmic mass density slightly greater, gravity's powerful grip would soon collapse all that mass into black holes and neutron stars. With a minimum density of 5 billion tons per teaspoonful, these black holes and neutron stars would not permit atoms to exist, much less life molecules.

These findings suggest a Creator's intentionality. They testify of a causal Agent who cares enough for humans to invest 13.73 billion years of time and 10 billion trillion stars' worth of matter and energy in preparing a just-right home. This evidence also verifies the Bible's bold statement, thousands of years earlier, that the stars add up to what was then an uncountable number (more than several billion) (see Gen. 13:16; 22:17; Jer. 33:22; Heb. 11:12).

Designed for Humans

Given the laws of physics and the gross features of the universe, formation of life-essential elements in adequate abundance took a long time.

The universe started with only one element, hydrogen. From three to three-and-a-half minutes after the beginning, the universe expanded through temperature and density conditions that sustained nuclear fusion. Nearly 25 percent of the hydrogen, by mass, converted to helium plus trace amounts of lithium and deuterium (heavy hydrogen).[28] From four minutes onward, nuclear furnaces in the cores of large stars produced the rest of the elements.[29]

Rocky planets couldn't form and life chemistry wasn't possible until at least two generations of stars had developed, burned, and exploded their nuclear ashes into interstellar space. Even then, adequate abundances of elements required some highly specialized circumstances.

Supernovae

First, production of the full range of life-essential elements in as short a time as 9.2 billion years (the time of Earth's formation) required the well-timed occurrence of three types of supernovae (relatively rare, massive stellar explosions). All three (a type I, a normal type II, and an especially rare species of type II) had to occur in proximity to one another. Each supernova produced a different suite of heavy elements.

Second, all three types had to detonate near the gas and dust cloud where the Sun had begun to coalesce. Yet a supernova exploding too close to this emerging solar nebula would have blown it apart, and no rocky planets capable of sustaining life could have formed. A supernova exploding too far from the solar nebula could not have provided enough enrichment of certain heavy elements critical for advanced life chemistry.

Third, the timing of the three supernovae eruptions had to be precise. If any of them had exploded too early or too late (relative to the emerging solar nebula), too few heavy elements would have been incorporated into the solar nebula.

The level of fine-tuning necessary to explain the localized availability and adequate quantities of all advanced-life-essential heavy elements so early in cosmic history defies reasonable chance probability. The odds of such a coincidence would be approximately the same as the odds of an explosion in a bicycle factory flinging out onto the sidewalk a block away, right in front of a cyclist, all the parts needed to assemble a new bike—without doing any harm or damage to the parts, the cyclist, or the sidewalk. This test indicates the validity of the RTB model's claim that the universe was supernaturally designed to make human life possible in as little as 13.73 billion years after the cosmic creation event.

Abundant Uranium and Thorium

As the universe proceeded through successive generations of stars, the abundance of most heavy elements steadily increased—with one exception. Radiometric elements increased or decreased depending on their decay rates.

Once the universe aged by a few billion years, ongoing cosmic expansion and the consumption of gas and dust by succeeding generations of stars slowed the star formation rate. That meant slower production of radiometric isotopes (nearly all atomic elements exist as a suite of isotopes—atoms with the same number of protons but different numbers of neutrons). Thus, depending on a particular radiometric isotope's half-life (time required for exactly one half of a certain amount of radiometric isotope to decay into daughter products), the production of that isotope

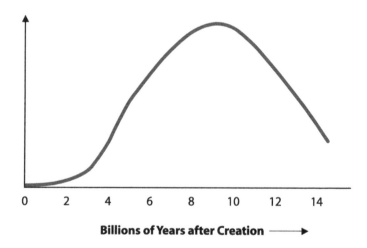

Billions of Years after Creation ⟶

Figure 7.5. Uranium and Thorium Abundances in the Milky Way Galaxy

As the Milky Way Galaxy aged, the rate at which it produced uranium and thorium peaked, then began to decline according to the rise and decline of the supernova eruption rate. However, because uranium and thorium undergo radiometric decay, the production of additional quantities of these elements in supernovae will eventually fail to compensate for their loss. The cosmic moment of their peak abundance coincided with the Earth's birth date. (Illustration by Jonathan Price) through stellar burnout events eventually failed to keep pace with the decay of previously existing amounts. Therefore, the abundance of each radiometric isotope steadily increased up to a peak value and thereafter continued to decline.

Several radioactive isotopes were essential to make a planet suitable for advanced life. Uranium-235, uranium-238, and thorium-232 played the most crucial roles (see chapter 10, pp. 154–56). Based on measurements of the cosmic expansion rate, astronomers have determined that the cosmic abundance of these elements collectively peaked when the universe was two-thirds its present age, some 4.57 billion years ago (see figure 7.5, p. 110). This date matches Earth's origin date (4.5662 ± 0.0001 billion years ago).[30]

According to RTB's creation model, the formation of the just-right radiometric isotopes at the just-right time, abundance, and location was not a series of baffling coincidences. A purposeful Creator would be expected to precisely time Earth's formation at the moment he engineered these radiometric isotopes to reach their collective peak abundance at the optimal galactic location for human life.

Habitat for Humanity

In 1961 Princeton physicist Robert Dicke noted that the universe couldn't contain physical life if any one of several physical constants differed in value by even a slight amount.[31] His discovery led to the development of the anthropic principle—the conclusion that the universe, Milky Way Galaxy, solar system, and Earth are all exquisitely fine-tuned so that human life can exist and flourish.

By the end of 2008, RTB's scientific team had identified 140 characteristics of the universe and laws of physics that must fall within narrow ranges for any kind of physical life to exist at any time in the universe's history (see Appendix B, part 1, "Fine-Tuning for Life in the Universe," pp. 259–60). In several cases, such as the ratio of electrons to protons in the universe, the ratio of the electromagnetic to the gravitational force constant, and the precise level of cosmic dark energy density, the required fine-tuning degree vastly exceeds the best levels of humanly achieved designs.

Astronomers can measure the Milky Way Galaxy and the solar system more precisely than they can the universe as a whole. When they do, they find even more evidence of supernatural design. Over nine hundred characteristics of the Milky Way Galaxy and solar system require fine-tuning to make advanced life possible (see Appendix B, part 4, "Probability Estimates on Different Size Scales for the Features Required by Advanced Life," pp. 229–30).

These characteristics demonstrate that even if the observable universe contains as many planets as stars, about 50 billion trillion, the possibility (without invoking divine miracles) for the existence of just one planet with the required conditions for advanced life falls below 1 in $10^{1,000}$.

Stated another way, the probability from a nontheistic perspective of finding a body anywhere in the observable universe with the necessary conditions to support advanced life is at least 10^{850} times more remote than the possibility that a blindfolded person could pick out a single marked electron randomly shuffled into a tightly packed pile of electrons that fills the entire universe, on the first try.

For the past fifty years as astronomers have learned more about the universe, the Milky Way Galaxy, Earth's solar system, and Earth, evidence for the anthropic principle has multiplied. With respect to RTB's creation model, in the years over which RTB has numerically tracked the accumulating evidence, new discoveries have continued to augment the plausibility of the biblical framework—including the Creator's powers, plans, and apparent purposes for the cosmos—at a breathtaking rate.[32] (For details and documentation for this accumulating evidence see chapters 8, 16, and 17 and Appendix B.)

Objective Cosmic Tests

The RTB creation model predicts that as astronomers learn more about the universe, Milky Way Galaxy, and solar system, the evidence for a Creator's fine-tuning should increase. Nontheistic models predict that as astronomers learn more, the evidence for fine-tuning should decrease. Some specific examples of predictions that can be tested for evidence of evolution or creation as new discoveries accumulate include:

> *If no Creator:* The number of cosmic, galactic, and solar system characteristics known to require fine-tuning for advanced life's existence will decrease.

If a Creator: The number of cosmic, galactic, and solar system characteristics known to require fine-tuning for advanced life's existence will increase.

If no Creator: The degree of fine-tuning apparently necessary for advanced life will decline.

If a Creator: The degree of fine-tuning apparently necessary for advanced life will increase.

If no Creator: Remaining evidences for fine-tuning will focus on life in general, not humans in particular.

If a Creator: Accumulating evidences for fine-tuning will be far more pronounced for humans than for life in general.

If no Creator: Remaining evidences for fine-tuning will be seen on only a few size scales.

If a Creator: Evidences for fine-tuning will be seen on all size scales: the universe, galaxy cluster, Milky Way Galaxy, solar system, Sun, Earth, Moon, Earth's surface, and Earth's life-forms.

If no Creator: Only some life on Earth will be found to serve the needs of humanity.

If a Creator: All life (both past and present) will be found to serve the needs and/or pleasures of humanity.

If no Creator: The Local Group, Milky Way Galaxy, Sun, solar system, Moon, and Earth will each prove to have many identified duplicates within the universe, "twins" manifesting all the characteristics necessary for sustaining advanced life.

If a Creator: The Local Group, Milky Way Galaxy, Sun, solar system, Moon, and Earth will be found to have no twins that manifest all the necessary characteristics for sustaining advanced life.

If no Creator: Evidence that the biblical Creator is the Designer of the universe and solar system for the benefit of humanity will become progressively weaker.

If a Creator: Evidence that the biblical Creator is the Designer of the universe and solar system for the benefit of humanity will become progressively stronger.

For a discussion and documentation on the results of these tests so far in the context of recent scientific discoveries related to the galaxies, stars, and planets, see chapters 8, 16, and 17 and Appendix B.

Several additional tests—such as the anthropic principle inequality, constant physical laws, ongoing cosmic expansion, and continual cosmic cooling—already supply substantial scientific support for RTB's biblical creation model.

So Much Time for Such a Brief Survival Window

Brandon Carter, the British mathematician who first used the term "anthropic principle" in the scientific literature,[33] observed a stunning temporal imbalance: the universe took billions of years to prepare for a species with the potential to survive no longer than a few million years. Carter called this imbalance between the minimum possible time required for the emergence of human life and the maximum time span for humanity's survival, the "anthropic principle inequality."[34]

Physicists John Barrow and Frank Tipler later showed that this inequality is far more extreme than originally thought. They calculated that human civilization with the benefits of some technology and organized social structure can last no longer than 41,000 years.[35] Furthermore, Barrow and Tipler demonstrated that the inequality exists for any conceivable intelligent physical species under any realistically possible life-support conditions.[36]

These conclusions were developed, in part, because it takes at least 9 billion years to form a stable planetary system with the right chemical and physical conditions for life. It takes at least another 4.5 billion years for a planet in that system to accumulate adequate biomass and biodiversity to support an advanced civilization's activities. The convergence of "just-right" conditions for an advanced species to thrive and civilize in as brief a time as 13.73 billion years reflects extraordinary, even miraculous, efficiency.[37]

Researchers also point out that the astrophysical, geophysical, and biological conditions necessary to sustain an intelligent civilized species do not last indefinitely without disruption. The Sun, like all other hydrogen-burning stars, continues to brighten during its most stable burning phase (see "A Brightening Sun," chapter 10, pp. 156–58). At the same time, Earth's rotation period lengthens, plate-tectonic activity declines, and atmospheric composition varies. At best, Earth can retain its advanced life-support capability for no more than an additional ten million years from now.[38] Any other possible life-support planet would experience similar life-challenging variations.

The time window for civilization is much narrower. Solar instability can severely impact civilization. Although the Sun has burned with extraordinary stability for the past 50,000 years, this stability can last only about another 50,000 years.[39] A nearby supernova eruption, a disturbance of Earth's benign climate, an asteroid collision, a social upheaval, an environmental disaster, mass extinction of one or more supporting species, a declining birth rate, or the accumulation of negative genetic mutations could easily send humanity back to the Stone Age.[40] Any of these events could even lead to human extinction.

These numbers underscore how extreme the anthropic inequality may be. They show that the *maximum* survival time for advanced physical life in a civilized state equals about one-millionth the *minimum* time required for development of its survival necessities. So why would a Creator invest so much time in such a short-lived species?

Consider how much time and money a hypothetical father might lavish on Christmas gifts for his young children, knowing in advance they may break some before the day is over. Given the high value this father places upon his children and the lessons he wants to teach them, his investment in time and money for gifts that may last only a few minutes or hours is understandable.

On a much grander scale, the cosmic Creator described in the Bible must place an extremely high value upon humans and their advanced civilization. Evidently their worth justifies his enormous investment of time and resources in a creation program for their specific benefit even though humanity can last only a very brief period of time. The anthropic principle inequality implies that the Creator's purposes for humanity must extend beyond the limits of the cosmos.[41]

Constant Physical Laws

About 2,600 years ago, the prophet Jeremiah described another cosmic feature—"fixed laws" to govern the entire universe (Jer. 33:25). Other Bible authors echoed this claim for constant physical laws (see chapter 6, pp. 79–80). Today this biblical prediction can be scientifically tested.

Physicists have calculated that physical life is impossible unless the universe is exceptionally uniform and homogeneous. As expected, astronomers see the same abundance of elements and density of matter and energy no matter where in the cosmos they look. Life also requires that virtually all constants of physics remain fixed to an extremely high degree throughout cosmic history, or at least since protons and neutrons formed.

When astronomers make direct measurements of the values of physical constants at various epochs in cosmic history, they find remarkable consistency. In some cases possible variations prove less than two parts per 10 trillion per year—over the past twelve billion years.[42] Laboratory measurements yield variation limits as small as two parts per quadrillion per year.[43]

Continual Cosmic Cooling

Biblical declarations of fixed physical laws and continual cosmic expansion imply yet another important testable feature. A universe continuously expanding under constant physical laws must grow progressively colder with age.

Radiation left over from the cosmic creation event (cosmic background radiation), when studied at great distances, and thus farther back in time, measures hotter than radiation that's closer (see figure 7.6, p. 117).[44] These measurements establish that the universe has continuously cooled from a near infinitely hot origin. In addition to anticipating many other important features of big bang cosmology, the Bible correctly predicted continual cosmic cooling.

Unique Observation Deck

Psalm 19:1–3 describes one of God's key purposes for creating the heavens: to make his existence and attributes visible to every human being.

> The heavens declare the glory of God;
>   the skies proclaim the work of his hands.
> Day after day they pour forth speech;
>   night after night they display knowledge.
> There is no speech or language
>   where their voice is not heard.

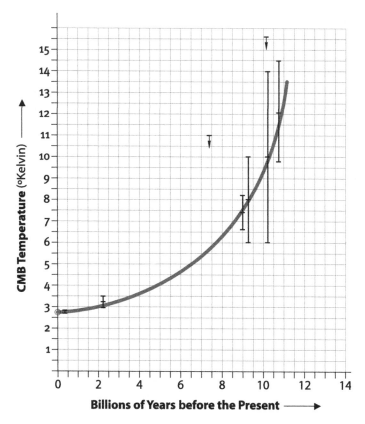

Figure 7.6. Evidence Supporting Hot Big Bang Creation Models

Today the temperature of radiation left over from the cosmic origin event measures 2.725° ± 0.001°C above absolute zero (-273.16°C). This graph shows temperature measurements of radiation from eight time periods in the universe's history. Each measurement (represented by a small cross with its accompanying error bar) indicates the temperature of the cosmic background radiation detected in a distant gas cloud. The downward arrows show upper-limit measurements. Superimposed on this graph is the temperature curve predicted by hot big bang models. (Illustration by Jonathan Price)

Once again, the Bible foretold what science discovered.

Perfect timing. Light, like everything else in the universe, is confined to the cosmic surface. Throughout the history of the universe, the speed of light has exceeded the speed of cosmic expansion. Thus the proportion of history visible to Earth-bound spectators has increased over time.

Eventually the entire history of the cosmos became visible. But it won't be for long.

As the cosmos ages, dark energy causes the universe's expansion to speed up.[45] It has already accelerated so much that objects formed immediately after the creation event are moving away from human observers at nearly the velocity of light. Someday dark energy will cause the expansion to accelerate beyond light's velocity. Then distant objects will no longer be visible from Earth's vantage point.

As the universe expands at progressively faster rates under the influence of dark energy, researchers will see increasingly less of cosmic history. Humanity lives at the only moment in cosmic history when the first stars, galaxies, and even cosmic background radiation can be observed. According to the Bible and RTB's creation model, the Creator perfectly timed humanity's arrival in cosmic history to facilitate discovery of his existence and attributes through observation and consideration of the heavens (see Ps. 19:1–4; 50:6; 97:6; Rom. 1:18–20).

Perfect place. At any other location in the Milky Way Galaxy, a spectator's view would be blocked by gas, dust, nebulae, nearby stars, star clusters, and/or galactic arms.[46] In almost every other medium-large spiral galaxy (the size required for life), nearby galaxies and/or galaxy clusters would obscure the view of a distant universe.[47] In every other location, knowledge of the deep history and structure of the universe remains hidden. Only from Earth can humanity see the magnificence of all cosmic creation.

Science Supports Scripture

Scientific discoveries about the origin and history of the universe point to the existence of a transcendent causal Agent. So does the Bible. The prophets Job, Isaiah, Jeremiah, and Zechariah, along with some of the psalmists, accurately described an expanding universe. Hundreds of finely tuned details in the cosmos make human life possible, suggesting the perfect plan and design of an all-knowing, all-powerful, intelligent Creator—the same as the God described in Scripture.

These cosmic tests affirm RTB's creation model while contradicting all previous nontheistic cosmic models, including those developed during the twentieth century. Pressured by the compelling cosmic evidence for a transcendent, personal Creator, twenty-first-century atheistic scientists have invented three different, highly imaginative alternate explanations for the universe. Chapter 14 tests the viability of these remaining atheistic explications.

The next chapter explores additional tools for testing the RTB cosmic creation model. While the universe as a whole is difficult to measure with any high degree of precision, many of its components—such as galaxies, stars, and planets—are close enough to invite comprehensive detailed observations. Further, while the sample size for the universe is only one, thanks to some amazing new instruments, astronomers now can accurately observe trillions of stars, millions of galaxies, and hundreds of planets. These new observations provide some of the most powerful scientific tests for evaluating the validity of different creation/evolution models.

8

Putting RTB's Model for Galaxies, Stars, and Planets to the Test

Though astronomy was my primary interest as a boy, all science fascinated me. One spring and summer, I experimented with a small vegetable garden to see if I could make crops grow faster. While tending my garden, I spent many hours observing the behavior of various birds and insects, partly motivated by a desire to prevent them from consuming my vegetables.

One afternoon I noticed an especially dense concentration of small ants on the sidewalk that divided our backyard. They all looked the same to me and seemed bent on one purpose. So I presumed they all belonged to one species.

On closer examination, however, I discovered that although the ants were the same size with the same morphological features, they manifested two distinct colors: black and red. And they were engaged in a pitched battle.

Looking even closer showed me another subtle but important difference. The red ants were using a different battle strategy than the black. In a microcosmic Battle of Marathon, the black ants followed the strategy of the Persians, marching forward in a strong central block. The red ones adopted the Greek strategy, meeting the enemy with a relatively thin line, one that steadily retreated under the pressure of the black advance.

Meanwhile, other red ants formed two strong blocks on the black's flanks. Though the red attacks were not as well coordinated and timed as the Greek assaults on the plains of Marathon, they nonetheless threw the black block into sufficient chaos to turn the battle's tide.

That afternoon taught me some important science lessons. What looks similar may not be, and a seemingly insignificant difference may prove important. Scientific testing needs to be as discriminating as possible.

Such discrimination—when applied to finding duplicates of galaxies, stars, and planets—yields potent tests for creation/evolution models. The RTB biblical model specifically predicts that a Creator supernaturally designed the Milky Way Galaxy, the Sun, and its system of planets, including Earth and its Moon, for the support of humans. Because he needed only one human-type species on one planet to fulfill his purposes,[1] these cosmic bodies (or sets of bodies) would each be expected to prove unique in possessing the necessary characteristics for sustaining advanced life. However, if there's nothing special about these features, astronomers should have no difficulty finding numerous duplicates with the same characteristics given the enormous populations of galaxies, stars, planets, and moons within the observable universe.

Are There Solar Twins?

Astronomers Jorge Meléndez and Iván Ramírez have spent most of their careers searching for a star that duplicates the Sun's capability to make intelligent life possible on a planet that orbits that particular star. They recently wrote:

> The question of whether the Sun is unique or not [is] a question that has important philosophical consequences. An anomalous Sun favors some forms of the anthropic principle.[2]

A unique Sun would support RTB's claim that the Sun was exquisitely designed by a supernatural, super-intelligent Creator to make human life possible.

Stars offer astronomers far more characteristics that can be accurately measured than galaxies and planets. In addition, because stars are so bright, nearby, and numerous, astronomers can compare our Sun's attributes with the properties of hundreds of thousands of stellar twin candidates. So the search for a solar twin provides the most definitive test of the idea that the Milky Way Galaxy, Sun, Earth, and Moon are all rare bodies.

For over fifty years, astronomers have scoured the Milky Way Galaxy in search of a star that qualifies as the Sun's twin. Given the Milky Way's life-friendly features and two hundred billion stars, the astronomical community expected to find many exact analogs. However, by October 2007, in spite of diligent searches spanning several decades, astronomers had found only two possibilities: 18 Scorpii and HD 98618.[3] Table 8.1 lists their observed properties:

Table 8.1: Two Stars Closely Matching the Sun

Characteristics	18 Scorpii	HD 98618
Mass	1.02	1.02
Luminosity	1.03	1.06
Metallicity	1.05	1.12
Age	0.85	0.91
Rotation	0.90	0.96
Temperature	1.01	1.01

Note: Each measurement is stated as a fraction of the solar value.

To anyone other than an astronomer, these stars might seem remarkably similar. But life requires a virtually identical twin. Because of obvious differences when compared to the Sun, Meléndez and Ramírez eventually dubbed the stars "quasi solar twins."[4] Not only do key features (luminosity, metallicity, and age) differ from the Sun, but both stars also possess a lithium abundance that's a factor of about three times higher than the Sun's.

Does a True Solar Twin Exist?

In a research paper published November 10, 2007, Meléndez and Ramírez claimed they had finally found a true solar counterpart.[5] They presented measurements on the star HIP 56948 showing a mass and temperature identical to the Sun's. In addition, the lithium abundance appeared nearly the same.

Meléndez and Ramirez identified HIP 56948 as a "true solar twin" by
searching through a sample of more than 100,000 stars in the Hipparcos
catalog of stars. This catalog lists accurate distance determinations, which
are crucial for establishing an individual star's precise properties. The
characteristics of HIP 56948 are listed in table 8.2 along with the features
of the two closest solar twins previously known.

Table 8.2: Three Solar "Twins" Compared to the Sun

Characteristics	18 Scorpii	HD 98618	HIP 56948
Mass	1.02	1.02	1.00
Luminosity	1.03	1.06	1.15
Metallicity	1.05	1.12	1.02
Age	0.85	0.91	1.26
Rotation	0.90	0.96	?
Temperature	1.01	1.01	1.00

Note: Each measurement is stated as a fraction of the solar value.

Unlike the quasi-solar twins, HIP 56948 exhibits a lithium abundance
indistinguishable from the Sun's, as well as a mass and temperature that
measure the same. Its metallicity is only slightly higher.

However, HIP 56948 is 1.2 billion years older and 15 percent more
luminous than the Sun. As long as a star has hydrogen to burn in its core,
it continues growing brighter as it ages. Such brightening happens as
nuclear burning fuses hydrogen into helium. The added helium increases
the star's core density. This increased density then causes nuclear fusion
to proceed with greater efficiency. A higher luminosity is consistent with
the age difference between the two stars.

The greater age and increased luminosity of HIP 56948 interfere with
its potential to support an advanced-life-carrying planet. If Earth's Sun
shone brighter by just 0.4 percent (as it will when it's only 0.2 percent
older), advanced life would become extinct.

Amazingly, Earth has sustained life for the past 3.8 billion years in spite
of the Sun becoming much brighter. The carefully timed introduction
of the just-right amounts and kinds of life and the just-right removal of
certain earlier life-forms gradually brought down the quantity of greenhouse gases in Earth's atmosphere to perfectly compensate for the Sun's

increasing luminosity (see chapter 10, pp. 156–58). Yet that compensation cannot continue much longer.

Greenhouse gases in Earth's atmosphere are already drawn down to a level just barely above the minimum necessary to permit the existence of photosynthetic life. Astronomers calculate that within the next 30 million years, either the Sun will heat Earth's surface beyond what life can tolerate, or the quantity of carbon dioxide and water vapor in Earth's atmosphere will dwindle to levels inadequate to support life capable of efficient photosynthesis.[6]

HIP 56948 more closely duplicates the Sun than 18 Scorpii or HD 98618. However, HIP 56948 must still be considered a quasi-solar twin. Its properties rule out the possibility of sustaining an advanced life-support planet in orbit. The Sun still lacks a true twin. The lack of an identical solar twin appears to affirm RTB's biblical model of the Sun's supernatural design for the specific benefit of humans.

The Sun's lack of a twin is not because twins of stars are rare. A great many other stars have such counterparts. In fact, 18 Scorpii and HD 98618 are duplicates in that all their observed properties are identical within the uncertainties of astronomers' measurements.

Are the Sun's Gas Giants Special Bodyguards?

Besides stars, the easiest kind of astronomical body to measure accurately is a gas giant planet. The first one found outside the solar system was discovered in 1995. Since then, astronomers have detected over three hundred. Not only can gas giants be easily detected, but scientists can also measure their mass, their orbital period, their orbital distance from their stars, the eccentricity (ellipticity) and inclination of their orbit, and sometimes even their radius.

For advanced life to be possible on any planet, it must be accompanied by a just-right suite of gas giants. These planets act as gravitational shields. Their large masses either absorb or deflect asteroids and comets that would otherwise collide with the life-support planet.

No single gas giant planet can provide adequate protection. It takes several to adequately cover all possible incoming collision routes.

For this shielding to be effective, the gas giant planets must orbit neither too near nor too far from the life-support planet. In addition, a gas giant must not orbit so closely that its gravity disturbs the life-support planet's orbit. Furthermore, to avoid disturbing that orbit, the inclination (tilt relative to the planetary system's plane) and eccentricity (degree of ellipticity) of the gas giant planets must be nearly zero.

If the masses of the gas giants are too great, their gravitational pull on the life-support planet will disrupt its orbit. However, if the masses are too small, the gas giant will neither deflect nor absorb sufficient numbers of incoming asteroids and comets.

Gas giant orbits must also not generate any significant mean-motion resonances (situations where one planet completes exactly one orbit for every two, three, four, or more orbits of another planet or completes exactly two, three, four, or more orbits for every two, three, four, or more orbits of another planet)—either with one another or with the life-support planet. Such resonances would result in orbital chaos.

No matter how carefully designed, a system of gas giant planets cannot protect a life-support planet from all possible collisions. Yet astronomers have found that a certain low frequency of just-right-sized asteroid and comet collisions with the life-support planet is crucial for maintaining life on that planet for billions of years. Such collisions, if carefully controlled and timed, can bring about the extinction of life-forms that might otherwise hinder the ongoing adjustment of Earth's atmosphere to compensate for the Sun's increasing luminosity and the layering of biodeposits essential for human civilization (see chapter 10, pp. 156–64). Billions of years of early life is essential to make advanced life possible.

All these exacting requirements (and possibly others yet undiscovered) leave few options for how a system of gas giant planets may be structured to make advanced life within that planetary system possible. Two teams of astronomers have shown that even the tiniest changes in the orbital features of any of our solar system's four gas giants could challenge the existence of advanced life on Earth.[7] At the same time, other research teams demonstrated that the primordial asteroid and comet belts of the solar system must be exquisitely fine-tuned for Jupiter, Saturn, Uranus, and Neptune to attain their orbital distances from the Sun and their extraordinary low inclination and eccentricity values.[8]

Out of more than three hundred extrasolar gas giant planets discovered so far, none exhibit anything close to these fine-tuned features. Not one exists in a single planetary system with all the advanced-life-essential parameters of the Sun's gas giant planets.

A new set of theoretical models for planet formation explains why the solar system's array of gas giant planets is so rare.[9] Depending on their birthing circumstances, many medium and small-sized stars, richly endowed with elements heavier than helium, will form a disk of gas and dust during their first few million years of existence.

Detailed numerical simulations of this process show that if the disk mass is low and the viscosity high, the disk will produce no gas giant planets at all. On the other hand, if the disk mass is high and its viscosity low, the disk will produce numerous gas giant planets with most, if not all, of them undergoing significant inward migration and acquiring large eccentricities in their orbits. During and after planet formation, the chaos generated by these events results in many of the planets either being ejected from the planetary system or being absorbed into the star.

The simulations demonstrate the exquisite fine-tuning required to form a set of gas giant planets akin to those in our solar system. For instance, the time required for the first gas giant planet to form had to equal the time for gas and dust to be depleted from the disk plus a specified tiny time difference. Thus, naturally forming planetary systems will rarely, if ever, duplicate the solar system's array of gas giants.

These results also matched the statistics for all the planets discovered beyond the solar system.

To date, there are 304 known extrasolar planetary systems. Of them, 303 contain a gas giant planet that either orbits its star closely (less than 3.5 times Earth's orbital distance from the Sun) or possesses a large orbital eccentricity.[10] Planets with these characteristics won't even permit a water-rich planet the size of Earth to form in their vicinity.[11]

So far, only one "Jupiter twin" has been discovered, HD 154345b.[12] This so-called twin of Jupiter orbits its star 20 percent closer than Jupiter does the Sun. It also lacks gas giant partners. Furthermore, its star is not even close to being a twin of the Sun. No advanced-life habitable planet is possible in the HD 154345 system.

Is a Search for Rocky Earth-Sized Planets Necessary?

Space agencies from nations around the world are lobbying their governments for expanded funding to sustain the search for rocky Earth-sized planets orbiting stars besides the Sun. Many scientists want to prove that the Milky Way Galaxy abounds with planets capable of supporting life. They claim that because such planets must be numerous, advanced life must be common, and no supernatural Creator is necessary to explain human existence.

The technology and manpower required to discover and determine the detailed characteristics of extrasolar planets the size of Earth and approximately matching Earth's orbit are orders of magnitude more costly than those necessary to determine the detailed features of planets like Jupiter and Saturn. Certainly the goal of learning about the physics and chemistry of Earth-sized planets is worthy in itself. However, if scientists want to experimentally determine the feasibility for the existence of bodies besides Earth with the capacity to support advanced life (apart from divine miracles), there is a much less-expensive way to proceed.

Astronomers can be confident that no advanced life is possible in the vicinity of an extrasolar star unless it possesses a planetary system that closely matches the features of Jupiter, Saturn, Uranus, and Neptune. Unless a true solar twin is found with four gas giant planets matching those detailed characteristics, there is no point in searching that system for a planet capable of sustaining advanced life. Nor should valuable telescope time be wasted in the search for electromagnetic signals from a hypothetical extraterrestrial intelligent civilization if no such star and suite of planets can be found.

Does a Milky Way Copy Exist?

Only galaxies that retain their spiral structure for many billions of years can possibly supply, at the right time and place, all the heavy elements advanced life needs. These requirements immediately eliminate about 94 percent of all galaxies as possible candidates for harboring advanced life.

Advanced life demands even more than just-right elements. It also needs a "habitable zone." That possibility exists only in spiral galaxies. The galactic habitable zone (see figure 8.1, p. 129) is the radial distance from the center of the galaxy where an adequate abundance of heavy elements exists for life, yet neither radiation nor stellar density pose a threat. Most spiral galaxies fail to provide such a zone.

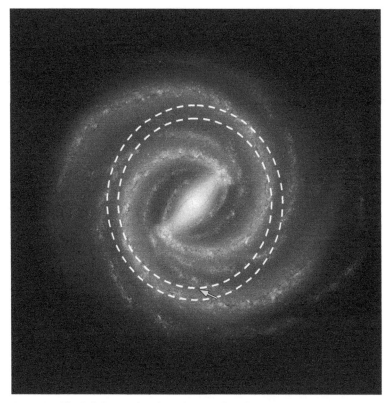

Figure 8.1. The Safe Spot within the Galactic Habitable Zone
This detailed reconstruction of the Milky Way Galaxy shows its spiral structure as well as the solar system's location within a narrow annulus (between the dotted circles). There it is protected from the dangers of the galactic core. That's also where the quantity and variety of heavy elements and long-lived radiometric isotopes required by advanced life are available. The solar system currently resides far from dangers to advanced life such as spiral arms, spurs, feathers, young supernova remnants, dense molecular clouds, and supergiant stars. (Image courtesy of NASA/JPL-Caltech)

In addition, advanced life is only possible in a spiral galaxy where the habitable zone coincides with the co-rotation distance. That's how far away from the galaxy's center a planetary system revolves around the galactic center at the same rate that the spiral arm structure rotates. A planetary system must be very close to this co-rotation distance to avoid frequently crossing the spiral arms. Only a tiny percentage of spiral galaxies manifest a habitable zone that coincides with this co-rotation distance.

Most spiral galaxies display extensive spiral substructure. Numerous spurs and feathers emanate out from the spiral arms. Advanced life can't tolerate proximity to any significant spiral arm substructures any more than it can survive being too close to a spiral arm. The Milky Way Galaxy not only has the just-right habitable zone but also is remarkably free of spurs and feathers.

Other wonders of the Milky Way Galaxy are the flatness of its spiral disk and the symmetry of its spiral arms. Unlike other spiral galaxies in its vicinity, there is no warp in the Milky Way Galaxy's spiral structure. Nor is there any distortion in its spiral arm pattern. The symmetry of its arms and its spiral arm pitch angle are ideal for advanced life.

All these features of the Milky Way Galaxy are just a few of more than a hundred highly improbable galactic characteristics that must be present for advanced life to be possible. The supernatural design predicted by RTB's biblical model explains why the Milky Way Galaxy is so perfectly fine-tuned for advanced life.

This conclusion can be experimentally tested by seeing if any other galaxy in the universe owns all of these advanced-life-essential traits. So far, astronomers find none. In fact, other spiral galaxies that come closest to matching the Milky Way Galaxy are noticeably lacking in these necessities (see figure 8.2, p. 131).

Is the Local Group Unique?

The Milky Way Galaxy resides in an unusual cluster of galaxies. Unlike typical clusters that contain thousands of densely packed galaxies, where several are giant or supergiant sized, the Local Group contains only about forty—two medium-sized (Andromeda and the Milky Way) and the rest small or dwarf. The Local Group's dwarf and subdwarf galaxies help sustain the Milky Way's spiral structure. (Unless the Milky Way Galaxy absorbs a small dwarf galaxy about once every half-billion to billion years, its spiral structure would collapse.)

Also less than typical, Local Group galaxies are spread apart. The lack of large, giant, and supergiant galaxies plus the distances between galaxies in the Local Group permits the Milky Way Galaxy's spiral structure to remain symmetrical and undisturbed.

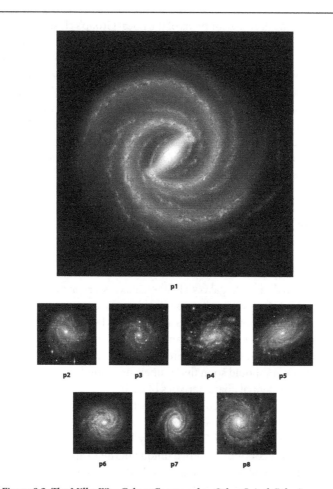

Figure 8.2. The Milky Way Galaxy Compared to Other Spiral Galaxies

The Milky Way Galaxy shows amazing symmetry in its spiral arm structure and little evidence of any recent internal or external major disturbance events, which sets it apart in its capacity to support advanced life. (Panel 1: Image courtesy of NASA/JPL-Caltech; Panel 2: Image courtesy of William Keel/University of Alabama; Panel 3: Image courtesy of Al Kelly [JSCAS/NASA] & Arne Henden [Flagstaff/USNO]; Panel 4: Image courtesy of NASA/JPL-Caltech/OCIW; Panel 5: Image courtesy of NASA/ESA, The Hubble Heritage Team and A. Riess [STScI]; Panel 6: Image courtesy of European Space Agency and Stephen Smartt [University of Cambridge]; Panel 7: Image courtesy of European Southern Observatory; Panel 8: Image courtesy of NASA, ESA, and the Hubble Heritage [STScI/AURA]-ESA/ Hubble Collaboration)

Searching the universe for twins of the Local Group's clusters of galaxies to test the idea of supernatural design will not be as easy as looking for duplicates of the Sun, Jupiter, Saturn, and the Milky Way. In most cases the greater distances from Earth challenge astronomers' ability to measure a galaxy cluster's traits with the required precision. The number, type, and distribution of dwarf and subdwarf galaxies, for instance, have not yet been well-determined for any cluster of galaxies beyond the Local Group. Nevertheless, even if the easy-to-see qualities are the only ones compared, no other known galaxy cluster comes anywhere near matching the advanced-life-essential attributes of the Local Group.

Predictive Tests

Uniqueness tests naturally lend themselves to more extensive testing. If a purposeful supernatural explanation for the advanced-life-essential features of Earth and its galaxy cluster, galaxy, star, planetary system, moon, and planetary surface has validity, then the uniqueness of each of these components should persist as astronomers learn more about their cosmic populations. On the other hand, if a strictly natural explanation for all the advanced-life-essential features of these components has validity, then astronomers should soon find numerous examples duplicating the advanced-life-essential characteristics of each.

RTB's creation model predicts that as astronomers continue to make discoveries about the populations of the various bodies that form the universe, Earth's own Local Group, Milky Way Galaxy, Sun, and planetary system will continue to prove unique in their capacity to support advanced life. So will the Moon and the Earth. A study of the origin of the Earth-Moon system, life's origin on Earth, and the possibility of life beyond Earth yield even more tests of RTB's model. They are explored in the next chapter.

9

PUTTING RTB'S MODEL FOR LIFE'S BEGINNING AND EXTRATERRESTRIAL HOMES TO THE TEST

Many a boy has used a magnifying glass to focus light and heat from the Sun onto some unsuspecting ant. I too was fascinated by a magnifier's capacity to concentrate heat. However, rather than seeing how many insects I could incinerate, I used mine to test how much heat it took to discourage bees from feasting on a dishful of a concentrated sugar solution.

Another test occurred to me during the course of this experiment. Occasionally I found a bee lying on the ground so motionless it appeared dead. Even when prodded with a stick, that bee would not move. However, if I focused sufficient heat on it with my magnifying glass, the bee crawled away from the heat, even though it couldn't fly.

This strange behavior motivated me to check out some library books. They described how gatherer bees take only enough honey from the hive to fuel their flight to a food source. Sometimes the bee runs out of energy. Then it stops flying and eventually becomes so motionless it appears dead. Even in that apparently dead state, however, a bee can be fully resuscitated if given some nectar.

Learning about bee behavior taught me important lessons about how scientists can use life's origins to test different creation/evolution models. Clearly, researchers must first determine what constitutes life and the conditions under which it can thrive.

The RTB creation model posits that life is extraordinarily complex. It claims Earth's first life arose and ultimately persisted not as a random naturalistic outcome but rather through supernatural intervention by the Creator. Again, keep in mind that the brief description here on life's origin and its possibility beyond Earth cannot equate to the extensive evaluations already in other RTB books, especially *Why the Universe Is the Way It Is* and *Origins of Life.*[1] However, a brief list of some of the model's distinctive features permits a significant evaluation.

Some Testable Features

RTB's model for life's beginnings and possible homes rests on the following biblical assertions and inferences. God personally shaped and crafted:

- *the universe* to produce all the ingredients necessary to sustain life, including humans. The heavens contain abundant evidence of God's fine-tuning for life's sake. Observers thus have the potential to uncover evidence of the supernatural, super-intelligent design of life's cosmic environment for humanity's specific benefit.
- *Earth* to provide for humanity's physical needs and well-being. Abundant evidence of the supernatural, super-intelligent design of Earth for the specific benefit and bountiful provision of the human species and its civilization can be discovered by humans.
- *all life* by supernaturally intervening early in Earth's history under relatively hostile conditions.
- *all life* at the optimal times and places and in the optimal forms and durations for the future benefit of humanity.
- *human life* for his good purposes (see chapter 12).

Chapters 7 and 8 briefly outlined the designs of the cosmic environment that made possible a planet like Earth with the capacity to support primitive life. Earth in its initial state, however, was far from conducive to sustain advanced life. It needed much additional crafting and design.

A Critical Collision

The atmosphere a planet accumulates during formation depends primarily on two factors: the planet's gravitational pull and the distance from its star. The greater the pull and distance, the thicker the atmosphere, and the more powerful the planet's capability to retain light-molecular-weight molecules long-term.

These conditions pose a serious challenge. For advanced life to be possible, abundant water vapor must be retained for several billion years. However, the high gravity and low temperature necessary for such retention would result in an atmosphere far too thick for life, much thicker than that of Venus. For Earth to possibly support advanced life, something had to blow away about 99 percent of this primordial atmosphere.

According to detailed computer modeling developed in 2004, when primordial Earth was only 30 to 50 million years old, a Mars-sized planet smashed into Earth at a 45-degree angle. This planet's speed upon impact was surprisingly slow (less than 4 kilometers per second).[2]

The collision:

- ejected Earth's thick, life-suffocating atmosphere. Some material eventually returned, forming a new atmosphere—one with the perfect air pressure for efficient lung performance, the ideal heat-trapping capability, and the just-right transparency for efficient photosynthesis.

- supplied the optimal chemical composition so the new atmosphere could be further transformed by simple life-forms into the appropriate composition to sustain advanced life.

- augmented Earth's mass and density enough to allow the atmosphere to retain a large, but not too large, quantity of water vapor for billions of years.

- raised the amount of iron in Earth's core close to the level necessary for a strong, enduring magnetic field (the remainder came from a later collision event—see pp. 138–40). This magnetic field shields life from deadly cosmic rays and solar X-rays.

- delivered just-right quantities of iron and other critical elements to Earth's core and mantle. These produced sufficiently long-lasting, continent-building plate tectonics at just-right levels. Finely tuned plate tectonics perform a crucial role in compensating for the Sun's increasing brightness.
- increased the iron content of Earth's crust, permitting a huge abundance of ocean life that can support advanced life.[3]
- salted Earth's interior with an abundance of long-lasting radio-isotopes, the heat from which drives most of Earth's tectonic activity and volcanism.[4]
- gradually slowed Earth's rotation to a rate that eventually permitted advanced life to thrive.
- stabilized Earth's rotation axis tilt, protecting the planet from rapid and extreme climatic variations.[5]
- formed Earth's moon.

Without the Moon, Earth could not sustain advanced life. Only a single massive moon has the gravitational strength to stabilize the tilt of a planet's rotation axis for an extended period. More than the mass, the ratio of the Moon's mass relative to Earth's mass is critical. Relative to its planet, the moon is fifty times more massive than any other known satellite.

A Moon Made for Man

Such an extraordinarily enormous mass ratio suggests purposeful design, especially when combined with several other extremely fine-tuned lunar features.[6] Dave Waltham, a British planetary scientist, decided to put this lunar anthropic principle to the test. He reasoned that if intended design for advanced life's benefit indeed explains the Moon's fine-tuned features, then this brand of the lunar anthropic principle should possess predictive power.[7]

Specifically, Waltham predicted that scientists should discover additional extraordinary fine-tuning of the Moon's characteristics targeting the needs of advanced life. Not content to wait, he launched his own search.

Waltham found that a moon's optimal mass for stabilizing Earth's rotation period would be one-half of our Moon's actual mass. In fact, Earth's moon is barely small enough. If its mass were only 2 percent greater (a radius of just an additional seven miles), the Moon would have pulled the tilt of Earth's rotation axis out of stability. At first this finding seemed to argue against design, but further study reversed that direction.

Waltham recognized that the Moon's large mass puts the brakes on Earth's rotation rate (via tidal friction). A moon less massive would take considerably longer than 4.5 billion years to slow Earth's rotation rate to the optimal twenty-four hours per day. Taking longer would have resulted in a brighter and less stable sun, one too luminous and unstable for the support of advanced life on Earth.

A more rapid rotation rate was not a good option either. Increased rotation speed would have led to greater temperature extremes and less evenly distributed rainfall on Earth.

The lunar anthropic principle yields additional predictive power. The Moon exhibits the just-right mass and mass density so that after 4.5 billion years of spiraling away from Earth, the Moon subtends in the sky (for Earth-based observers) the same angular diameter as does the Sun. These identical diameters make perfect solar eclipses possible. Such eclipses helped emerging civilizations build accurate historical records and later permitted both an easy test of general relativity and certain breakthroughs in understanding solar physics.

The Moon-forming collision event resulted in a planet whose surface gravity and temperature, atmospheric composition and pressure, iron abundance, tectonics, volcanism, rotation rate, decline in rotation rate, stable rotation axis tilt, and perfect solar eclipses are *all* in the just-right range to support advanced life.[8] What could have been a catastrophic collision for Earth, upon closer look, affirms the RTB model's claim of a Creator's purposeful intent.

This last point can also be framed as a set of additional predictive tests. Naturalistic models for the universe and life's history would predict that as astronomers discover extrasolar bodies as small as Earth and its Moon and learn more about the physics of planet-and-moon formation, relatively simple naturalistic explanations will emerge for how the Earth-Moon system formed and acquired its capacity to support advanced life. The RTB creation model predicts the opposite. It predicts that increasing knowledge will show that strict analogs to the Earth-Moon system demand even more fine-tuning than evident today and that these analogs in other planetary systems will prove extremely rare or nonexistent.

A Beneficial Late Bombardment

Not only was primordial Earth's atmosphere deadly, but so were the primordial solar system's asteroids and comets. A steady stream of potential life-exterminating collision events pelted Earth during its early days (see figure 9.1 below).

These asteroids and comets, nevertheless, played a crucial role. As they gravitationally interacted with Jupiter, Saturn, Uranus, and Neptune, the asteroids and comets caused all four planets to migrate outward from their birthplace and assume much more circular orbits. These new locations and orbital features proved essential for the support of advanced life on Earth (see chapter 8, pp. 125–28).

This primordial asteroid-comet belt prepared Earth for advanced life in another important way. Because Saturn was closer to the densest part of the belt than Jupiter, Saturn moved outward faster. When its orbit reached a point where Saturn made exactly one orbit of the Sun for every two orbits of Jupiter, the resulting 1:2 resonance destabilized the entire belt of asteroids and comets. Many of them were pushed out into the much more distant Oort cloud, while others hurtled into the inner solar system causing the Late Heavy Bombardment.[9]

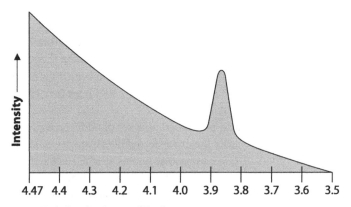

Figure 9.1. Early Bombardment of Earth

Large asteroids and comets pummeled the entire inner solar system (from Mars to Mercury) between 4.57 and 3.5 billion years ago. The intensity declined exponentially during that time—except for during the Late Heavy Bombardment (3.9 to 3.8 billion years ago). Triggered by an orbital resonance between Jupiter and Saturn, this event destabilized the Kuiper Belt's asteroids and comets.[10] (Illustration by Jonathan Price)

Astronomers have calculated that between 3.9 and 3.8 billion years ago, the Late Heavy Bombardment pummeled Earth with roughly 17,000 collisions.[11] These collisions deposited a total of 400,000 pounds of extra-terrestrial material per square yard (220,000 kilograms per meter squared) over the entire surface of Earth.[12]

This destabilization event reduced the size of the asteroid-comet belt to just 1 percent of its former magnitude. What remained of the belt moved out beyond Neptune's orbit. Now neither the belt's size nor its position poses a serious threat to advanced life on Earth.

Recently geophysicists have reproduced the temperature and pressure conditions of Earth's mantle and core in laboratory experiments.[13] Their results demonstrate that the Late Heavy Bombardment heated Earth's surface so that an ocean of hot magma several hundred kilometers deep covered the entire planet. In addition, their calculations and experiments showed that the very large size and high oxygen content of Earth's core—critical factors for the long-term maintenance of Earth's life-essential magnetic and tectonic characteristics—resulted from this deep magma ocean.

Like the earlier collision event that produced the Moon, the Late Heavy Bombardment required precise fine-tuning. One enormous blast, by itself, was insufficient to prepare Earth for advanced life. Both collision events had to be carefully fine-tuned and timed to ensure that Earth formed a core with the just-right chemical composition and size to maintain the magnetic field and plate tectonics advanced life requires.

The timing of the Late Heavy Bombardment implies that life's origin on Earth occurred within a geological instant. Carbon-13 to carbon-12 ratio analysis of ancient carbonaceous material, along with an abundance analysis of the decay products from uranium and thorium oxide precipitates, establishes that life was abundant on Earth as far back as 3.8 billion years ago.[14]

Carbon-13 to carbon-12 ratio analysis, plus nitrogen-15 to nitrogen-14 ratio analysis on ancient carbonaceous material, further establishes that a primordial soup, or mineral substrate of prebiotic molecules, never existed on Earth.[15] The Late Heavy Bombardment did not end until about 3.8 billion years ago. Therefore, Earth transitioned from a life-exterminating to a life-abundant state in less than a few million years.

The RTB biblical creation model explains the two collision events as the handiwork of God, who chose in the context of his physical laws to prepare Earth as quickly as possible for an array of abundant simple life-forms that over the next few billion years established an environment suitable for advanced life. The geologically instantaneous nature of life's origin—without the presence of prebiotics—and the abundance and diversity of life 3.8 billion years ago seriously challenge all materialistic/naturalistic models. These findings fit well, however, with a Creator's plan to create humans as well as develop the possibility of advanced civilization and technology as quickly as possible.

Building-Block Paradoxes

From a naturalistic perspective, the origin of life required a site where amino acids (building blocks of proteins) and nucleotides (building blocks of DNA and RNA) could be efficiently concentrated and assembled. One problem, however, is that both oxygen and ultraviolet radiation are toxic to this prebiotic chemistry. They powerfully shut down any possible synthesis of amino acids and nucleotides.

This oxygen-ultraviolet paradox explains why Earth contains no record of any prebiotics. The presence of oxygen halts prebiotic chemistry, whereas the lack of oxygen means no ozone shield could form in Earth's atmosphere to prevent the penetration of ultraviolet radiation from the Sun.

A few astronomers have speculated that perhaps some regions within dense interstellar molecular clouds might lack both oxygen and ultraviolet radiation and, thus, might conceivably permit prebiotics to form. However, no amino acids, nucleotides, or even the pentose sugars and nitrogenous bases that make up parts of the nucleotides have been found there. Repeated claims for the detection of the simplest amino acid (glycine)[16] have proved false, as have claims for the detection of the simplest nitrogenous base (pyrimidine).[17]

A few meteorites contain up to six of the twenty biologically required amino acids at levels of several parts per million or less. One meteorite, the Murchison, contains three nitrogenous bases (at a few parts per billion).[18] However, research shows that some of these amino acids and nitrogenous bases may not be indigenous to the meteorites, but rather may result from terrestrial contamination (contact with the remains of life on Earth).[19] Furthermore, astronomers have found no amino acids or nitrogenous bases in comets, the source of the meteorites in question.[20]

Astronomers do detect all the chemical precursors for both amino acids and nitrogenous bases in both comets and interstellar molecular clouds. Thus it's simply a matter of better technology and more time before they actually discover the existence of amino acids and nitrogenous bases in those locations. However, current measurements using existing technology already establish that maximum abundance levels for amino acids, nitrogenous bases, and pentose sugars in comets and interstellar molecular clouds fall orders of magnitude below what any naturalistic origin-of-life scenario would require.

The absence of significant concentrations of prebiotics on Earth or anywhere in the Milky Way Galaxy[21] appears to rule out the possibility of life's spontaneous emergence. Yet life appeared—suddenly and early in Earth's history.[22] RTB's creation model both anticipates and explains this scenario.

On One Hand or the Other

Naturalistic models for life's origin also require a site where amino acids and pentose sugars of a single orientation (right or left) can be selected from the normal random mix of left- and right-handed configurations. Amino acids can link together to form protein chains only when the group is entirely one-handed (homochiral)—either all right or all left. Likewise, nucleotides can link together to form DNA or RNA only when the pentose sugars are all the same handedness.

No known natural mechanism exists on Earth, past or present, for generating this homochirality.[23] While some individual mineral crystals produce limited right- or left-handed enrichment (at best, about 10 percent), any natural ensemble of mineral crystals contains roughly the same number of crystals favoring production of left-handed configurations as it does those favoring right.[24]

Even under highly complex and carefully controlled laboratory conditions roughly simulating a realistic natural environment, chemists have struggled to produce homochiral amino acids. Only experiments exploiting 100 percent circularly polarized ultraviolet (UV) light have led to positive results. But even then, only a 20 percent excess of left-handed amino acids could be generated.[25] The cost, however, was the destruction of nearly all the original amino acids. For every 2 percent excess generated, half or more of the amino acids in the original mixture were destroyed.[26]

The only known natural source of circularly polarized UV light resides far from Earth—in the synchrotron radiation emitted by a few neutron stars and in regions just outside some black holes. At best, such light is only slightly more than 40 percent circularly polarized and only for brief periods.[27] Experiments simulating the synchrotron radiation emitted by neutron stars produced a mere 1.12 percent excess of homochiral amino acids.[28] These experiments, however, used 100 percent circularly polarized light at only one wavelength.

Neutron stars and the regions around black holes emit light across a broad spectrum, bringing the Kuhn-Condon rule into play. This rule notes that while one wavelength of circularly polarized UV light destroys more left-handed amino acids than right, a different wavelength has the opposite effect.[29] Thus, a broad light band will fail to produce any significant homochirality.

The lack of discernible natural mechanisms for generating homochiral amino acids and pentose sugars remains devastating to naturalistic models. Theistic evolutionists who hold that God's creative activity manifests itself only and always through natural processes face the same intractable problem. RTB's biblical creation model proposes that a purposeful Creator intervened to produce the otherwise impossible homochirality essential for construction of life molecules.

Is There Life from Beyond?

A relatively new discipline tackles the daunting problems facing naturalistic scenarios for life's origin. Astrobiology is concerned with life beyond Earth. So far, no life of any kind has been found or even shown possible in alternate places.

Potential indigenous life sites already ruled out by astrobiologists include:

• other solar system bodies
• interplanetary gas and dust
• interplanetary rocks and comets
• interstellar gas and dust
• interstellar rocks

In none of these places could life have originated through natural means (see "So Why Do NASA and ESA Keep Looking for Life on Mars?"). Nor could any of them have been vehicles that carried life from a distant planet or moon to Earth.[30]

The lack of any naturally occurring life-transport mechanism to carry life from some hypothesized distant site has led some prominent origin-of-life researchers to suggest life arose through "directed panspermia."

This hypothesis proposes that intelligent aliens intentionally seeded Earth with life, bringing it here on a spacecraft about 3.8 billion years ago.[31]

The directed panspermia proposal collides with two insurmountable barriers. First, the laws of physics and the cosmic space-time dimensions

So Why Do NASA and ESA Keep Looking for Life on Mars?

As impossible as it is to explain life's origin on Earth from a naturalistic perspective, trying to explain it on Mars is even more challenging. Mars is subject to the same oxygen-ultraviolet paradox and homochirality problems as Earth. In addition, Mars has such a rarified atmosphere that the freezing point of water is identical to the boiling point. This characteristic implies that water can remain liquid on the Martian surface for only a few seconds at most. Compounding these problems are the much more corrosive chemical environment and much harsher radiation environment on Mars.

In addition, Mars, unlike Earth, suffered a carbonate catastrophe. The Late Heavy Bombardment 3.85 billion years ago brought a lot of water and carbon dioxide to Mars. They reacted with Mars's surface rocks to form carbonates. This carbonate production rapidly depleted the Martian atmosphere of carbon dioxide and water. Thus Mars was swiftly and permanently transformed into a dry, cold wasteland.

These facts seem to have done little to dampen the enthusiasm of many at NASA (National Aeronautics and Space Administration) and ESA (European Space Agency) in their search for life on Mars and other solar system bodies. The primary rationale is that scientists observe extremophiles on Earth—a few hardy life-forms surviving under extremely hostile conditions. So researchers reason that if life can survive under harsh conditions on Earth, why not under harsh conditions on Mars?

This thinking commits at least one fallacy—extremophiles are irrelevant to the origin of life. The harsh conditions under which extremophiles survive pose orders of magnitude greater difficulty for a naturalistic origin-of-life model than the conditions under which ordinary life thrives.[32]

would have prevented physical aliens, no matter how well-funded or technologically advanced, from safely traversing the interstellar distances in any reasonable time period. Either too much time would transpire to allow life onboard to survive or radiation, interstellar dust and debris, and long-term wear and stress on the spacecraft and its occupants would have destroyed them in transit.[33]

Second, at the time life appeared on Earth, the universe was only 9.9 billion years old—far too young for an advanced physical species to have emerged and developed technological sophistication by any conceivable natural means. The building blocks of advanced life and the resources to sustain advanced civilization simply didn't exist during that early epoch.

Fundamentally, directed panspermia suggests no solution to the origin-of-life problem. The hypothesis merely transfers the concerns to a different time and place.

A few scientists have proposed another exotic alternative as the answer to the origin-of-life question. They hypothesize the existence of a yet undiscovered, self-organizing, complexity-enhancing physical law as the "cause" of life.[34] Such a law, however, directly contradicts the second law of thermodynamics, which says that all systems in the universe proceed toward increasing disorder and decreasing complexity. Although isolated departures from thermodynamic equilibrium can occur, the more extreme the departure, the more rapid the return to equilibrium. For anything as complex as a simple bacterium, the return-time would be so fast as to be indistinguishable from zero.

The anthropic principle rules out any possibility of a self-organizing, complexity-enhancing law of physics as the cause of life. For stars and planets to form and for any kind of physical life to be possible anywhere and at any time in the universe, the cosmos must be both homogeneous and uniform to a very high degree. Thus all parts of the universe must also be subject to a very high measure of entropy (increasing disorder).

Despite ample funding, astrobiology has yet to produce any evidence for indigenous extraterrestrial life. Eventually, however, researchers will find life or more likely life's remains on other solar system bodies.

Over the course of life's history (3.8 billion years), impacts by meteorites massive enough to generate large craters (a few kilometers or more across) would have blasted hundreds of millions of tons of Earth rocks and soil beyond Earth's gravity and scattered them throughout the solar system.[35] This debris, containing thousands of tons of organisms and their remains, landed on nearby planets and their moons. Table 9.1 shows the estimated amounts.[36]

Table 9.1: Delivery of Earth Material to Other Solar System Bodies

Solar System Body	Estimated Amount of Earth Material (grams per sq. kilometer)
Moon	200,000
Venus	3.1
Mercury	3.3
Mars	1.0
Jupiter	0.09
Saturn	0.01

Some of Earth's microorganisms may even have been temporarily viable on Mars and Earth's moon. Because of their proximity to Earth, a remote possibility exists that Earth life could have arrived on the Moon or Mars aboard a speck of meteoritic material before the harsh lunar or Martian conditions killed it.

Are There Repeated Origins?

The RTB biblical model predicts that life may have originated by the Creator's hand more than once, before and/or after the Late Heavy Bombardment. Figure 9.1 (p. 138) illustrates the bombardment by large asteroids and comets during the first billion years of Earth's history that kept conditions unstable for life.

Clearly the Moon-forming collision that occurred about 4.50 billion years ago and the Late Heavy Bombardment about 3.85 billion years ago made the entire planet temporarily uninhabitable for any conceivable life-form. While several other extermination events likely occurred between these two milestones, relatively life-benign conditions may have existed for brief interludes between them.

Indeed, scientists have recovered a few zircon crystals dating to various epochs between 4.4 and 3.9 billion years ago with oxygen-18 to oxygen-16 ratios indicating Earth possessed a watery ocean for at least a few brief periods.[37] The existence of intermittent oceans during that time means early life could have existed periodically before being destroyed.

Some 4.25-billion-year-old zircons found in Western Australia show the same low carbon-13 to carbon-12 ratios as seen in the decayed remains of life.[38] However, the ratios are not unambiguous evidence for very early life. Some nonbiotic reactions involving carbon oxides, methane, hydrogen, and water produce the same results, results that also are exhibited in some interplanetary dust particles.

These multiple origins of early life could have accomplished one or more possible long-range purposes that included:

- consuming at least some of the greenhouse gases (carbon dioxide, water vapor, and/or methane) from Earth's interior and/or their input from comet collisions to help prevent a buildup that would have permanently made Earth too hot for life.
- helping to fill Earth's early oxygen sinks (oxygen-consuming mineral reservoirs) so humans could arrive at the best possible time for the launch and maintenance of advanced civilization.
- getting a head start on boosting atmospheric and oceanic oxygen levels.
- correcting the potential imbalance caused by the young Sun's cooling (due to solar mass loss) through the creation of methanogenic bacteria. These bacteria produce methane, a powerful greenhouse gas.

Discoveries confirming multiple origins of life on Earth would pose no problem for RTB's creation model. This approach could easily suit the purposes and powers of the biblical Creator. By contrast, such findings would only exacerbate the already intractable problems naturalistic models face. Instead of needing to explain only one "virtually impossible" origin of life, they would need to explain several.

An Impossible Planet Made Possible

RTB's creation model acknowledges the purposefully orchestrated and timed sequence of probability-defying events as the efficiently and effectively engineered and timed work of the biblical Creator. This model proposes that he prepared Earth for the just-right simple life-forms that established, at just-right epochs, an environment fit for advanced life and human civilization. The next chapter evaluates how well RTB's creation model explains life's history on Earth.

10

PUTTING RTB'S CREATION MODEL FOR LIFE'S HISTORY TO THE TEST

The scree and talus slopes in British Columbia make it one of my favorite mountaineering areas. These deep piles of pebbles (scree) or rocks (talus) permit my boots to sink into that loose conglomerate of stones, giving me the necessary traction to climb many a spectacular peak. How deep I sink determines my climbing rate. It also determines how steep a slope I can safely climb.

The unpredictable weather in that region motivated me to test both the degree of my safety and climbing speeds on various kinds of scree and talus under varying conditions. I quickly discovered that the weight of my backpack, steepness of the slope, size and shape of the pebbles or rocks and their depth, as well as the amount of moisture on them, are the most important factors. It only took a couple of climbing seasons before I could look at a slope and determine whether I could complete the ascent without risk of injury. I also learned to calculate fairly accurately how long that climb might take.

How much time the Creator took, given his chosen physical laws, to prepare Earth for advanced life can also be calculated. Many factors weigh in.

New understanding of Earth and life's history reveals crucial and intricate preparations for humanity's benefit. The RTB creation model proposes that the cosmic Creator supernaturally intervened on frequent occasions to transform the earthly environment into a habitat suitable for progressively more advanced species of life. Once again, there's no way all the specific details for this particular portion of RTB's biblical model can be included. Many of them, however, have been presented in other RTB books, especially *Origins of Life*.[1] However, a brief list of a few of the model's distinctives that pertain to life's history permits some specific scientific evaluations and tests.

Some Testable Features

RTB's creation model, as pertaining to life's history on Earth and the preparations of its habitat, is based on the following biblically derived premises. God personally shaped and crafted:

* *Earth* (including its interior, exterior, and atmosphere) over the entire history of life to provide all the needs of every life-form.
* *the physical environment* for life and the precisely timed layering of life for humanity's benefit in a way that reveals abundant and increasing evidence of the Creator's involvement. He gave humans the potential to uncover accumulating evidence for the supernatural, super-intelligent design of the planet and its creatures over Earth's entire history.
* *life in a progression from relatively simple to radically advanced.* Research is expected to increasingly confirm this pattern in life's history.
* *life with optimal designs.* Research should reveal increasing evidence of this optimization at all levels: in life's molecules, cells, tissues, organs, appendages, organisms, species, and ecologies. Because what is optimal for one species also may be optimal for others, investigators should find common design features.
* *life with optimized ecological relationships.* All life—bacteria, detritivores (organisms that feed on the remains of life), plants, herbivores, carnivores, and parasites—was designed to interrelate in ways that enhance the quality of life for all species.
* *Earth* and all its life to supply everything for the launch and maintenance of global human civilization.

* *life in such a way as to hold all authority over it.* The Creator determined when various life-forms were to enter and leave Earth's habitats. Researchers can expect to find evidence that the timing of origination and extinction events in the fossil record follows a strategic plan that prepared for humanity's future needs and well-being. Each species of life began at the best possible time for the launch and spread of civilization.

This creation model anticipates a different scenario from prominent naturalistic models for life's history on Earth. These naturalistic models rest on the premise that life descended from the last universal common ancestor (LUCA). This single life-form is presumed much simpler than any existing today.

RTB's model, however, claims that the biblically stated plans and purposes of the Creator for humanity imply that he created first life as soon as early Earth was prepared for it. It also implies that life appeared suddenly in as great an abundance and diversity as the planet permitted.

Early, Diverse, and Complex

Evidence now shows the simultaneous appearance of multiple distinct complex unicellular life-forms rather than a single ultra-simple organism. This ensemble likely included (at minimum) both oxygenic and anoxygenic photosynthetic life, sulfate-reducing microbes, and a diversity of other chemoautotrophs (microbes that exploit high-energy chemicals to sustain metabolic reactions). Each primordial life-form played a crucial role in preparing the way, with remarkable efficiency and speed, for the eventual appearance of more advanced animals. Ultimately humans appeared on the scene and civilization rapidly emerged.

Not So Simple Genes

Genomics research reveals that no organism, not even a simple parasite (dependent on other species for some of its life-critical functions), can survive without at least 250 functioning gene products.[2]

When geochemists found evidence for uranium/thorium fractionation precipitates in rocks older than 3.7 billion years, it showed Earth's first life was far more complex. This discovery indicated that oxygen-exploiting photosynthetic bacteria were already prolific at that early date.[3] Such bacteria require more than 1,700 gene products[4]—350 more than the simplest independent (nonparasitic) organisms alive today.[5]

Naturalistic explanations for Earth's first life demand that such life be orders of magnitude simpler and less diverse than the simplest independent life-forms on Earth today. However, the sudden simultaneous appearance of highly diverse and not-so-simple life-forms as early as 3.8 billion years ago is consistent with the work of a supernatural, super-intelligent Being, aggressively preparing Earth for humanity and civilization.

Transforming Vital Poisons

The primordial salting of Earth with heavy elements produced globally distributed deposits of arsenic, boron, chlorine, chromium, cobalt, copper, fluorine, iodine, iron, manganese, molybdenum, nickel, phosphorous, potassium, selenium, sulfur, tin, vanadium, and zinc—all of which are among life's vital "poisons."[6] Though advanced life requires minimum amounts of these elements in the environment in soluble forms, too much of any one of them in a soluble form would prove deadly.

Early in life's history, sulfate-reducing bacteria directly participated in re-forming and redistributing heavy elements that otherwise would have thwarted the future existence of advanced life. Following the re-formation and redistribution, the just-right kinds and quantities of sulfate-reducing and photosynthetic bacteria remained to perfectly regulate several life-sustaining processes, such as the sulfur and carbon cycles.[7]

Sulfate-reducing bacteria remove toxic concentrations of certain elements from water. For example, some species of bacteria consume water-soluble zinc and manufacture pure sphalerite (ZnS) from it.[8] This sphalerite is insoluble and, therefore, nontoxic for advanced life. Moreover, when sufficiently large, dense populations of these bacteria die and settle onto ocean and lake bottoms, they precipitate highly economic ZnS ore deposits.

Researchers now recognize that sulfate-reducing bacteria supplied much, if not all, of the concentrated (thus economic to mine) ore deposits of iron, magnesium, zinc, and lead. Ores of trace metals such as silver, arsenic, selenium, and other vital poisons may similarly owe their concentrations to sulfate-reducing bacteria.

The dominance of sulfate-reducing bacteria for nearly a billion years or more early in life's history paved the way for advanced life, especially humans—not in a random way but in what appears to be a purposeful, carefully timed manner. From 2.9 billion years ago to the present, the abundance and diversity of sulfate-reducing bacteria declined to the just-right levels to maintain the delicate balance necessary to nourish advanced life but not harm it. Today the release into the environment through erosion forces of soluble vital poisons is perfectly balanced by the removal of soluble vital poisons by sulfate-reducing bacteria. In addition, it took the easy-to-mine vital-poison ores produced over the past few billion years by sulfate-reducing bacteria to equip humanity for global high-technology civilization.

Preparing the Land

Earth's early landmasses were hot and soil-deficient. Because cryptogamic colonies can withstand these harsh conditions, they took hold as soon as the first barren continental masses appeared. These microbial colonies effectively limited erosion and at the same time enhanced chemical conditioning of the soil. They also cooled the environment and oxygenated the atmosphere.

Analyses of this cryptogamic crust material—soils comprised of photosynthetic or oxygen-producing bacteria, fungi, mosses, sand, and clay existing together in symbiotic relationships—reveal that these microbial soils transformed both the temperature and chemistry of Earth's early landmasses. Over 2 to 3 billion years, cryptogamic colonies transformed Earth's landmasses into the large accumulations of stable, nutrient-rich soil that vascular plants (higher plants with conducting tissue consisting primarily of xylem and phloem) require.[9] This preparation helps explain the long wait—roughly 3.3 billion years—for the arrival of the first advanced life-forms. It suggests careful planning for later life's needs.

Raising the Continents

Though cryptogamic colonies need only a few small islands to survive, advanced life needed continents. A combination of both large continents and large oceans were also necessary for regulating Earth's surface and atmosphere to compensate for the Sun's increasing brightness (see pp. 156–58). However, continents were not a given. Earth would have remained a permanent water world, with water covering its entire surface, if not for powerful and sustained plate tectonics.

Continents formed out of light silicate rocks that "floated" above the denser basaltic rocks comprising ocean floors. The separation of Earth's primordial crust into silicates and basalts occurred through the dynamics of crustal plate pressures and movements.

Stable, long-standing plate tectonics required three things: (1) a powerful, long-lasting source of radioactive decay in Earth's interior, (2) a stable efficient dynamo (electric generator) in Earth's core, and (3) an abundant supply of liquid water on Earth's surface. Each of these essentials had to exist at a precisely fine-tuned level.

For example, an abundance of long-lived radioactive elements requires (among other things) a concert of highly unlikely, perfectly timed and placed supernova events, as well as the amazingly fine-tuned collision that formed the Moon. The stability and efficiency of Earth's dynamo depends on the exact regulation of at least seven major geophysical features:

1. Relative abundances of silicon, iron, and sulfur in Earth's solid inner core
2. Viscosities at the boundaries between this solid inner core and the liquid outer core and between the liquid outer core and the mantle
3. Ratio of Earth's inner core to outer core radii
4. Ratio of the inner core to outer core magnetic diffusivity (measure of how well a magnetic field diffuses throughout a conducting medium)
5. Magnetic Reynolds number (a measure of viscous flow behavior) for the outer core
6. Gravitational torques from the Sun and Moon
7. Earth's core precession frequency[10]

The intricate process of continent building began with the decay of radioactive elements in Earth's interior. This release of energy provided enough heat to generate convective cells throughout Earth's mantle. These cells are giant eddies that circulate in the mantle from just above Earth's core to just under Earth's crust. Different eddies associate with different crust regions. At the boundaries of these regions, subduction (the sliding of one crustal plate under another) can occur, but *only* if a huge amount of high-density, low-temperature liquid water was available to lubricate the sliding.

Subduction is governed by the rate at which minerals in the area where two underwater plates come together (the subduction zone) chemically react with water to form hydrated minerals.[11] The hydration process in the downward-moving slabs leads to production of a talc layer that reduces and stabilizes the sliding friction between adjoining plates. A just-right level of lubrication permits efficient movement of one tectonic plate under another.

At these subduction zones, some basaltic slabs become hydrated. This lowers the newly hydrated minerals' melting point. Once enough of these silicates began to float above the nonhydrated basalts, Earth's mountains and continents began forming. Given their lower melting point, the silicates stayed liquid at depths closer to the surface, thereby facilitating the formation of volcanoes.

The ongoing development of mountains and volcanoes resulted in landmasses poking up above the water's surface. With yet more time, these landmasses grew to become continents (see figure 10.1, p. 156). However, they had to continue growing at the just-right rates throughout life's history for the Sun's increasing luminosity to be properly compensated.

For there to be any hope of removing enough greenhouse gases from Earth's atmosphere (pp. 158–61) to compensate for the Sun's increasing luminosity, continental landmass buildup through plate tectonics had to initially exceed and later at least keep up with the reduction of continental landmasses through erosion. However, the energy release from radioactive decay (the primary driving force behind plate tectonics and continental buildup) declines over time. The plate-tectonic movement level today is only about a fifth of what it was when life first appeared.

The same collision that helped enrich Earth with radioactive elements also produced its gigantic moon. The Moon acts as a tidal brake on Earth, gradually slowing its rotation rate. A slower rotation rate meant less erosion. Thus, the decline in the rate of continent buildup was accompanied by a decline in the rate of continent erosion.

So many factors had to be fined-tuned to sustain stable silicate continents—not to mention oceans—at levels that perfectly compensated for the Sun's luminosity variations that defining their existence as a miracle seems fully justified. Even nontheistic scientists acknowledge Earth's long-lasting, large continents and oceans as truly amazing.[12] Earth may indeed be the only planet to possess such features.

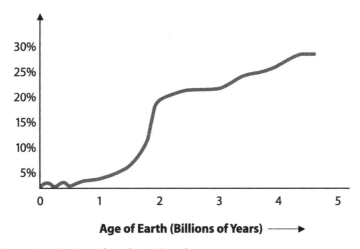

Figure 10.1. Continental Landmass Growth

For the first 750 million years of its history, Earth alternated between total and near total water coverage, with just a few small islands occasionally popping up above sea level. Later, as a result of ongoing plate tectonic activity, continental landmass grew relatively rapidly. Today, continental buildup through tectonic activity is only slightly greater than continental shrinkage due to erosion. (Illustration by Jonathan Price)

A Brightening Sun

Most evolutionary models make a foundational assumption that the Sun provided stable temperature conditions on Earth throughout the past 3 to 4 billion years. However, astronomers now recognize that the Sun's luminosity (brightness) has varied by as much as 15 percent. The need to compensate for such changes helps explain why the fossil record looks the way it does. In addition, it discloses how much foresight and planning went into the frequent but intermittent eradications and introductions of life on Earth.

Astronomers have learned that the Sun shed between 4 and 7 percent of its primordial mass during its first 1.0 to 1.5 billion years.[13] Because the Sun's luminosity is proportional to slightly less than the fourth power of its mass, its brightness during that era declined by about 15 percent. Since then, however, the Sun's luminosity has steadily increased.

This increased brightness results from the Sun's nuclear burning that turns hydrogen into helium. The extra helium then increases the Sun's core density, which causes a higher core temperature. That hotter temperature augments the nuclear burning rate. Over the last 3.5 to 3 billion years, the Sun's luminosity has increased by about 15 percent.[14]

The initial drop in the Sun's brightness followed by its gradual increase should have destroyed any chance for life's tenure on Earth. Life cannot tolerate even a 1 percent change in luminosity.[15]

Yet these dramatic changes obviously did *not* sterilize Earth. The capacity for Earth's atmosphere to trap heat (the greenhouse effect) had a modulating effect on the Sun's luminosity as it impacted Earth's surface. A faint Sun could be compensated for by a more-efficient greenhouse effect in the atmosphere, while a less-efficient greenhouse effect could compensate for a brighter Sun.

At the time of life's origin 3.8 billion years ago, the Sun would have been considerably fainter than today, but Earth's atmosphere then was much

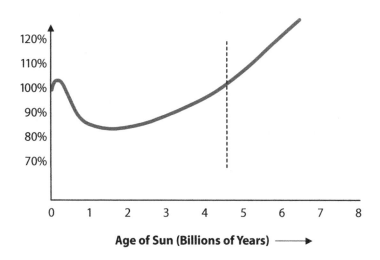

Figure 10.2. Sun's Luminosity History

The Sun's luminosity continues to increase and will eventually make Earth uninhabitable. (Illustration by Jonathan Price)

richer in greenhouse gases, carbon dioxide, methane, and water vapor. Consequently, Earth's surface would have been considerably warmer.

During roughly the first half billion years of life's history, life progressed from unicellular organisms well-suited for relatively high heat (50–80°C, 120–175°F) to those better equipped for more moderate temperatures (0–20°C, 32–68°F). Given the frequent mass extinction events (such as asteroid and comet collisions, supernova eruptions, gamma-ray bursts, and solar flares) at the time of Earth's early life, species driven to extinction may have been replaced with new species better suited to the cooler conditions brought on by the Sun's declining luminosity.

By itself, however, the replacement of heat-loving microbial species with microbes designed for lower temperatures would not have been sufficient to accommodate the Sun's decreasing luminosity. A more important factor would have been outgassing from volcanic eruptions as they pumped just-right quantities of additional greenhouse gases into the atmosphere.

The numbers of just-right outcomes converging at the just-right times to compensate for the youthful Sun's decreasing brightness seriously strain naturalistic models. Unless the just-right life-forms appeared at just-right times, life would have been quickly extinguished. This problem could also occur if just-right life-forms weren't removed at just-right times. Finally, the amount and kind of volcanic outgassing had to be just-right throughout the time the Sun was losing mass. This much exactness is perfectly consistent with a super-intelligent, super-powerful Creator who knows both the present and future details of the Sun's and Earth's interior physics.

The Sun's transition from dimming to brightening some 3.5 to 3 billion years ago necessitated a directional shift in the type of life and in life's adaptation. A not-so-simple reversal back to heat-loving life-forms would have extended life's survivability on Earth by a few tens of millions of years at most. But this reversal also would have switched life's progression from more to less complex life. A different but much more elaborate strategy was needed.

Regulating the Greenhouse Gases

Maintenance of necessary temperature conditions to sustain progressively more advanced life required the removal of greenhouse gases from Earth's atmosphere in direct proportion to the increase in the Sun's luminosity. The erosion of silicates (the main components of continental landmasses) and the burial of organic carbon accomplished this intricate regulation.

In the erosion process rain, streams, and mist catalyze the chemical reaction between silicates and atmospheric carbon dioxide (a greenhouse gas). The end products are carbonates and silicon dioxide (sand). To get the necessary amount of exposed silicates, efficient plate tectonics had to build up islands and continents (see pp. 153–56). The silicate erosion rate depends on seven factors:

1. Earth's rotation rate
2. Average global rainfall
3. Average global temperature
4. Chemical composition of Earth's atmosphere
5. Total area of Earth's landmasses
6. Average slope of Earth's landmasses
7. Quantities and types of land plants

Photosynthetic plants, bacteria, and methanotrophs (methane-consuming bacteria) take carbon dioxide, water, and methane from the atmosphere and chemically transform them into sugars, starches, fats, proteins, and carbonates. If these components get buried (by erosion, tectonics, and/or volcanism) before they decay or get eaten by other organisms, then greenhouse gases are converted into biodeposits through physical and chemical processes operating in Earth's crust.

The end products of greenhouse gas removal—coal, oil, natural gas, limestone, marble, gypsum, phosphates, and sand—are all valuable resources for launching and sustaining human civilization. Without billions of years of greenhouse gas removal from Earth's atmosphere and the conversion of such gas into biodeposits, human civilization never would have achieved its current level of technology.

Though the required proportions differed in the past, today about 80 percent of greenhouse gas removal takes place through silicate erosion and 20 percent through organic material burial. Fine-tuning this removal to compensate for the increase in solar luminosity demands the fine-tuning of all seven factors governing silicate erosion plus all the factors governing the abundance, diversity, growth, decay, extinction, and burial of organisms. Furthermore, all this fine-tuning had to be exquisitely timed and regulated throughout the past 3.5 to 3 billion years.

This continual planning and fine-tuning over an extended time period challenges any reasonable naturalistic explanation. On the other hand, it validates RTB's biblical premise that life's causal Agent anticipated the future physical and chemical conditions of the Sun and Earth in intricate detail—not to mention the Moon, the prime regulator of Earth's rotation rate. Exquisite fine-tuning also fits well with the biblically stated purposes for God's creating the just-right life-forms at just-right times (and removing life-forms no longer appropriate) to sustain a habitable Earth and prepare the environment for humanity's arrival. It provides insight into why the fossil record looks the way it does.

Pumping Oxygen

The extremely high abundance of free oxygen in its atmosphere sets Earth apart from all other heavenly bodies. Scientists know only one way for a planet or moon to gain such a large amount of free oxygen—through the long-term activity of superabundant photosynthetic life. Yet even with the help of photosynthetic life, oxygenating a planet's atmosphere to the level where it can support advanced life is very difficult.

The role cryptogamic colonies played in oxygenating Earth's atmosphere, while significant, is minor compared to that of photosynthetic bacteria in the oceans. The abundance of marine bacteria is so enormous it could have transformed Earth's atmosphere from 1 or 2 percent oxygen to about 20 percent oxygen in only a few million years, perhaps even less. At the same time, however, Earth's oxygen sinks swallowed up so much oxygen as to slow that process by 3 billion years.

Erosion of the earliest rocks delivered unoxidized iron and sulfur to the ocean, where oxygen from photosynthesis reacted with them to form oxide deposits. It took several global cycles of erosion, oxidation, deposition, and tectonic uplift to fully oxidize the iron and sulfur.

Earth's mantle, the layer between Earth's crust and core, gobbled up even more oxygen. Only after several global cycles of volcanic eruption, erosion, oxidation, and tectonic subduction of crustal plates into the mantle, then more volcanic eruptions, did the unoxidized mantle minerals become fully oxidized.

Geochemical analysis of deep-water marine sediments indicates that the oceans became fully aerobic (fully oxygenated) sometime between 1.0 and 0.54 billion years ago.[16] The timing of Earth's oceanic and atmospheric oxygenation (see figure 10.3) helps explain the timing of the explosive appearances of life—the sudden, widespread, and extremely diverse origins of more than forty phyla of complex animals.

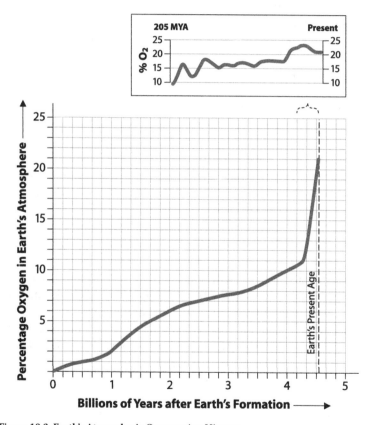

Figure 10.3. Earth's Atmospheric Oxygenation History

The larger graph shows the increasing abundance of oxygen in Earth's atmosphere over the past 4.1 billion years. An insert shows the increase over the past 200 million years.[17] Note that the explosive emergence of complex, large-bodied animals occurs at the moment oxygen increases to a level adequate to support these creatures. (Illustration by Jonathan Price)

No naturalistic model, as yet, reasonably explains biology's big bangs. However, these explosions fit several premises of RTB's creation model.

Biology's Big Bangs

Between 600 and 800 million years ago, Earth experienced several "snowball" events where ice ages extended to within a few degrees from the equator. Though Earth's climate later warmed, until about 580 million years ago, the oceans remained too salty (too full of sulfides), too oxygen poor, and too deficient in molybdenum to make the support of complex life possible. Microbes and colonies of microbes were the only life able to survive.

Then two explosive events marked the appearance of complex multicellular life. The first, the Avalon explosion, occurred 575 million years ago.[18] This event brought about the Ediacara life-forms, which included a variety of sponges and jellyfish. All the basic body plans or phyla for the Ediacara were fully present. No new phyla appeared during the subsequent 32 million years. Toward the end of that time, however, the Ediacara experienced a serious decline.

Following the Ediacarian decline, a second, much more dramatic outburst of complex life-forms occurred 543 million years ago. In a time window narrower than 2 to 3 million years (possibly much briefer), during the Cambrian explosion, some forty or more phyla of complex animals appeared (none related to the Ediacara), including at least twenty-four of the thirty animal phyla that remain on Earth today.

In both cases, not only did complex phyla show up out of nowhere, virtually all at once, but so did complete ecologies. Predator-prey relationships, for example, did not develop gradually. They were optimized right from the start. Furthermore, the most advanced phylum ever to appear, the chordates (including such vertebrates as jawless fish), are found at the very base of the Cambrian explosion fossil record.

A naturalistic evolutionary perspective would anticipate the ongoing appearance of new phyla at a relatively high and constant rate. However, only five or six new phyla have appeared during the past 540 million years, and about fifteen phyla have disappeared—taking the idea of evolution in the opposite direction of what naturalistic models predict.

Both the Avalon and Cambrian explosions fit RTB's biblical model, which proposes that the Creator worked efficiently to rapidly prepare a home for humanity. A huge array of highly diverse, complex plants and animals living in optimized ecological relationships and densely packing Earth for a little more than a half billion years perfectly suits humanity's needs. These life systems loaded Earth's crust with sufficient fossil fuels and other biodeposits to catapult humans toward a technologically advanced civilization.

Fill 'Er Up

Both sedimentation and plate tectonics bury large amounts of organic material. Heat, pressure, and time transform this matter into kerogen (high molecular weight tars). More time and heat convert a small fraction of it into petroleum.[19] Yet more time, plus microbial activity, degrades the petroleum, turning it into methane (natural gas).[20]

Upon death and burial, certain organisms are more likely than others to yield kerogen. Swarms of small-bodied animals inhabiting large shallow seas right after the Cambrian explosion were the most efficient producers.

In the context of providing humanity with the richest possible reserves of fossil hydrocarbons, a fixed period of time had to transpire between the epochs when efficient kerogen producers were dominant and the appearance of humans. Not enough time would have produced too little petroleum. Too much time would have degraded most or all of the petroleum into methane.

More was needed than the burial of particular organisms and their progressive conversion into kerogen, petroleum, and methane to produce easily exploitable fossil hydrocarbon reserves. Certain sedimentation processes laid down porous reservoir rocks. These were later overlaid with fine-grained rocks with low permeability (sealer rocks). Finally, specific tectonic forces formed caps under which fossil hydrocarbons could collect.[21]

With inadequate time, too few and too small reservoirs would have formed. However, other tectonic and erosion processes would eventually cause these reservoirs to leak. If too much time transpired, the fossil hydrocarbon reservoirs would empty out.

Both methane and kerogen play important roles in sustaining modern civilization. However, they don't compare to petroleum, especially in the plastics industry. While technology is advanced enough now that it might survive without petroleum, it is doubtful a high-tech society would have arisen at all without easy access to large amounts of this commodity.

Humans indeed arrived at the best possible fossil hydrocarbon moment. Such optimized timing for both the Cambrian explosion and humanity's arrival, though unexpected in naturalistic models, validates the predictions of RTB's creation model.

Natural Degeneration

Geneticists observe that deleterious mutations outnumber beneficial mutations by at least as much as ten thousand to one, and in some species by as much as ten million to one. Neutral or slightly deleterious mutations vastly outnumber both the beneficial and clearly deleterious mutations. However, because the fraction of the genome acknowledged as functional is rapidly increasing (see chapter 13, pp. 200–202), the number of neutral mutations is dropping, while the quantity of recognized deleterious mutations is rising.

By themselves, these statistics seriously challenge both naturalistic and theistic evolutionary models. While natural selection would tend to move the genetic variation within a species toward the beneficial mutations, the ongoing generation of many more deleterious and slightly deleterious mutations much more strongly pulls the species toward degeneration.

Given the high mutation rate for most species,[22] natural selection cannot be expected to remove both the deleterious and near neutral mutations as quickly as they arise. Nor can it effectively separate the good from the bad and near neutral mutations. Everything in the natural realm, including the genomes of all life-forms, is subject to the law of entropy.[23] As a result, genetic decay appears inevitable.

Out with the Old, In with the New

A species can only evolve into a distinctly different species if it can naturally select a sufficient number of beneficial mutations and somehow amplify independently arising beneficial mutations into functional assemblies before being driven to extinction. Instead, a combination of accumulated harmful mutations, physical changes in its environment, reproductive failures, and competition from other species sharing the same habitat drives a species to extinction.

Additional risks come from within the physical environment. These include a declining rotation rate of Earth, increasing solar luminosity, tidal pattern changes, changing chemical compositions of the atmosphere and oceans, changing biodeposits, nearby supernova eruptions, nearby gamma-ray bursts, asteroid and comet collisions, solar flaring, volcanic eruptions, earthquakes, storms, wildfires, climate cycles, and changes in ocean and air currents. Can any species survive long enough to gain important new functions through naturally selected beneficial mutations before the onslaught of deleterious mutations and environmental stresses wipes it out?

Every species races an evolutionary clock. Certain characteristics of a particular species determine its odds of winning:

- population size
- average body size
- average generation span (time between birth and the capacity to give birth)
- abundance, variety, longevity, and stability of food sources
- average number of progeny per adult
- level and duration of parental care and training required for independence
- complexity of morphology
- complexity of biochemistry
- protein-to-body-mass ratio
- metabolic rate
- hibernation and aestivation (summer dormancy or torpor) level
- average life span
- habitat size
- ecological diversity of habitat
- complexity of social structures
- complexity of symbiotic relationships with other species

Direct field observations reveal substantial real-time evolutionary change for several viral and bacterial species. Among ant and termite species with populations of more than a quadrillion individuals, significant change remains debatable. For animal species numbering less than a quadrillion individuals, with average body sizes larger than one centimeter and generation time greater than three months, biologists have yet to observe any significant evolutionary alteration, other than extinctions.[24]

This significant change is defined as generating a new species that under no set of circumstances can be made to interbreed with the species from which it arose. If the evolutionary limits stated previously are valid, biologists should be discovering new bacterial "species" (definitions of a species are difficult to apply at the bacterial level) at a rate that roughly equals or exceeds one per year. Yet during the past 150 years biologists have failed to observe—in real time—the emergence of even one truly new bacterial species (as opposed to a "species" whose distinct characteristics can easily be bred out). Such observational failure implies the evolutionary limits stated above are not severe enough.

The exceptionally benign climate and freedom from the environmental hazards which life has enjoyed over the past few millennia add to the case for even more severe evolutionary limits. Factoring in the usual hazards, naturalism's odds for progression become even slimmer.

RTB's creation model based on biblical predictions explains the fossil record enigma: Speciation and extinction remained roughly balanced before humanity's appearance, but with the arrival of humans, real speciation suddenly ended. Speciation became overwhelmed by extinctions after humans arrived—even apart from human encroachment or abuse. According to Genesis 1, the Creator actively and purposefully built life's diversity as part of his preparation for humanity in six "days" (eras of creation). Once he created the first humans, he ceased making new kinds of life and no longer replaced extinct life-forms. The Creator then began his seventh day (an era of rest).

Psalm 104 declares that all life God creates on Earth eventually dies out and that God re-creates new life to replace it. The extinctions and the replacements occurred at levels and rates just right to compensate for the Sun's changing luminosity and to maintain God's planned progression of life.

Purposeful Transitions

Naturalists frequently point to "transitional forms" as "proof" for their explanation of life's history.[25] The similar bone structures of certain large mammals, in particular whales and horses, through many millions of years show an apparent progression that seems to indicate such animals naturally evolved.

Whales and horses, however, are not even in the evolutionary race. As previously explained: the smaller the population, the larger the body size, the longer the generation time, and the fewer progeny per adult, the less likely any new functions from beneficial mutations and the more likely a downward spiral to extinction. Horse and whale species manifest no realistic probability of evolutionary advance. Neither can survive any longer than several million years before experiencing complete extinction.

RTB's biblical model proposes that the Creator had a particular purpose in the ecosystem for each of the many apparent transitions for whales and horses. Due to a rapid extinction rate, it appears the Creator frequently created new species as replacements. The fossil record confirms this observation. Creatures such as cockroaches, with long extinction times, manifest either no transitions or very few. God seldom needed to intervene to preserve them.

Naturalistic models would predict transitional forms among tiny-bodied simple life-forms vastly outnumbering those among large-bodied complex life. RTB's creation model predicts the reverse: far more "transitional" forms for large-bodied complex life than for tiny-bodied simple life.

Design Convergences

Support for RTB's biblical model also comes from observations that species unrelated in the "evolutionary tree" often manifest identical anatomical and physiological features. Examples include the limb structures of bats and flying lemurs, the brain structure for vocalization in hummingbirds, parrots, and songbirds, and the anatomy of modern wolves and extinct Tasmanian wolves.

Naturalists attempt to explain such design convergence as the result of nearly identical environmental, predatory, and competitive pressures on unrelated species. They propose natural selection shaped these species in identical ways.

This explanation poses at least two problems, however. First, given that naturalistic evolution supposedly happened in response to a large number of unpredictable and often dissimilar events, design convergence resulting from natural process should be extremely rare. Yet design convergence outcomes permeate the fossil record.

Second, design convergence appears in species from radically different habitats facing widely diverse survival stresses. Different habitats and different survival stresses imply dissimilar bases for natural selection.

The chameleon (a reptile) and the sandlance (a fish) are an example.[26] Both have eyes that move independently; when one eye is in motion the other can remain motionless. Both use the cornea rather than the lens of the eye to focus on objects. Both have skin coverings for their eyes that make them less conspicuous to prey and predators. Both have the same kind of tongue and the same kind of tongue-launching mechanism for snagging prey. Yet, these creatures exist in drastically distinct habitats and remain far apart on any workable evolutionary chart.

My colleague biochemist Fazale Rana offers over a hundred examples of design convergence at the molecular level.[27] Paleontologist Simon Conway Morris, in his book *Life's Solution*, described dozens more at the organismal level.[28]

Still, strict evolutionists, when they observe a tree frog ideally suited for its environment, assert that natural selection—environmental, predatory, and competitive pressures repeatedly operating on random inheritable variations over long eras of time—led to this relationship. Evolutionists claim that chance governs the evolutionary process at its most fundamental level, so repeated evolutionary events will result in dramatically different outcomes. This concept of historical contingency is the theme of paleontologist Stephen Jay Gould's book *Wonderful Life*:

> No finale can be specified at the start, none would ever occur a second time in the same way, because any pathway proceeds through thousands of improbable stages. Alter any early event, ever so slightly, and without apparent importance at the time, and evolution cascades into a radically different channel.[29]

Conway Morris disagrees with Gould that evolution is fundamentally unpredictable and that if the "tape of life" were replayed from some point in the distant past, the outcome would be far different from the one we see today.[30] He claims that while the possible evolutionary routes are near infinite in number, because of some hidden law or mechanism of nature, the number of outcomes must be extremely limited to explain all the examples of design convergence. This debate instigated an elegant experiment.

A Decisive Test

Recently a team of microbiologists at Michigan State University completed an experiment to adjudicate the Gould–Conway Morris debate.[31] Over a twenty-year period, they observed 44,000 generations of twelve different populations of E. coli bacteria. Each population was raised in a glucose-poor, citrate-rich environment, and each population experienced billions of mutations. However, the capacity to feed on citrate evolved in only one population, at the cost of efficient glucose feeding, and not until after 31,500 generations had transpired.

At regular intervals over the twenty-year period, the team placed samples from each population into a state of suspended animation. Thus the researchers could take the one "successful" population and go back to the 30,000th, the 29,500th, the 29,000th (and so forth) generations and test whether the revived samples ever duplicated the citrate feeding capability as they evolved.

Such duplications were never observed for any sample that predated the 15,000th generation. Therefore, the team concluded that "evolution of this phenotype was contingent on the particular history of that population."[32] In other words, they proved Gould right and Conway Morris wrong.

Replaying the tape of life will not produce identical evolutionary outcomes, even under repeated highly controlled natural conditions. Still, Conway Morris's observation that nature presents dozens of examples of repeated design outcomes also remains correct. The Michigan State team's experiments merely proved that no natural law or process explains the repeated outcomes.

Many science commentators in reference to the research team's results trumpeted the team's success in evolving at least some of their E. coli from glucose feeding toward citrate feeding. They claimed the result proved the Darwinian model correct.

The result, however, is not that dramatic. It is a microevolution example, no more impressive than gonorrhea evolving resistance to penicillin.

The *E. coli* bacteria in the Michigan State experiment did not evolve biochemical machinery to metabolize citrate. *E. coli* already possessed that machinery. What the *E. coli* bacteria initially lacked were membrane pore structures that would permit them to draw in citrate from outside. Microevolutionary changes in those pore structures under extreme environmental pressure is what allowed a portion of one of the twelve populations to transition from glucose to citrate feeding.

The Michigan State experiment's significance must not be overlooked, however. Darwinian models cannot survive the proof that natural biological processes only produce nonrepeatable outcomes while nature's record offers hundreds of examples of repeated design outcomes among Earth's life-forms and life's molecular machinery.

The RTB creation model explains the observation of multiple examples of design convergence as the Creator's efficient use of optimal design templates. Such investigation of design convergence by biologists and paleontologists has barely begun. Likewise, research at the biomolecular level is just starting.

Naturalistic models predict that examples of design convergence, both organismal and biomolecular, should prove nonexistent or extremely rare. Further, they expect currently established examples to prove flawed. By contrast, RTB's creation model predicts future research will uncover many more examples of design convergence, more that, like the chameleon and sandlance, reveal the convergence of many different intricately complex mechanisms.

However, the RTB model predicts that researchers will find no, or very few, examples of repeated design outcomes arising after the appearance of the first humans. Because in RTB's model God rests from his creation work after he creates humans, repeated design outcome events should be restricted to prehuman eras.

Life's Crucial Role

Without abundant diverse life on Earth, greenhouse gases couldn't have been converted to rich biodeposits. Without abundant life on the islands and continental landmasses, the quantity of silicates and carbon dioxide converted into carbonates and sand wouldn't have helped launch or sustain civilization. Maintenance of these "just rights" and many more required the support of just-right ecological balances. The life-forms needed for reduction of atmospheric greenhouse gases to precisely compensate for the Sun's increasing luminosity depended on the existence of other diverse species, all perfectly placed, timed, and proportioned. The pattern of life observed in the fossil record—which species existed when, where, and for how long—reflects a delicate, step-by-step balancing of nature. The scientific evidence based on observable, objective criteria contradicts the random timing, placement, and diversity proposed by naturalistic models.

At various levels of complexity, life appeared as soon as Earth was ready. Optimal ecological relationships always existed.

Life influences the amount of heat and light Earth's surface reflects into outer space.[33] That amount determines whether Earth remains inhabitable or experiences a runaway freeze-up or a runaway boil-off. The kinds and quantities of life on Earth's continental landmasses impact the cycling of silica, a substance that buffers soil acidification, regulates atmospheric carbon dioxide, and provides an important nutrient for both marine and terrestrial life-forms.[34]

Each new discovery adds more detail to the spectacular view of an intentional, anticipatory, carefully orchestrated plan, a plan perfectly timed to prepare Earth for advanced life. The next chapter shows how RTB's model unfolds for birds, mammals, and vascular plants as well as the soulish qualities demonstrated by the animals so many of us love.

11

PUTTING RTB'S CREATION MODEL FOR ADVANCED LIFE TO THE TEST

My firstborn son was only six months old when he began learning the testing principle. On walks around the neighborhood, we encountered a variety of animals. Through his own brand of testing, Joel discovered the difference between dog breeds. A friendly German shepherd quickly turned hostile after my son stuck his finger up the dog's nostril. But a pair of keeshonds warmly greeted Joel, no matter how much he pestered them. Joel also learned that repeated visits to three geese that guarded their yard eventually transformed their intimidating attacks into enthusiastic greetings.

During the next few years, my son tested his presumption that every animal could be turned into a pet. For a while our home resembled a zoo. Amphibians, reptiles, fish, and insects seemed to be everywhere. Joel soon learned, however, that these creatures treated him no differently than any other animal they randomly encountered.

On the other hand, my son found that he could experience an emotionally fulfilling relationship with virtually any bird or mammal species. Yet the kind of relationship varied greatly from species to species. A dog is far easier to hug than a goose.

Scientists too have begun to discover that not all animals can be treated as purely physical entities. There seems to be more to the way certain bird and mammal species interact with humans than mere physical attributes.

RTB's creation model asserts that the Creator personally intervened to create all advanced life species that have existed on Earth. Though only a small portion of RTB's creation model that pertains to advanced life is included here,[1] listing a few of its key distinctives from a biblical viewpoint will permit some specific scientific evaluations and tests.

Some Testable Features

The RTB creation model for advanced life is based on the following biblical premises:

- God created three distinct forms of life: first, purely physical; second, life both physical and soulish (manifesting mind, will, and emotions); and finally, one species with body, soul, and spirit.
- As with the origin of first life, the appearance of the first soulish life and the first spirit life was sudden and miraculous.
- God created soulish life with the capacity to form emotional relationships not only with members of its own species but also with humans.
- God endowed each soulish species with specific capacities to serve or please humans. These capacities are diverse.
- The soulish capacity to serve and/or please humans implies that different soulish species will share many physical attributes. However, the most physically similar soulish species often manifest markedly different soulish ways of serving or pleasing humans.

Advanced Plants for Advanced Animals

Lignified tissues in vascular plants conduct water, minerals, and photosynthetic products throughout the organism. This system permits these plants to grow large and produce abundant and varied food sources for animals. It also allows vascular plants to thrive under much drier conditions.

These plants appeared as soon as warm wet swamps ceased to dominate Earth's landmasses about 350 million years ago. Vascular plants expedited silicate erosion much more effectively than other plants.[2] This feature proved critical because as Earth aged and rotated more slowly, silicate erosion by wind and water declined and plate-tectonic activity significantly subsided. Progressively more advanced vascular plants appeared at the just-right times and in the just-right amounts to maintain silicate erosion at high enough levels to ensure that just-right levels of greenhouse gases were extracted from Earth's atmosphere to perfectly compensate for the ongoing increase in solar luminosity.

As the planet continued drying out, forests appeared about 300 million years ago. Seed plants followed, and by 140 million years ago the first flowering plants appeared. Accompanying each advance among vascular plants were simultaneous advances in the size, complexity, and diversity of animals.

Evolutionary models predict that vascular plants don't waste energy to make excess food. They also predict that any food made by plants is strictly for the purposes of distributing its seeds to other soils. Yet vascular plants produce huge quantities of food for Earth's advanced life. Some altruistic vascular plants even make and give away food that in no way assists the plants to reproduce.

The perfectly timed appearances of the first and progressively more advanced vascular plants testifies of careful planning and design for the benefit of all life—most especially for birds, mammals, and humans.

Man's Best Friends

Most of Earth's species can be explained in purely physical terms. But birds and mammals are different. In addition to their physical features, they manifest the capacity to express emotions and form lifelong nurturing relationships.

These animals exhibit a freedom to choose apart from instinct. They possess a mind capable of exploring new experiences and solving problems. Such creatures bond with members of their own species and can form relationships with members of other bird and mammal species. Most especially, soulish animals can form emotional attachments with humans.

Typically creation/evolution discussions largely ignore the issue of how soulishness originated. When pressed, naturalists and most theistic evolutionists insist that physical explanations exist for every soulish attribute. Yet they cannot describe where these soulish attributes came from.

The biblical usage of the Hebrew word *nepesh* (Gen. 1:20–25; Job 39) however, refers to the unique attributes of birds and mammals as soulishness. Use of the Hebrew verb *bārā'* in Genesis 1:21 indicates that the origin of soulishness is just as miraculous as the origin of the universe and of Earth's first life.[3] RTB's creation model predicts the behavior described in Scripture. The Creator designed soulish animals to meet many of the needs and pleasures of humankind.

Size Matters

Evolutionary biologists have long observed in the fossil record that large-bodied species and genera have much higher origination and extinction rates than other animals. This disparity is especially dramatic for land mammal species[4] and yields one of the more potent tools for putting different creation/evolution models to the test.

A study of four thousand land mammal species spanning a body-mass range from 2 grams to 4,000 kilograms showed that the potential of extinction risk against six established predictors (environmental and species intrinsic traits) becomes greater with increasing body mass.[5] In particular, a sharp increase in extinction risk occurs at a body mass of three kilograms. Above this size "extinction risk begins to be compounded by the cumulative effects of multiple threatening factors."[6]

An independent study established a much greater accumulation of deleterious mutations for large body–sized mammals.[7] The two studies combined establish that land mammals with large body sizes possess extinction rates much higher than those for smaller animals. Meanwhile, molecular studies demonstrate that larger animals with their lower metabolic rates and longer generation times have much slower rates of evolution.[8]

The bottom line is that large-bodied land mammals experience extinction rates far higher than the most optimistic naturalistic speciation rates. Consequently, large body–sized mammals cannot be the product of natural process or theistic evolution. Such high-extinction rates and slow-evolution rates also falsify young-earth creationism with its appeal to the rapid evolution of large-bodied animals after Adam's sin and the flood.[9]

These results, however, are entirely consistent with the RTB creation model. RTB's model explains the very high origination rate seen in the fossil record for mammals compared to the presently observed zero origination rate as an outworking of the Genesis 1 creation week. For six creation eras (as seen in the fossil record), God replaced extinct species with new ones. During the seventh era (the time since the creation of humans), God rests.

To Serve and to Please

All bird and mammal species predate humans. Yet many of them appear specifically designed to either benefit the needs of humanity or bring people pleasure. Furthermore, each of these species appears designed in distinctly different ways to carry out these purposes.

Study of Genesis 1 in several biblical translations reveals that before God created humans, he made three different kinds of land mammals to help meet humanity's needs. He made short-legged mammals—rodents, hares, and weasels—that supplied an important source of clothing for early humans. Two different kinds of mammals had long legs: wild creatures and beasts.

Wild Animals

Carnivores, though difficult to tame, can make excellent household pets. Unlike herbivores, they don't need to spend nearly all their waking hours eating and digesting. So they can focus more intently and for longer periods of time on serving and pleasing their human owners. For instance, dogs (bred from wolves, foxes, jackals, and dingos) often form such strong emotional bonds with their owners that they will sacrifice their health and even their lives to serve them.

Recognizing this characteristic, many hospitals and care facilities encourage interactions with dogs and other animals to bring comfort and pleasure to patients. Household pets, such as cats (bred from the Near Eastern wildcat), also play an increasingly important role in stress relief as the demands upon humans continue to grow with technology.

Gentle Beasts

Herbivores are mammals that sustain humanity's agricultural enterprises. The first such beasts domesticated on a large scale were goats.[10] It's easy to see why. Even goats that have never seen a human will readily approach and follow one. They can eat almost anything and thrive in virtually all climate conditions. These mammals provide their owners with a wide range of agricultural products for very little cost. Goats seem perfectly designed to catapult the first humans into animal husbandry. Besides goats, many other bird and mammal species seem much better designed to meet humanity's needs than even their own.

Evolutionary models are hard pressed to explain why all these creatures were so wonderfully designed to enhance the technology and quality of life for a species that did not yet exist.

RTB's biblical creation model, on the other hand, anticipates that every bird and mammal species will show evidence of being designed in some specific manner to either serve the needs of humans or please them through their entertainment, companionship, and comfort. The RTB creation model predicts that the more research is done on the behavior of birds and mammals, the more such design for humanity's benefit will become evident.

Soulish Diversity

The wide variety of ways in which birds and mammals express their soulish characteristics presents problems for any naturalist and most theistic evolutionary models. For such models to have credibility, bird and mammal species that are physically similar to one another should also be soulishly similar. The following example is only one of many that challenge this premise.

Donkeys, horses, and zebras are physically so similar that humans have easily crossbred them to make mules, zorses, and zebrasses. Their soulish characteristics, however, are markedly different.

Horses can form strong emotional bonds with their human owners. They will forgive cruelty. If treated well, they'll sacrifice their own needs and even their lives to protect their owners. Loyalty to their human owners can be so strong that they will charge into battle with them.

Donkeys are extremely adaptable. Like horses, they can form a lifelong emotional bond with a human. However, if a human loses his donkey, the donkey can take care of itself under almost any circumstances. It easily transitions from domestication to living in the wild and from living in the wild back to domestication. Unlike the horse, the donkey hates danger and provides useful service in warning its human owner of impending risks.

Zebras are much more difficult to domesticate, harness, and ride than either horses or donkeys. However, they are more alert to imminent danger and much hardier. In the wild, zebras form dense herds providing human hunters an easy, productive source of food and leather.

As difficult as it is for naturalists to build a phylogenetic tree for the physical attributes of different species, no such attempt has ever been tried for the soulish characteristics of birds or mammals. Rather, each bird and mammal species appears to possess independently designed soulish attributes so that each species in its own distinct way can serve and please humans. RTB's creation model predicts that more research will uncover yet more ways that birds and mammals were designed in advance to meet human needs and pleasures.

A Distinct Creation

Birds and mammals share the property with humans that their creation combined something old with something brand new. Physicality existed in amphibians. Yet, as my son Joel found out, that didn't make them very good companions. It was the soulish quality introduced in birds and mammals that fulfilled my son's desire for animal playmates.

In human beings, still another quality is introduced—a spirit. The next chapter shows how the past decade's discoveries have yielded a spectacular array of tests for distinguishing between competing models for the origin and history of humanity.

12

Putting RTB's Creation Model for the Origin and History of Humanity to the Test

In one of my freshman physics lab classes, we did a set of experiments with a magnetron oscillator. The goal was to determine the oscillator's efficiency by measuring how quickly it could bring a small vial of ice water to a boil. I was amazed at how fast the oscillator worked and longed to test its capability on real food. So did my friends.

After creating a diversion to distract the attention of the lab proctors, we chopped a wiener in half, wrapped it in paper, then popped it into the magnetron cavity.

The oscillator worked great. We had stumbled upon a microwave oven more than a dozen years before one hit the market. If we'd focused our energies on development and marketing instead of preparations for grad school, we all could have been rich.

In science, sometimes the focus on one particular agenda can derail or delay a wealth of knowledge and understanding about important discoveries. Dramatic examples of such stalled efforts have occurred in human origin research.

One impediment has been use of the term "human." The assumption that there's nothing extraordinary about present-day humans relative to other primates led anthropologists to use "human" to refer to the broad category of bipedal primates, or hominids, including a number of archaic species distinct from modern humans. To avoid any confusion, in RTB's creation model (and this book) the term "human" refers only to modern humanity (*Homo sapiens sapiens*), while "hominid" is used to designate nonhuman bipedal primates.

It's no exaggeration that more has been discovered about human origins in the past ten years than in the previous ten thousand. That fact makes it impossible for this book to supply an extensive appraisal such as the one detailed in *Who Was Adam?*[1] However, evaluating the way a few characteristics of RTB's human origins model and its predictions fit with recent discoveries helps test the model's scientific viability.

Some Testable Features

The RTB creation model for the origin and development of humanity and of global civilization is based (in part) on these biblical premises:

- God created humans in a deliberate, miraculous act.
- Adam and Eve are historical individuals from whom all humanity descends.
- The first man and woman lived in a particular locale, referred to as the Garden of Eden, somewhere near the juncture of Africa, Asia, and Europe in the relatively recent past (less than 100,000 years ago).
- Humans are qualitatively different from all other animals, including the great apes and hominids.
- Humanity is Earth's only life-form, past or present, to exhibit spiritual qualities characterized as "the image of God." Manifestations of this spiritual nature include the capacity to evaluate past actions, contemplate the future, consider what lies beyond death, comprehend and attempt to maintain moral and ethical standards, seek connection with a higher Being or Force, engage in worship, express curiosity and creativity about matters beyond the immediate environment and survival needs, and seek ultimate hope, purpose, and destiny.

- After the flood of Noah destroyed all humans and the soulish creatures associated with them, except those on Noah's ark, humans quickly spread from in or near the Middle East into the rest of Africa, Asia, Europe, Australia, and eventually the Americas. During this global migration, human population and civilization grew rapidly.

- God gifted humans from the outset with unique intellectual and physical attributes useful only in a high-tech civilization.

Winning the Origins Lottery

Nontheistic models adhere to a central premise that humans arose by strictly natural unguided steps from a bacterial life-form that sprang into being 3.8 billion years ago. Famed evolutionary biologist Francisco Ayala, an advocate for the hypothesis that natural selection and mutations can efficiently generate distinctly different species, nevertheless calculated the probability that humans (or a similarly intelligent species) arose from single-celled organisms as a possibility so small ($10^{-1,000,000}$) that it might as well be zero (roughly equivalent to the likelihood of winning the California lottery 150,000 consecutive times with the purchase of just one ticket each time).[2] He and other evolutionary biologists agree that natural selection and mutations could have yielded any of a virtually infinite number of other outcomes.

Astrophysicists Brandon Carter, John Barrow, and Frank Tipler produced an even smaller probability. Not only does the presumed natural evolution of an intelligent species necessitate a stunningly large number of improbable biological events, it also demands unlikely changes in the physics, geology, and chemistry of Earth and the solar system. For a species as technically capable as humans to arise from a suite of bacterial species in ten billion years or less, the probability was determined at $10^{-24,000,000}$.[3] For comparison, the probability of randomly picking a single marked proton out of all the protons in the observable universe is 10^{-79}.

The calculations done by Ayala, Carter, Barrow, and Tipler were performed to prove the impossibility that other intelligent species exist in the universe. At the same time, however, such odds demonstrate the impossibility that any intelligent life, including humans, originated by naturalistic means.

Crucial Tests

The origin of humanity is a critical distinguishing factor for creation/ evolution models. Findings that prove humans emerged naturally from previously existing species in various regions rather than from one couple living in one region within the last 100,000 years would certainly deal RTB's biblical model a severe blow. The model could also be falsified if researchers decisively demonstrated that humans possess no unique characteristics unaccounted for by superior intelligence alone.

Evolutionary models, by contrast, claim that humans arose naturally from previously existing species and thus differ from those species only in the degree of their common attributes. As a result, incontrovertible evidence that humans possess unique attributes or that no direct genetic link with earlier species exists would invalidate key evolutionary premises.

Scientific discoveries about the origin of humanity could also falsify young-earth creationist and many theistic evolution models that identify Neanderthals, archaic *Homo sapiens*, and *Homo erectus* as fully human offspring of Adam and Eve. Any evidence definitively establishing that Neanderthals and other *Homo* species are unrelated to humans would seriously undermine these positions.

Until recently, anthropologists lacked any definitive evidence of how humans originated. However, DNA recovery efforts, new archaeological finds, and new fossils have changed the situation, making validation or falsification of competing models possible.

True or False? The Answer's in the DNA

Most DNA is recombined or shuffled like a deck of cards during sexual reproduction. Exceptions are mitochondrial DNA (mtDNA) and parts of Y-chromosomal DNA. Everyone inherits mtDNA exclusively from his or her mother. Every male inherits Y chromosomes exclusively from his father.

An offspring's mtDNA or Y chromosomes only vary from the parents' when the inherited genes undergo a mutation. Thus, measurements of mtDNA and Y-chromosomal diversity in a population, plus its changes over time, become markers for any evolutionary effects.

Mitochondrial DNA has been recovered and analyzed from fifteen Neanderthal specimens that span the Neanderthals' entire geographical range (Europe and west Asia) as well as a large part of their history.[4] This DNA collection shows little variation and no perceptible correlation with either the geographical location or date. Neanderthal DNA remained remarkably constant throughout that species' range and history.

Geneticists have recovered mtDNA from humans dating as far back as 25,000 years.[5] The range of diversity for human mtDNA does not overlap Neanderthal in any way. This observation, coupled with marked differences in their mtDNA, establishes beyond a reasonable doubt that Neanderthals made no contribution to the human gene pool. They have been eliminated as a possible ancestor.

Dates for *Homo erectus* range from 1.8 to 0.5 million years ago, with some evidence suggesting dates as recent as 100,000 years ago. Given the rate of DNA decay, these dates leave little hope of recovering *Homo erectus* DNA pristine enough for meaningful comparisons with either Neanderthals or humans. Nevertheless, *Homo erectus* fossils are sufficiently abundant for testing this hominid's role, if any, in humanity's lineage.

Finding Fossils

A discovery that the most ancient fossils for *Homo erectus* are indistinguishable from the most recent shows that *Homo erectus* remained static, experiencing no more significant change with respect to time than either Neanderthals or humans. Because *Homo erectus* manifests morphological features radically different from either humans or Neanderthals and because all three species experienced no observable evolutionary change, it is highly unlikely that *Homo erectus* was the ancestor of Neanderthals, archaic *Homo sapiens*, or modern humans.

An appeal to earlier hominids as possible links to humanity faces the same problem. All these species manifest morphological features even more radically distinct from humans than *Homo erectus*. Given that earlier hominids presumably would not evolve any faster than *Homo erectus*, Neanderthals, or humans (see chapter 10, pp. 164–67, for the reasons), it seems very unlikely that the earlier creatures naturally acquired the necessary morphological changes during the limited time available prior to their extinction.

Where fossil evidence exists, it shows that individuals within different hominid species mature much faster than humans. For example, the skull of a one-year-old *Homo erectus* revealed a brain size of about 84 percent of an adult's.[6] This compares with about 80 percent for a one-year-old modern ape and only 50 percent for a one-year-old human.

Likewise, comparisons of Neanderthal skulls from individuals ranging in age from six months to young adulthood show much faster cranio-facial maturation and dental development than humans.[7] Long-lasting childhood and adolescence during which the brain continues to grow and develop appears to be a unique hallmark of humans. This distinctive provides additional support for the conclusion that hominids did not give rise to humanity.

Locating the First Humans

Mitochondrial DNA also allows scientists to investigate the originators of the human race, where they came from, and approximately when. This mtDNA evidence establishes that humans descended from one woman (or a very few women) in a single location.[8] Likewise, Y-chromosomal evidence confirms that humanity descended from one man (or a very few men) from the same location.[9] With obvious biblical overtones, ge-neticists refer to humanity's mtDNA ancestor as mitochondrial Eve, and to the Y-chromosome ancestor as Y-chromosomal Adam. Scientists call the location where they originated the Garden of Eden.

According to the analysis this location is in eastern Africa, not Mesopotamia, the traditional biblical site. Both locations, however, are questionable.

The Bible mentions four rivers coming out of Eden: the Pishon, Gihon, Tigris, and Euphrates (see Gen. 2:10–14). The Pishon is said to flow through Havilah, the Gihon through Cush, and the Tigris through eastern Asshur. Most scholars identify Havilah as central Arabia, Cush as eastern Africa, and Asshur as Mesopotamia.

Geologist Ward Sanford has identified two ancient riverbeds that flow into the southern part of the Persian Gulf near the border between Qatar and the United Arab Emirates.[10] One riverbed extends into central Arabia, the other into its southernmost tip.

Sanford points out that both the Persian Gulf and the Red Sea could have been dry during the biblical timing for Adam and Eve's creation (see pp. 189–90). Placing the Garden of Eden in the southeastern part of the current Persian Gulf could indeed have placed it at the juncture of the four rivers. With the Red Sea dry (or almost), it would have been easy for part of Adam's family, or Noah's, to migrate up the Gihon into present-day Yemen and Ethiopia.

The mtDNA and Y-chromosome identification of the east African site is based on the observation that the people living there manifested the greatest genetic diversity of all humanity's ethnic groups and on the assumption that human migration and mating was random. These practices, however, were far from haphazard. Both the Bible (see Gen. 10:1–11:9) and archaeological evidence testify to the early rapid migration of humanity from a single location to many distant lands.[11] Then people ceased migrating and settled in their chosen destinations.

Africans especially avoided random mating. For example, nineteenth-century European explorers were surprised to observe pygmy tribes in central Africa living next to tribes of extraordinarily tall people. Given that not all human groups migrated and mated like other species, the genetic evidence for human origins simply identifies the single location for humanity's origin as somewhere near northeastern Africa, which could include any region near the juncture of Asia, Europe, and Africa.

Compare and Contrast DNA Similarities

Many evolutionary biologists argue that the DNA similarity among various species shows that all species are related through evolutionary descent. They further claim that the remarkable likeness between human and chimpanzee DNA proves the two species share a common ancestor in the relatively recent past.

RTB's biblical creation model, however, predicts an even greater DNA similarity between species than the evolutionary model (see chapter 6, p. 86). The Bible implies that God employed the best possible designs in his creatures. An optimal design for one species often proves just right for others.

Morphologically, humans resemble chimpanzees more than any other current species. Their average body weight is similar. So is the structure of all major organs inside the main body cavity. Therefore, from a biblical perspective, it's not at all surprising that human and chimpanzee DNA show remarkable similarity.

New research, however, indicates that the widely advertised 98 to 99 percent similarity between chimpanzee and human DNA is greatly exaggerated. Such claims were based on small segments of the human and chimpanzee genomes where common sense dictates that similarities would be the greatest. While comparisons between the complete human and chimpanzee genomes have yet to be done, the most complete analyses performed so far show that the similarity is closer to 85 to 90 percent.[12]

Dissimilarity is especially pronounced for gene expression patterns governing brain structure and activity. The human brain, unlike that of chimpanzees or any other species, possesses structures that sustain spiritual activity, meditation, analysis, mathematics, logic, complex language development, and communication. Gene expression patterns responsible for these structures are unique to humans.[13]

RTB's creation model predicts that as geneticists look deeper into the genomes of the great apes and hominids that preceded humanity (see "Why Did God Create Hominids?" p. 189), research will continue confirming that humans are genetically distinct. RTB's model also predicts that future genetic research will show that the Creator made appropriate use of similar or identical genetic designs for humans that had already been optimized for other species.

Solving the Birth Date Mysteries

During the past decade anthropologists, archaeologists, geneticists, and geochemists have developed a diverse collection of tools for dating humanity's origin. Consequently, humanity's birth date is no longer a complete mystery.

DNA date. Geneticists have calculated the date for the first Y-chromosomal man between 42,000 to 60,000 years ago.[14] For the first mtDNA woman, the date reflects a much wider error bar, 170,000 ± 50,000 years ago.[15] This mtDNA date assumes universal homoplasmy (that all humans possess only one set of mtDNA). However, studies show that 10 to 20 percent of the human population possesses two sets of mtDNA (heteroplasmy), and nearly 1 percent has three sets (triplasmy).[16]

Calculations based on these new findings place the date for the first mtDNA woman closer to 50,000 years ago, in line with the Y-chromosome date.[17] It also corresponds with the biblical date for Adam and Eve's creation based on reasonable calibration of the Genesis genealogies.[18] The dates for the explosive emergence of advanced art, advanced tools, complex language, clothing, and jewelry corroborate this timing.

Why Did God Create Hominids?

The Bible does not mention any of the hominids that preceded humanity. This omission is consistent with the biblical practice of avoiding references to natural phenomena that only some readers over the centuries would find familiar.

Scripture does address human responsibility for the natural realm (see Gen. 1:28–30), however, and warns of the negative impact of human sin upon other creatures (Gen. 3:17, 9:2). Because God gave soulish animals (birds and mammals) the desire to interact with humans, the evil that people manifested could have had a devastating impact. According to Genesis 9:2, God took protective action: "The fear and dread of you will fall upon all the beasts of the earth and all the birds of the air."

From a biblical perspective, God possesses complete knowledge of the future. He knew before creating any hominids that future humans would rebel against his authority and become selfish and dangerously harmful to each other and the environment. The many bird and mammal species driven to extinction sadly testifies to such abuse. Of the 15,000 to 20,000 bird species present at the time of humanity's origin, only about 9,000 remain. Of approximately 8,000 land mammal species, only about 4,000 are left.[19]

Humans have devastated the very creatures God supplied to improve humanity's quality of life. Perhaps this impact would have been even worse had God not created a series of progressively more advanced hominids.

Large-bodied mammal extinction studies support this premise. In Africa, where several hominid species predated humanity, the extinction rate for large mammals during the human occupation period is 14 percent. In North and South America and Australia, where no such hominids preceded humans, the large-mammal extinction rate during the human occupation periods stands at 73, 79, and 86 percent, respectively.[20]

In such places as Africa, the fossil record reveals a sequence of hominids that spanned several million years, with each successive species slightly more capable of hunting birds and mammals than the previous. This increasing exposure to gradually improved predation skills may have allowed birds and mammals to adapt step-by-step to the shock of a sinful super-predator.

Family history date. Though they acknowledge gaps in the biblical genealogies, Bible scholars disagree on how many and how wide. Genealogies in Genesis 5 and 11 trace human history from Adam to Abraham. Biblical and extra-biblical historical records independently establish that Abraham, the father of both Jews and Arabs, lived about four thousand years ago.

Carbon-14 dating places the breaking of the Bering land bridge (that once connected Asia to North America) at about 11,000 years ago.[21] Genesis 10:25 declares that the world was divided in the time of Peleg, a patriarch mentioned near the midpoint in the Genesis 11 genealogy. Given that life spans declined geometrically from around 950 years for the earlier patriarchs to about 120 years for the latter, and given that each patriarch's life span listed in the Genesis 5 and 11 genealogies is proportional to the actual passage of time (a reasonable though unproved assumption), extrapolation from the fixed dates for Abraham and Peleg indicate that Adam lived approximately 50,000 years ago.

Technology explosion date. Until about 50,000 years ago, the most advanced tools constructed by hominids were little more than flake fragments created by striking a core rock with a hammer stone.[22] These shards were useful for scraping, among other things.

Then, between 50,000 and 40,000 years ago, a technological quantum leap occurred.[23] Early humans used wood, bones, stones, leather, sinews and ivory to manufacture tools. These people carved, polished, and assembled raw materials into sophisticated implements that included axes, awls, knives, hammers, fishhooks, harpoons, needles, and shovels.

Cultural explosion date. The technology big bang coincided with a burst of clothing,[24] jewelry, and other cultural innovations. No evidence has yet been found for the fabrication of any of these trappings by hominids. For humans, however, jewelry and clothing burst into the archaeological record all at once. At most ancient human sites, the amount of jewelry outweighs the quantity of tools. The number of seashells used exclusively for making jewelry outweighs the evidence of shellfish used for food.[25]

Archaeological research reveals other coincidental events: the sudden, widespread appearance of advanced art, musical instruments, complex language, and religious ceremonies and practices.[26]

All of these cultural explosions date to about 40,000 years ago, timing consistent with a human origin date roughly 50,000 years ago. Significant population growth and societal development had to occur for deposition of enough archaeological evidence for modern scientists to discover.

Overqualified

For tens of thousands of years, innate talents beyond obvious purpose or advantage vastly over-endowed humans for their simple hunter/gatherer or agricultural lifestyle. Many examples could be cited, but dexterity and intellectual capacity alone set *Homo sapiens sapiens* apart from other hominids and animals.

Dexterity. The design and agility of the human hand certainly gave humans an early survival advantage. Humans could craft more elegant tools and weapons than hominids. However, the ability to type faster than 100 words per minute offered no obvious advantage until it met the corporate world. Likewise, the ability to play a Liszt concerto had no benefit until the invention of the modern piano.

Intellectual capacity. The intelligence quotient of the human brain gave *Homo sapiens sapiens* a huge survival advantage, providing the ability to invent new implements for hunting, agriculture, cooking, and building. Yet not until a few hundred years ago was any use found for the phenomenal capacity of the human brain to tackle higher mathematical functions such as nonlinear tensor calculus, relativistic quantum theory, and higher-dimensional geometry.

Humans pay a price for their higher mathematical skills. The main reason people are weaker and slower than similar-sized animals is that 35 percent of the human body's blood flow serves the brain. Complex brain structure is needed to support the capacity for higher mathematics—as well as meditation, analysis, prayer, logic, and complex languages. Brain structures devoted in animals to supporting more muscles and acute senses of smell, hearing, touch, and/or taste must be sacrificed. (A larger human brain was not an option because the required blood flow already put the brain in danger of overheating.)

Assessment. These extra abilities are costly. They take energy, time, muscles, nerves, and blood flow to support. From a naturalistic perspective, such resources could otherwise be channeled to features providing immediate survival advantages. Also, no known natural mechanism exists for generating costly abilities that offer no immediate or short-term advantages to the species.

Some biologists propose that certain currently worthless by-products of evolutionary change might remain long enough to become useful for a future challenge or application.[27] However, naturalistic evolutionary principles permit such survival only if the cost to individuals is low and the wait time for a different application is short. In the examples cited, the cost would have been high and the wait time long.

Many other endowments also equip humanity for maximum performance in a high-tech environment. Unlike any other species of life, humans seem to have been equipped in advance for a future role far different from the one fulfilled when they first appeared.

From a naturalistic perspective, perhaps one, but not all, of humanity's over-endowments might appear as a random genetic accident in a single individual. However, the evolutionary forces and mechanisms that characterize all naturalistic models would quickly eliminate such immediately unusable but costly accidents. On the other hand, such extensive equipping of humans in advance for distant future needs and the preservation of such capacities validates RTB's creation model.

Humanity's Time Window

RTB's creation model predicts dates not only for the beginning of human life, but for the end of it as well. The time span between them is relatively short. The Bible implies that humanity lasts only tens of thousands of years, as opposed to millions or billions (see 1 Thess. 4:13–5:11; 2 Thessalonians 2),[28] and now science can test that prediction.

Greenhouse gases in Earth's atmosphere currently warm Earth's surface temperatures by 60°F (33°C) above what they might be otherwise. This warming makes human life possible. The Sun, however, grows progressively brighter as it continues to burn or fuse hydrogen into helium. Removing increasing amounts of greenhouse gases from the atmosphere (as in the past) could compensate for the extra potentially deadly solar heat Earth will receive in the future (see pp. 156–58). However, this process cannot persist much longer.

Water vapor and carbon dioxide are the dominant greenhouse gases in Earth's atmosphere today. Significant water vapor reduction would dramatically reduce the amount of rainfall. Sufficient reduction to compensate for the Sun's future brightening would turn all the continents and islands into parched deserts.

Carbon dioxide plays a much bigger greenhouse role. To adequately compensate for a brightening Sun, atmospheric carbon dioxide must be reduced. (The current carbon dioxide level is 385 parts per million, up from 284 parts per million in 1832.[29]) As this level declines, so does photosynthetic plant production. If the atmospheric carbon dioxide level falls below about 175 parts per million, photosynthetic life will die, and the death of most (if not all) animal life would quickly follow.

For the past three billion years, greenhouse gases in Earth's atmosphere were steadily reduced so that life remained abundant despite a brightening Sun. However, continued reduction of greenhouse gases extends life's time window by only another 0.02 billion years. A nearby supernova eruption, climatic perturbation, war, social or environmental upheaval, mass extinction of supporting species, declining birth rate, or the accumulation of negative mutations could drive humans to extinction in just tens of thousands of years.

Humanity's arrival so near the inevitable end of all life on Earth is either a dreadful but meaningless fact or part of the Creator's plan. By appearing toward the end of life's history, humans reap the benefit of nearly 4 billion years' worth of biodeposits as RTB's biblical model predicts.

A look around the cities and transportation arteries that link them reveals that the raw materials for their construction came from biodeposits—concrete, iron, zinc, chromium, molybdenum, limestone, marble, bricks, mortar, asphalt, timber, paper, plastics, and so forth. Nearly all the energy that drives civilization comes from biodeposits such as coal, oil, natural gas, wood, and kerogen. In addition, biodeposits supply nearly all the fertilizers that support agricultural production. More importantly, according to RTB's creation model, human life continues beyond Earth's demise.[30]

Unmistakable Fingerprints

Humanity belongs in a category all its own. Scientific testing of evidence for human origins from a variety of disciplines shows that the timing, DNA, fossil, and cultural evidence, among many other recent discoveries, all validate RTB's biblical model. The evidence all points toward a purposeful creation that culminates with human beings.

For RTB's biblical creation model to gain full respect among naturalists and others, however, it must address difficult *why* questions concerning a Creator's intentions. In the next chapter, answers to these challenges provide yet another means for testing.

13

PUTTING RTB's CREATION MODEL TO THE "WHY" QUESTION TEST

One day in grade school, I watched as each of my classmates went to the nurse's office. Over half came back with white envelopes for their parents. Then came my turn. The nurse asked how many colds I'd had in the past year. After I told her "one," she sent me back to class without an envelope. Arriving home, however, I found that both my sisters had them.

Throughout British Columbia's public school system, students were receiving envelopes that contained orders for the surgical removal of tonsils and adenoids. I couldn't help but wonder why.

Evidently the scientific community had pronounced adenoids and tonsils as useless organs—accumulated junk from the evolutionary process. Apparently evolution had cluttered the human body with useless organs. Tonsils, adenoids, and the appendix, along with other "mistakes" including the S-shaped backbone and the tailbone, were cited as examples.

But I'd been taught that natural selection was supposed to weed out useless and faulty features. Why, I puzzled, would so many useless and faulty organs persist? And why were so many people convinced that the human body is filled with flawed or worthless structures?

Asking similar *why* questions has helped the scholars at RTB expand and refine their creation model. Exploring the why of a phenomenon often leads to increased understanding of it. Important questions related to biblical creation models include why, if an all-powerful Creator exists, would he:

- let millions of generations and species of plants and animals die before making humans?
- make so many bacteria, trilobites, and dinosaurs?
- make so many different hominid species before creating humans?
- imbue Earth with such high levels of erosion?

These questions have been addressed briefly in chapters 7–12. More thorough discussions of each can be found in other RTB books.[1] *Why the Universe Is the Way It Is* specifically addresses many additional questions, including why would an all-loving, all-knowing, all-powerful Creator:

- take ten billion years to prepare the cosmos for life?
- take more than four billion years to prepare Earth for human life?
- fill the universe with so much empty space?
- make the universe so predominantly dark?
- make so many lifeless galaxies, stars, planets, and moons?
- choose the physical laws that he did?
- choose the cosmic space-time dimensions that he did?
- endow the universe with so much decay?
- cause humans to suffer so much?
- grant humans such a very brief window of time in which they can exist?

Other important questions have also refined and expanded RTB's creation model. These include, why would:

- a loving Creator make carnivores, detritivores, and parasites?
- an intelligent, supernatural Creator make "junk DNA"?
- "bad designs" exist in nature?

- a caring Creator expose all his creatures to so many destructive "acts of God" such as earthquakes, hurricanes, tornadoes, volcanic eruptions, floods, drought, and wildfires?

Admittedly these questions deserve a more thorough treatment than space here permits, but brief answers show additional ways to evaluate RTB's creation model.

From the Beginning

Many people romanticize Adam and Eve and all the animals who roamed an earthly paradise free of pain, decay, suffering, and death. Then, in an instant, Adam's bite of a forbidden fruit ruined everything. But that image distorts both biblical and scientific reality.

The Bible certainly teaches that Adam's rebellion intensified pain, multiplied work, and visited death upon all humanity (see Gen. 3:16–24). It does not suggest, however, that pain, decay, and physical (as distinct from spiritual) death didn't exist prior to human sin.

Herbivores, Carnivores, Parasites, and Detritivores

Biblical accounts of nature, particularly those in Job and Psalms, describe various species of life as fulfilling vital roles for other species in ecological systems. As part of God's provision and care for life, he designed elegant ecologies that included, yet minimized, pain and death (see Job 38:34–39:40; Ps. 104:10–28; 145:7–16; 147:8–18).

Herbivore Contributions

Nature observers note the strange fact that many plants vastly outproduce what they need to survive. Herbivores eat that overage. As they digest their food and excrete their wastes, nutrients are transformed and transported to other places in ways that benefit the environment.

Herbivore consumption of plant parts prevents plants from depleting their nutrient base to a point that threatens the plant's existence, population level, habitat spread, genetic vitality, and/or general health. Herbivores also benefit plant populations by spreading seeds over a wide area, sometimes introducing them to new ecosystems. Herbivores benefit other creatures in providing concentrated nutrient-rich food sources.

Carnivore Contributions

Much in the same way as plants need herbivores to maintain their vitality, herbivores need carnivores. In the wild, carnivores (unlike human hunters) hunt and kill only the sick, injured, weak, or unwary. By removing these animals from herbivore flocks or herds, carnivores alleviate herbivore suffering and prevent their populations from becoming dangerously diseased and genetically weakened.

Carnivores also reduce the problem of an overpopulation of herbivores exhausting their own food supplies, then starving to death. The Australian rabbit epidemic in the 1800s illustrates the problem. Twelve rabbits from England were brought to Australia with the hope of providing her citizens with some easy-to-hunt game. However, Australia's human population was nowhere near as dense as England's. Nor were its animal predators as well-adapted to hunting rabbits. Lacking adequate predators, the rabbit population multiplied out of control. They stripped the landscape of vegetation, causing great hardship for native herbivores and for the country's sheep and cattle industry.

The rabbits themselves then suffered as overpopulation caused frequent cycles of starvation. In addition, the survival of sick individuals led to disease epidemics.

Optimal ecological designs established circles of life that both prevented species from over-consumption and ensured that life-essential nutrients cycle efficiently throughout the environment. This protection of the food supplies and nutrient bases minimized suffering and death for all species.

Parasite Contributions

Many parasites also perform useful purposes. Unlike carnivores, most parasites do not kill their "prey." Those that do, do so slowly. Many parasites bring no irritation, discomfort, or lack of vitality to their hosts. Some protect their hosts from potentially harmful parasites. The overuse of antibacterial soap in America, for example, removes benign bacteria from the bodies of many Americans, leaving them open to dermal infections.

Parasites can protect their hosts from much more serious calamities than dermatitis. Parasite-induced diarrhea has been virtually eradicated from the world's more advanced nations. The cost, however, has been high rates of colon cancer. Meanwhile, people who experience frequent bouts of such diarrhea rarely, if ever, die from colon cancer.

Some parasites distract their hosts from overeating. Others encourage certain species to temporarily leave a particular habitat, thereby giving another species a reprieve from competition.

Research may never fully reveal all the good that parasites accomplish in the balance of nature. But a true story illustrates some of the ways they benefit Earth's life and resources.[2]

Famed Harvard anatomy professor Dr. Étienne Léopold Trouvelot made a hobby of studying exotic insects. One afternoon in 1868, a few prized European gypsy moths escaped from his home laboratory. Unchecked by any local predators, this species' population ballooned to pandemic proportions. Within several years deciduous forests across New England, then over most of the eastern United States, were stripped of every leaf. The destruction of the forests brought about disease and starvation for hundreds of species dependent on the forests, including the gypsy moths.

For the first few decades nothing could slow or stop the moths—except the lack of food. After each destructive episode, the forests took decades to recover, but when the trees came back, so did the moths. Each cycle produced a progressively weaker gene pool for all the involved plant and animal species.

When local carnivores, primarily birds and mice, finally adapted to the gypsy moths as a new food source, the degree of devastation decreased. But even then, it did not end.

Finally, when researchers introduced a European virus specific to the gypsy moth, some significant headway was made toward solving the problem. Yet it wasn't until 1989 that the destructive cycles finally came to an end. Success came through the introduction of a second European parasite, this time a fungus. Only when several carnivore species and at least two parasite species began feeding on gypsy moths were North American deciduous forests ensured of remaining extensive enough and healthy enough to sustain hundreds of species, including the gypsy moths, with an optimal quality of life.

The lack of appropriate parasites results in loss and increased suffering for every species. An adequate number and diversity of parasites keeps nature in balance.

Detritivore Contributions

Creatures such as earthworms, woodlice, millipedes, and bottom-feeders (in a marine environment) provide a valuable service by eating the remains of dead organisms. For example, these detritivores prevent leaf litter from becoming so thick that seeds can't reach the soil and germinate. Without them, many poisons from dead plants, fungi, and animals would leach into the soil.

Most importantly, detritivores convert dead organisms and the waste products of living organisms into nutrients critical for the support of all life. Detritivores keep nutrient recycling from becoming so limited as to force a serious reduction in Earth's biomass and biodiversity and, thereby reducing the quality of all life.

From an evolutionary perspective, optimal ecological relationships—plants, herbivores, carnivores, parasites, and detritivores in well-balanced relationships, with no species dominating the habitat to the detriment of others—would be unexpected. Either these relationships would not develop at all, or they would develop very slowly and haltingly.

The coexistence of well-designed carnivores, parasites, and detritivores comports with the notion that a caring, powerful Creator planned for them. A biblical perspective anticipates creation of life with optimal ecological relationships right from the start. So far, fossil record research on mass origination events confirms that complex optimal ecologies arose virtually intact. The RTB creation model predicts that future research into fossil record origination events will provide further validation.

Junk DNA

In complex plants, fungi, and animals, only 5 to 20 percent of the DNA carries code for making proteins. Only about 3 percent of the DNA in humans codes for proteins. Geneticists have long referred to the DNA that does not code for protein production as "junk."

An evolutionary perspective expects undirected biochemical processes and random molecular events to have transformed functional DNA segments into useless artifacts. These obsolete components tag along from generation to generation in the genome (an organism's total nuclear DNA content) due to their physical attachment to the functional strands of the DNA.[3]

For decades this explanation satisfied curiosity. Many scientists considered junk DNA powerful evidence for naturalistic evolution.[4] When identical segments of junk DNA appeared (often in the same genome location) in a set of species that from an evolutionary perspective are related to one another, evolutionists drew what they considered an obvious conclusion: respective junk DNA segments arose prior to these organisms' divergence from a shared ancestor.[5]

An assumption that the nonprotein-coding part of the genome served no purpose caused researchers to abandon study of its features for nearly three decades. Then a team of physicists made an observation that revived interest. They noticed that the quantity of "junk" in a species' genome was proportional to that species' degree of advancement.

The physicists performed a computer analysis and, in 1994, published their results. They found that what had long been labeled junk DNA carries the same complex patterns of communication found in human speech.[6] In fact, the researchers found that junk DNA has an even higher linguistic complexity than protein-coding DNA. This breakthrough and later analyses of genomes drew teams of geneticists worldwide into a veritable frenzy to uncover the hidden designs and functions of the DNA portions once thought useless.[7]

This flurry of research has revealed five kinds of noncoding (for proteins) DNA. Each plays an important role in the vitality and function of the organisms in which they reside (see "Useful 'Junk,'" p. 202). However, much of this research is so recent that a considerable quantity of what has long been termed "junk" has yet to be studied.

The RTB creation model anticipates that future research into the remaining "junk" DNA will provide further evidence of purpose and design. It does not, however, propose that all DNA must serve a functional purpose. RTB's biblical model acknowledges that the optimal DNA designs present at the time God created a species will, thereafter, gradually degrade as a consequence of natural mutations. Therefore, depending on how long a particular species has existed, a small amount of real junk DNA is to be expected.

Useful "Junk"

After more than thirty years of referring to DNA that does not code for the manufacture of proteins as "junk," geneticists have discovered five kinds of nonprotein-coding DNA—pseudogenes, SINES, LINES, endogenous retroviruses, and LTRs—that perform life-critical functions.

Pseudogenes got their name from the assumption that certain DNA segments are the dead, useless remains of genes that many generations ago coded for proteins. Recent experiments, however, show that many pseudogenes are not useless. When certain pseudogenes were turned off, the organism suffered either fatal or injurious consequences.[8] Geneticists now realize that these pseudogenes somehow protected the protein-coding genes from breakdown or malfunction. Other pseudogenes were found to actually encode for functional proteins.[9] Still other pseudogenes were misidentified and later discovered to encode for the construction of molecules once thought to serve no purpose.[10]

SINES is an acronym for short-interspersed nuclear elements. Emerging research shows that these DNA elements serve at least two distinct purposes. Some help protect the cell when it experiences stress.[11] Others help regulate the expression of the protein-coding genes.[12]

LINES is an acronym for long-interspersed nuclear elements. Recent findings show that some LINES play a central role in X-chromosome inactivation.[13] When such inactivation fails, serious genetic disorders result.[14] Another discovered LINES function is to turn off one of the two protein-coding genes inherited from an individual's parents.[15]

Endogenous Retroviruses were once presumed by evolutionists to be the product of retroviral infections. Scientists hypothesized that retroviral DNA becomes incorporated into the host's genome. New research, however, shows that many endogenous retroviruses protect the organism from retroviral infections by disrupting the life cycle of invading retroviruses.[16] Others function as protein-coding genes.[17]

LTRs, an acronym for long-terminal repeats, were once thought to originate from endogenous retroviruses. Recent studies show that several LTRs play crucial roles in protecting organisms from retroviral attacks.[18] Other research demonstrates that some LTRs help regulate the expression of certain protein-coding genes.[19]

Far from being junk, nonprotein-coding DNA serves many amazing life-beneficial purposes. These purposes would never have been discovered and understood if geneticists had continued to study only protein-coding DNA.

"Bad" Designs Becoming Good

For more than a century, evolutionists have argued that if a caring, powerful God were behind Earth's life, organisms would be free of inferior designs. That bad designs are most apparent in late-arriving, large-bodied animal species seems to indicate that bad designs accumulated as a result of evolutionary processes. But did they?

The Panda's "Clumsy" Thumb

Perhaps the most famous examples of so-called "bad designs" in nature are those identified by Stephen Jay Gould in his book *The Panda's Thumb*. Gould viewed the giant panda's thumb as a clumsy contraption, an evolutionary adaptation of wrist bone material, not the work of a divine Designer.[20]

While rebuttals to this argument have been published since the mid-1980s,[21] a study reported in 1999 offers the most rigorous response. Six Japanese biologists used three-dimensional computed axial tomography and magnetic resonance imaging (CAT and MRI scans) to determine that "the radial sesamoid bone and accessory carpal bone form a double pincer-like apparatus in the medial and lateral sides of the hand, respectively, enabling the panda to manipulate objects with great dexterity."[22]

In the close of their paper, the Japanese biologists concluded, "The hand of the giant panda has a much more refined grasping mechanism than has been suggested in previous morphological models."[23] Their conclusions were confirmed by field observations of three pandas. Those studies showed the wrist flexion and manipulation of the double-pincer capacities are essential aspects of the panda's specialized food gathering and feeding.

Why Some Parts of the Human Body Appear Useless

Not too long ago, in the same way the removal of tonsils and adenoids was common when I was a child, surgeons routinely removed the appendix during abdominal surgery. They presumed, as they were taught, that the appendix was a useless by-product of humanity's evolutionary history. These practices stopped with the discovery that the tonsils, adenoids, and appendix play important roles in the human immune system.

Likewise, textbooks on anatomy once claimed that the "tailbone" at the base of the human spine was a useless residual of humanity's descent from long-tailed primates. As a result of research into the engineering dynamics of the human spine, anatomists now recognize that the human tailbone and in fact all the bones of the human spine, as well as its S-shape, are exquisitely designed to facilitate extended periods of running, walking, standing, sitting, and load carrying.

Questions about the design of the panda's thumb and the human appendix, spine, and tailbone should caution scientists against jumping too quickly to an evolutionary conclusion whenever some aspect of anatomy seems superfluous. The RTB creation model anticipates that future research into the anatomy of complex physical features will reveal increasing, rather than decreasing, evidence for exquisite design and functionality.

Natural Catastrophes

No doubt hurricanes, tornadoes, volcanoes, earthquakes, wildfires, ice ages, floods, and droughts cause inestimable damage and untold suffering to plants, animals, and humans. How could a good God allow such devastating forces to destroy his creation?

Why We Need Hurricanes and Tornadoes

The number and intensity of hurricanes and tornadoes depends on several factors. These include the strength and paths of ocean currents; the size, orientation, and shapes of continental landmasses and islands; the extent, average height, and orientation of mountain ranges; and Earth's rotation rate.

Any Creator powerful enough to create the universe could completely rid Earth of hurricanes and tornadoes. The costs, however, would include at least one or more of the following: less rainfall, less evenly distributed rainfall, a lesser amount or lower quality of living space on the landmasses, or more extreme temperature differences between day and night. Even with fewer or less intense hurricanes and tornadoes, these same factors would still exist, though the costs might be lower. Still, the present level of hurricane and tornado activity yields the most optimal balance between advanced-life productivity and collateral damage.

The RTB creation model goes beyond noting that while hurricanes and tornadoes are bad, the alternatives are worse. This model claims that hurricanes and tornadoes also serve several good purposes. For example, hurricanes significantly increase chlorophyll concentrations along continental shelves.[24] Such enrichment benefits certain continental shelf life-forms.

Hurricanes linger over oceans far longer than over land. Their powerful winds lift huge quantities of sea-salt aerosols from the oceans. These aerosols make up a large fraction of cloud nuclei that in turn play a critical role in raindrop formation.[25] Thus, hurricanes (and to a lesser degree tornadoes) ensure enough rain to support a large and diverse population of land life.

These aerosols and the clouds that form from them also efficiently scatter solar radiation. So hurricanes act as Earth's thermostat, fulfilling a life-essential role.[26] When tropical oceans get too hot, they generate hurricanes. The sea-salt aerosols produced by hurricanes cool the tropical oceans to a benign temperature. To a lesser degree, tornadoes also cool certain continental landmasses that have become too hot.

Why We Need Earthquakes and Volcanoes

Plate-tectonic activity, which gives rise to earthquakes, plays a critical role in building islands and continents, compensating for the Sun's increasing luminosity and maintaining life-essential chemical cycles (see p. 155). It also provides an ongoing supply of nutrients to surface soils.

The maintenance of these life-essential processes early in Earth's history required much greater tectonic upheaval. Today, the level of activity is only about a fifth of what it was when Earth's first life came on the scene. As with hurricanes and tornadoes, scientists note that the human race appeared on Earth at the ideal tectonic moment. Earthquake activity today is high enough to sustain adequate levels of various surface nutrients but low enough to allow for a global, high-tech civilization.

Why We Need Ice Ages

For some time geologists have noted that the large, fast-moving glaciers predominant during ice ages contributed to the formation of many of Earth's richest ore deposits. Geographers observe that ice ages and their resultant glacial sculpting of Earth's crust are responsible for carving excellent harbors, fertile valleys, and gorgeous lakes on high-latitude landmasses. All provide value for a growing technological society.

Why We Need Wildfires

No one needs a scientist to prove that life would be severely impacted if wildfires were more frequent and widespread. Scientists, however, have identified the two primary factors that determine how fires start and burn: the quantity of atmospheric oxygen and the electric discharge rate (rate of lightning strikes). If these were greater by even a small percentage, fires would seriously limit the level of human civilization and technology. However, if they were less, human metabolic levels and nitrogen fixation levels would drop.

Soil studies reveal that humanity would be in serious trouble without *enough* forest and grass fires.[27] Fires eliminate dead vegetation on the forest floor that inhibits growth. Burning off this organic litter gives seeds and seedlings greater access to the mineral soil beneath, enhancing their chance of germination.

Old forests also accumulate certain plant- and microbe-suppressing agents. Burning stimulates essential microbial activities, such as nitrification of the soil. The lightning that starts many fires contributes by generating nitrogen fixation from the atmosphere.

A by-product of forest and grass fires is charcoal, which benefits the soil by absorbing tannins and other plant- and microbe-inhibiting chemicals that have settled there. During and after a fire, charcoal breaks down into fine dust and ash easily transported by wind and water to areas adjoining the burn area. This chemically inert matter greatly enhances the soil's water retention capacity and can even transform sandy soil into a clay-like material.[28] Further, this dust and ash can form new wetlands. They also help develop peat bogs and, thus, coal formation.

Like charcoal filters used in water purification systems, the benefits of soil charcoal dwindle with time. Studies of Swedish forests indicate that these advantages drop to one-eighth their original level in one hundred years. After two hundred years, no measurable benefit remains.

Studies in American forests demonstrate that more frequent fires do much less damage than fires separated by a century or more. These findings have led researchers to estimate that Earth's biomass and biodiversity are maximized if forests and grasslands burn every twenty to one hundred years—precisely the natural rate ecologists measure for much of the planet.

In response to the question, "Couldn't an all-powerful Creator alter cosmic and terrestrial physics so that humans could exist without such things as hurricanes, earthquakes, volcanoes, wildfires, and ice ages?" science answers, "Yes, he could. But doing so could thwart several of his purposes for creating the universe, Earth, life, and human life in the first place" (see chapter 6, pp. 73–74). The Bible implies that God will one day create a realm where no such phenomena ever occur, but only *after* evil is permanently and finally done away with.[29]

Why Questions for Evolutionists and Creationists

Creation advocates are not the only ones called upon to answer *why* questions. Any viable scientific model, whether for creation or evolution, attempting to explain life's history must find credible answers to such questions as:

- Why does the structure of the universe, including its physical laws and constants, appear to be planned billions of years in advance for the arrival and benefit of the human species?
- Why are Earth's continents and oceans and the elements they contain optimal for advanced life?
- Why are so-called transitional life-forms most abundant among species with the lowest probability to survive mutational and environmental changes and least abundant among species with the highest probabilities to survive such changes?
- Why does life's timing, quantity, type, and diversity throughout the past 3.8 billion years consistently anticipate the needs of future species, including humans?
- Why does life's quantity, kind, and diversity always precisely compensate for changes in the Sun's luminosity?
- Why are the laws of physics optimized to restrain the expression of evil?
- Why are the exquisitely fine-tuned characteristics of the universe and solar system that make a home for humanity possible identi-

cal to the exquisitely fine-tuned cosmic and solar system characteristics that allow humans to observe the universe's origin and development?

• Why do so many plants and animals exhibit altruistic behavior?

• Why are there so many examples in nature of the sudden appearance of multiple-partner symbiosis?

• Why do humans everywhere distinguish between right and wrong, good and evil?

• Why do humans alone, among all species on Earth, search for a sense of hope, purpose, and destiny?

Attempts to develop credible answers to these challenging questions provide new opportunities to craft more complete and detailed models and to learn more about our world and humanity in the process.

Testing a Model's Strengths

The most discriminating tests of differing models lie in the discipline of cosmology. Especially productive tests come from *why* questions posed by a number of best-selling authors as they give a scientific response to the "overwhelming impression of design" observed in the cosmic characteristics that make human life possible. These tests are developed in the next chapter.

14

PUTTING NEW ATHEIST COSMIC MODELS TO THE TEST

My toughest class ever was an undergrad experimental physics lab. After months of grueling assignments, we faced a two-part final exam. No books, notes, or instruments were allowed—only a pen, blank scratchpad, and slide rule, plus the tools provided.

The first part consisted of a seemingly impossible test. We had four hours to perform an experiment, with less than half the necessary equipment. Our professor expected us to be resourceful. We could use our tongues as a heat source, our heartbeats as a stopwatch, and a balloon as a beaker.

The second part posed an even more difficult challenge for some. In this four-hour session we found lab tables loaded with all kinds of instruments. Fortunately, I quickly realized almost all the stuff on my table was irrelevant. We were expected to spot unproductive or extraneous research tools and eliminate them.

The ability to identify futile scientific and philosophical arguments is equally crucial for making scientific progress. When leading proponents of a model use irrelevant evidences and/or arguments, their efforts hinder science and confuse the public. But when such attempts are exposed, they can reveal a model's weaknesses.

Some recent attempts by scientists promoting materialistic interpretations of the natural realm indulge in this type of bewildering practice. Compounding the confusion is the unprecedented publicity and promotion devoted to these efforts.

Where's the Delusion?

Arguably the most famous living atheist is Oxford biologist Richard Dawkins. His book *The God Delusion* sold 1.5 million copies its first year and remained on the *New York Times* nonfiction best-seller list for fifty-one consecutive weeks. In the fourth chapter Dawkins presents his "central argument" against the existence of God.[1] While acknowledging "the complex, improbable appearance of design in the universe,"[2] he dismisses "the natural temptation . . . to attribute the appearance of design to actual design."[3]

Dawkins claims that an appeal to God to explain the extreme statistical improbability of the universe, solar system, and Earth manifesting so many amazingly fine-tuned characteristics for life simply introduces something far less statistically probable.[4] Therefore, Dawkins concludes that "God almost certainly does not exist."[5] Reinforcing this conclusion, he claims he has "yet to hear a theologian give a convincing answer despite numerous opportunities and invitations to do so."[6]

Dawkins and his followers seem to believe they have discovered a new scientific argument against God's existence. However, this recently sensationalized approach has been around for thousands of years. The improbability argument is simply another way of asking, "If God created the universe, who created God?"

Its fallacy lies in the presumption that the causal Agent who brought about the universe must be subject to the same materialist limitations as the universe. God, indeed, would be even more statistically improbable than the finely tuned universe, Milky Way Galaxy, solar system, and Earth *if* confined to one dimension of time that can neither be stopped nor reversed.

Where's the Reality?

Unwittingly, this atheistic argument makes a powerful case in favor of RTB's biblical creation model. From the properties of cosmic time, it follows that any entity or system confined to cosmic time must have a beginning—a caused origin.

Science has now verified the Bible's ancient claim that the universe's causal Agent exists and operates from outside the universe. The space-time theorems of general relativity and the proven reliability of general relativity to accurately describe cosmic dynamics (see pp. 96–98) establish that the universe's causal Agent is not bound by space, time, matter, energy, or the physical laws in any way. All these entities were created by a Source beyond themselves.

In the universe, cause-and-effect relationships cannot occur apart from time (see chapter 7, pp. 96–98). Thus, in creating the space-time dimensions of the universe, its causal Agent, in effect, operated in what can be considered the equivalent of an additional time dimension.

Using the equivalent of two time dimensions, the universe's Creator could perform an infinite number of cause-and-effect operations along an infinitely extended timeline that never crosses or touches this universe's timeline. In our time context, the Creator would have no beginning or end. That causal Agent would not have been created.

The Creator would not have been created in any time context because the space-time theorems establish that in creating a time dimension at will, this Being's causal capabilities are in no way restricted or limited by time. Statistical improbability does not apply to a Being who always was, is, and will be.[7]

Where Did Complexity Come From?

In his book *God: The Failed Hypothesis*, physicist Victor Stenger (an atheist) concedes that the natural realm is burgeoning with countless examples of apparent design. However, Stenger claims all these examples can be attributed not to a Creator but rather to "self-organization."[8] He argues that people are deluded into thinking "mindless natural processes are unable to account for the complex world we see around us," failing to realize that "simplicity easily begets complexity."[9]

Stenger draws his evidence for naturally arising complexity from previous analysis developed by chemist Nobel laureate Ilya Prigogine. In his book *Order Out of Chaos*, Prigogine presents several examples of seemingly chaotic systems evolving a high degree of order without the apparent interference of an experimenter's involvement.[10] The examples, however, are limited to pattern generation such as that seen in snowflakes. Some order is generated, but little in the way of complexity, information, or specified purpose.

Biologist Stuart Kauffman of the Sante Fe Institute proposes that an undiscovered law of nature spontaneously brings about self-sustaining self-organization.[11] He calls this hidden law the "fourth law of thermodynamics."[12] This hypothetical law, however, would violate the second law of thermodynamics, which states everything in nature tends toward decay.

Are There Infinite Possibilities?

Evidence for cosmic fine-tuning has reached the proverbial "tipping point." With few exceptions, physicists and astronomers involved in researching the universe's features agree with their distinguished colleague Paul Davies: "The impression of design is overwhelming."[13]

Many physicists and astronomers, however, resist belief in a personal Designer. Instead, they suggest that if multiple universes exist (by "multiple" they mean an infinite number), each with different characteristics from the others, it's mathematically possible, by chance alone, that one of the universes would exhibit all the just-right features for life, including humans.

One problem with this "multiverse" appeal is that no basis can be cited to explain why the infinite number of universes would all be different from one another. They might all be the same, or only a certain range of differences might be represented. For every conceivable variation in just one law of physics, one constant of physics, or one cosmic gross characteristic to be fully represented, an infinite number of an infinite number of universes (∞^∞ or infinity to the infinity power) might be required.

A second problem with the multiverse appeal is that it potentially explains too much. Any improbable outcome can be attributed to chance. For example, in a truly infinite number of an infinite number of universes, where all the different universes manifest distinct properties and where every conceivable value for every property is manifested, not only would there be the possibility of a planet sufficiently like Earth that it could sustain advanced life, but, in addition, there would be an infinite number of planets like Earth.

On the infinite number of Earth-like planets, there would be an infinite number of seashores with an infinite number of different possible patterns appearing in the sand. Within the infinite number of sand patterns would be an infinite number of markings appearing identical to all the letters and spaces on this page. No meaning, logic, or purpose could be assigned then to any achievement by any sentient being.

How about a Little Less than Infinity?

Recognizing the illogic of appealing to such an infinite number of an infinite number of universes, many nontheists suggest an extremely large number instead. One string theory version allows for as many as 10^{500} different possible solutions that, in principle, could describe 10^{500} different universes. Thus, some cosmologists hypothesize that our universe is the one lucky chance out of all these options that manifests all the features required to support intelligent life.[14]

The problem with such a proposal, however, is that 10^{500} differently structured universes would not be enough. The actual scientific evidence accumulated so far shows that even if that many universes did exist, where all of them had the *same* laws and constants of physics and the *same* gross features as our universe, there would still be much less than one chance in 10^{500} that even one body would be found anywhere within all those universes possessing all the known characteristics necessary for the support of advanced life (see chapters 8 and 17 and Appendix B).

Why Now?

Scientists didn't begin to present serious models for an infinite number of physically distinct universes beyond our own until after Freeman Dyson claimed that "the universe in some sense must have known that we were coming"[15] and Stephen Hawking announced that "it would be very difficult to explain why the universe should have begun in just this way except as the act of a God who intended to create beings like us."[16]

Interesting timing, to say the least. It seems the idea of a potent, science-based case for intentionality with its implied challenge to atheism prompted the emergence of this theoretical innovation.

All Size Scales Great and Small

Evidence for the purposeful manufacture of the natural realm for the specific benefit of life, and humanity in particular, abounds on *all* size scales. It's not just the universe as a whole that manifests design. Scientists find overwhelming design evidence no matter what volume size they investigate—the universe, our galaxy cluster, galaxy, planetary system, star, planet, planetary surface, cell, atom, and fundamental particles (see chapter 8 and Appendix B). On each of these size scales, evidence for extreme fine-tuning on the behalf of life and humanity persists.

Furthermore, the degree of design seen on any particular size scale is proportional to the researchers' technological capabilities to detect and measure the various features observable at that size scale. In other words, the more cosmic or galactic details astronomers discover, the more fine-tuning evidence they see. The same outcome occurs for living cells, subatomic particles, and all the rest. If everywhere scientists *can* measure design they *do* detect design—and if the degree of detected design consistently increases with their measuring capabilities—it seems irrational to discount all this design evidence by appealing to that which never can be detected or measured.

According to general relativity (the best-proven principle in all physics), the space-time surface of one universe, where physical observers currently reside, can never overlap the space-time surface of any other possibly existing universe. So an appeal to the multiverse proposes the existence of something beyond the matter, energy, space, and time of our universe. It appeals to something beyond what anyone can possibly measure or detect, even theoretically.

The irony is that such a multiverse hypothesis points to a "transcendent" explanation for the design that researchers observe throughout the universe. In essence, it echoes a statement about the universe from Hebrews 11:3: "What is seen was not made out of what was visible." Thus, the multiverse proposition is actually an appeal to the supernatural.

Multiverse models are purely speculative, not based upon any measurable or scientifically testable evidence. Thus, while any cosmic model may be extended hypothetically into some kind of multiverse model, any *multi*verse hypothesis ultimately reduces to a *uni*verse model when the science community insists on measurable evidence to support that hypothesis. And that data maintains the integrity of the scientific method.

The multiverse appeals to the supernatural in another way. Every reasonable (life-supportable) multiverse model is just as subject to the space-time theorems as any other physical life-supportable universe model. A transcendent causal Agent is required either way.

Nothing New under the Sun

It's important to note that the multiverse concept, at least in some contexts, is neither novel nor necessarily anti-theistic. In previous centuries, theologians often debated whether the universe may be infinite by virtue of its Source. Some argued that an infinite Creator would be satisfied with nothing less. Even those who take a minimalist perspective on God's creative activity must concede there may be more to what God created than just the universe in which humanity resides.

When the writer of Hebrews says the universe was not made from that which can be detected, he leaves no clue as to what that undetectable something (or nothing) may be. Hebrews may leave open the possibility that God created other universes. The Bible speaks of other "realms," where angels exist and where people will reside, both spiritually and physically, after this universe passes away.

Revelation, Scripture's final book, describes the new creation, a "new heaven and a new earth" (21:1), and a "new Jerusalem" (3:12; 21:2) with unique physical features this current universe cannot accommodate. When Revelation says God's people will rule over "nations" (21:24; 22:2), it leaves open the possibility that the new creation may include a multiplicity of separate dimensional realms.

The Gambler's Fallacy

On a more practical level, the multiverse theorist commits a variation of the "gambler's fallacy." The following scenario illustrates the problem.

A person stands in front of an audience flipping a coin 100,000 times. If each toss yields the same result—say, heads—what would be a reasonable conclusion? Logic says the coin is weighted, the tosser is using a trick, or the coin is two-headed. Whatever the case, no one would likely bet on "tails" for the next toss—unless he commits the gambler's fallacy.

Such a gamble takes into consideration the possibility that outside the auditorium $2^{100,000}$ (that's 100,000 multiples of 2 x 2 x 2 x . . .) people are all tossing coins 100,000 times each. The laws of probability predict that one of those flippers would toss 100,000 consecutive heads strictly by chance. Thus, a gambler might conclude that the coin and its tosser inside the auditorium may be fair and, therefore, decide to call tails for the 100,001st flip.

The person placing that bet commits at least three significant errors. He has no evidence of $2^{100,000}$ tossers outside the auditorium or, even if they do exist, that they are flipping coins. Even more, he has no evidence that the coin-flipping results outside the auditorium differ from those observed inside.

With a sample size of only one, the rational conclusion is that the coin has been purposed or designed to land heads up. Only a nonrational conviction that coins *cannot* be designed or tweaked to come up heads every time would prompt someone to bet on tails.

In the case of the universe, the measurable sample size is one and always will be one. As the details of that single sample are probed, scientists see a dramatically increasing number of markers indicating intricate, orchestrated design for life's and humanity's sake. The evidence shouts humans were meant to be here. So why would anyone bet otherwise? The only reason appears to be an unshakable commitment to an a priori assumption that no universe can possibly be attributed to a transcendent Designer.

One could argue that the gambler's greatest error was a failure to carefully investigate the properties of the coin before placing his bet. He should have tested whether the coin possessed any previously undiscovered characteristics that might favor the "heads" outcome.

Astronomers and others need not make the gambler's error concerning the universe. One way they can test theistic universe models against nontheistic multiverse models is to examine the observable parts of the universe in more detail to determine whether such research turns up additional fine-tuning evidence for the possible support of advanced life.

Such examination is a prediction, really a contrast between two predictions. The RTB creation model predicts that kind of examination will reveal an even greater and more comprehensive impression of supernatural, super-intelligent design of the universe for the specific benefit of humanity. Naturalistic cosmic models predict the opposite—that evidence for design will grow weaker.

This enterprise of generating second tiers of tests through predictions can be extended throughout all research disciplines. Chapters 16 and 17 develop many such predictive tests. But first it's important to understand the attempts of some creationist and evolutionist organizations to use the political and legal system to avoid the testing process. The next chapter analyzes how these attempts have fared in light of landmark court decisions and how the courts reaffirmed the testing process.

15

PUTTING RTB'S CREATION MODEL TO THE U.S. CONSTITUTION TEST

During the early days of perestroika, the Soviet World Lab invited me to give a series of lectures on recent developments in cosmology. Because my presentation included confirmations of a particular set of big bang models, I expected some resistance. But I received none. That was surprising considering the obvious implications of a transcendent personal Creator for an audience that included a few hundred scientists as well as some Communist party leaders.

Afterward, many individuals told me how much they appreciated all the scientific tests I presented for the existence of the Bible's God. They confided that the Soviet government's long-standing prohibition of any public discussion of big bang cosmology, along with a policy forcing scientists to attend weekly indoctrination in atheism, had already persuaded them that a Creator or causal Agent must exist.

Unlike the Soviet Communist party, the United States government has no policy of forcing a state belief system upon its citizenry. Nevertheless, several institutions and citizens' groups have sought political and legal recourse to compel their particular creation/evolution model upon the public.

Numerous court cases have been centered around creation/evolution issues, and there's no apparent end to this litigation in sight.[1] The legal battle began during the famous Scopes Trial of 1925 when evolutionists insisted on the right to teach their view in public schools. Creation advocates fought hard against the teaching of naturalism and initially succeeded, but eventually evolutionists prevailed.

Gradually the right to teach any form of creation or divine design in the classroom disappeared. Or did it?

Over the past several decades, in attempts to change the situation, young-earth creationists have taken political action. Many have lobbied their local school boards and state legislatures demanding "equal access." These creationists insist that whenever and wherever evolutionary theory is taught in public education, creationism must be taught at an equivalent content level.

Examining the Constitution along with the legal history of the equal access court cases clarifies key creation/evolution issues and charts a path for putting creation/evolution models to the test. Doing so also unfolds the best course of action for educators and researchers.

First Amendment Court Cases

The U.S. Constitution's First Amendment has been a critical element in court decisions handed down since *Tennessee v. John T. Scopes*. The First Amendment states:

> Congress shall make no law respecting an establishment of religion, or prohibiting the free exercise thereof; or abridging the freedom of speech, or of the press; or the right of the people peaceably to assemble, and to petition the Government for a redress of grievances.

Philosopher Robert Pennock notes that creation opponents universally insist that "teaching Creation in the public schools would violate the First Amendment's establishment clause."[2] Two nonprofit organizations, Americans United for Separation of Church and State and People for the American Way, have interpreted this conclusion as a mandate to establish an impenetrable wall of separation between religion and the state.[3]

The mainstream perception that teaching any aspect of creation in public education is forbidden by the Constitution rests on four court decisions: *Epperson v. Arkansas* (1968), *McLean v. Arkansas* (1981), *Aguillard v. Treen* (1983), and *Edwards v. Aguillard* (1987). In all four cases, "creation teaching" collided with the First Amendment's establishment clause—but for reasons different than most people think.

Epperson v. Arkansas (1968)

In 1968, public high school biology teacher Susan Epperson (Central High School in Little Rock, Arkansas) brought suit against an old anti-evolution statute. The law prevented teachers in state-supported schools or universities from teaching or using a textbook teaching "that mankind ascended or descended from a lower order of animals."[4] The State Chancery Court found in favor of Epperson based on the free-speech clauses in both the First and Fourteenth Amendments of the United States Constitution.

Upon appeal, however, the State Supreme Court upheld the anti-evolution statute as within Arkansas' power to specify public education curriculum. When the case was appealed again, the United States Supreme Court ruled in favor of Epperson. In support of their ruling, the justices noted:

1. Arkansas had no scientific reason—in fact, no reason at all—for upholding its anti-evolution statute other than its observation that a particular religious group considered evolution theory to conflict with its interpretation of man's origin as set forth in the opening chapters of Genesis.[5]
2. Arkansas' right to prescribe public education curriculum does not include the right to prohibit the teaching of scientific data, theory, or doctrine simply because it might offend someone's religious beliefs.[6]

In siding with Epperson, the United States Supreme Court sent a strong message that a particular religious viewpoint could not, by itself, be used to hinder the advance of scientific knowledge and understanding.

Although a case can be made that America's founding fathers intended for the nation's governmental organization, policies, and laws to be under the authority of the God of the Bible and to reflect Christian principles (see "What Did the U.S. Founding Fathers Intend?" p. 222), these initial

What Did the U.S. Founding Fathers Intend?

Many people, beside People for the American Way and Americans United for Separation of Church and State, take Thomas Jefferson's comment about "building a wall of separation between church and state" to imply that the government, government officials, and schoolteachers must avoid any public practice, teaching, or support of religious views. However, two facts make this interpretation questionable: (1) Jefferson originally wrote his statement to reassure Baptists in Connecticut that their right to publicly practice and teach their religious views both inside and outside their churches was protected by the U.S. Constitution, and (2) Jefferson, in his official capacity as the United States President, closed his letter with a prayer to the God of the Bible.[7]

While the founding fathers of the United States did not want a federally sponsored church, they opposed "a wall of separation" between God and state—specifically between religion and public life, between almighty God and political concerns. The Declaration of Independence itself makes four direct references to the biblical God.[8]

George Washington, in his capacity as the nation's first president, issued a proclamation of national thanksgiving. He and both houses of Congress recommended to the people of the United States "a day of public thanksgiving and prayer to be observed by acknowledging with grateful hearts the many signal favors of Almighty God."[9]

The U.S. Senate has always had a chaplain paid by the U.S. government. This chaplain has always been a Christian who opens each Senate session with prayer.[10] Likewise, the U.S. military, from the earliest days of the Revolutionary War to the present, has provided chaplains.[11]

lawmakers did not encourage or permit public instruction of unscientific teachings.[12]

McLean v. Arkansas (1981)

In 1981, the Arkansas legislature passed a law mandating that whenever "evolution-science" was taught in public schools, "creation-science" must be taught as well (for definitions, see "Balanced Treatment for Creation-Science and Evolution-Science Act," p. 223). This Balanced Treatment Act appealed to the freedom clauses in the U.S. Constitution and its amendments.

Concerned about the damage young-earth creation teaching would do to the credibility of the Christian faith, science education, and scientific research, the Rev. Bill McLean and a coalition of scientists and science

Balanced Treatment for Creation-Science and Evolution-Science Act

The governor of Arkansas signed Act 590 of 1981 into law to balance

treatment of creation-science and evolution-science in public schools: to protect academic freedom by providing student choice; to ensure freedom of religious exercise; to guarantee freedom of belief and speech; to prevent establishment of religion; to prohibit religious instruction concerning origins; to bar discrimination on the basis of creationist or evolutionist belief; to provide definitions and clarifications; to declare the legislative purpose and legislative findings of fact; to provide for severability of provisions; to provide for repeal of contrary laws; and to set forth an effective date.[13]

"Creation-science" and "evolution-science" are defined in the Act as follows:[14]

   a. "Creation-science" means the scientific evidences for creation and inferences from those scientific evidences. Creation-science includes the scientific evidences and related inferences that indicate: (1) Sudden creation of the universe, energy, and life from nothing; (2) The insufficiency of mutation and natural selection in bringing about development of all living kinds from a single organism; (3) Changes only within fixed limits of originally created kinds of plants and animals; (4) Separate ancestry for man and apes; (5) Explanation of earth's geology by catastrophism, including the occurrence of a worldwide flood; and (6) A relatively recent inception of the earth and living kinds.
   b. "Evolution-science" means the scientific evidences for evolution and inferences from those scientific evidences. Evolution-science includes the scientific evidences and related inferences that indicate: (1) Emergence by naturalistic processes of the universe from disordered matter and emergence of life from nonlife; (2) The sufficiency of mutation and natural selection in bringing about development of present living kinds from simple earlier kinds; (3) Emergence by mutation and natural selection of present living kinds from simple earlier kinds; (4) Emergence of man from a common ancestor with apes; (5) Explanation of the earth's geology and the evolutionary sequence by uniformitarianism; and (6) An inception several billion years ago of the earth and somewhat later of life.

educators filed suit. The Arkansas Court quickly observed that the act mandated a contrived dualism, the dogmatic claim that only two possibilities existed for explaining the history of the universe, Earth, and life: atheistic materialism and young-earth creationism.[15]

The court ruled, therefore, that the exclusion of other possible explanations, by themselves, violated the freedom clauses the act supposedly sought to defend. Ironically, two witnesses (for the defense of the act), Norman Geisler and Chandra Wickramasinghe, presented two different explanations (old-earth creationism and pantheism/deism) for life's origin and history.

The court noted that the freedom clauses in the United States Constitution and its amendments already allowed for religious ideas and concepts to be taught in public education *provided such ideas and concepts have at least some demonstrable secular merit and academic integrity.* If the defendants' young-earth creationism could show a value independent of its particular religious perspective, then public education access for this specific brand of creation science could not be denied. Consequently, the court focused on the scientific credibility of young-earth creationism.

The scientists who testified for the plaintiff declared (without exception or equivocation) that they could find no merit, credibility, or integrity in the brand of creation science promoted by the defendants. In response to the question, "Are you aware of any scientific evidence to indicate the earth is no more than ten million years old?" Brent Dalrymple of the U.S. Geological Survey replied, "None whatsoever."[16]

When asked, "In your professional opinion, are [*sic*] the creation scientists' assertions of a young-earth been falsified?" Dalrymple stated, "Absolutely, I'd put them in the same category as the flat-earth hypothesis and the hypothesis that the Sun goes around the earth. I think those are all absurd, completely disproved hypotheses."[17]

In a surprising move, the defense chose not to place on the witness stand either of the two current leading young-earth creation scientists from the Institute for Creation Research, Henry Morris and Duane Gish. Apparently the defense believed that neither Morris nor Gish could withstand cross-examination.[18] Instead, the defense called British cosmologist and origin-of-life researcher Chandra Wickramasinghe to testify on behalf of the "creation-science" position.

In a prepared statement, Wickramasinghe explained to the court why he and a number of his colleagues rejected Darwinian evolution as a valid scientific explanation for either life's origin or its history.[19] However, under cross-examination, Wickramasinghe fully corroborated the testimony of the plaintiff's science expert witnesses that "no rational scientist would believe the earth's geology could be explained by reference to a worldwide flood or that the earth was less than one million years old."[20] Afterward

Judge William Overton wrote, "The Court is at a loss to understand why Dr. Wickramasinghe was called in [sic] behalf of the defendants."[21]

Once it had determined that young-earth creation science "has no scientific merit or educational value as science,"[22] the court was forced to evaluate the worth of the Balanced Treatment Act on religious merit alone. Unfortunately for the defense, several Christian theologians and clergy representing a wide spectrum of denominations, including Presbyterians and Southern Baptists, testified to their disagreement with the defendants' interpretation of the biblical creation accounts.[23] Consequently, the court determined that the act violated the United States Constitution's First Amendment.

In the Court's opinion, the Act would force upon public education students and teachers one particular creation perspective to the exclusion of all others.[24] Therefore, the conclusion that the act violated the First Amendment was inescapable.

Aguillard v. Treen (1983)

In spite of (or perhaps because of) what happened in Arkansas, the Lousiana state legislature in 1982 passed a Balanced Treatment Law (later dubbed the "Creationism Act") virtually identical to the one overturned in Judge Overton's court. As in Arkansas, a suit was filed within months of the law's passage.

In 1985, U.S. District Judge Adrian Duplantier declared Louisiana's law null and void by summary judgment, that is, without benefit of a trial. He agreed with Overton that the young-earth creation science mandated by that law was not science but rather a particular religious dogma. Duplantier refused to consider any of the thousand-plus pages of scientific documentation (pro and con) filed in the case.

The decision that Louisiana's Balanced Treatment Law violated the U.S. Constitution's First Amendment then went to the U.S. Court of Appeals, where a panel of fifteen judges voted (eight to seven) in favor of upholding Duplantier's verdict. Because of the close vote, the state of Louisiana filed a "jurisdictional statement" with the U.S. Supreme Court, arguing that the Balanced Treatment Law and the lower court's response established a substantial federal question. The U.S. Supreme Court justices concurred and agreed to hear the case, which had become *Edwards v. Aguillard*.[25]

Edwards v. Aguillard (1987)

The most famous young-earth creationism court battle is *Edwards v. Aguillard*, the U.S. Supreme Court's judgment on Louisiana's "Creationism Act." The Supreme Court justices declared this act superfluous in that it did nothing to "further its stated secular purpose of protecting academic freedom."[26] Specifically, the justices pointed out that the act failed to "further the goal of 'teaching all of the evidence.'" They added that "requiring the teaching of creation science with evolution does not give schoolteachers a flexibility that they did not already possess to supplant the present science curriculum with the presentation of theories, besides evolution, about the origin of life."[27]

According to the justices, the act would have actually diminished academic freedom. They wrote that "under the Act's requirements, teachers who were once free to teach any and all facets of this [creation/evolution] subject are now unable to do so."[28]

The Supreme Court justices also challenged the fairness concept of equal access. They observed that:

> the Act evinces a discriminatory preference for the teaching of creation science and against the teaching of evolution by requiring that curriculum guides be developed and resource services supplied for teaching creationism, but not for teaching evolution, by limiting membership on the resource panel to "creation scientists," and by forbidding school boards to discriminate against anyone who "chooses to be a creation scientist" or to teach creation science, while failing to protect those who choose to teach other theories or who refuse to teach creation science.[29]

Most telling of all, the Supreme Court justices concluded that the "appellants had failed to raise a genuine issue of material fact"[30] or to establish that their viewpoint "constitutes a true scientific theory."[31] Consequently, the court held that "the Act is facially invalid as violative of the Establishment Clause of the First Amendment, because it lacks a clear secular purpose."[32] The panel further pronounced that "while the Court is normally deferential to a State's articulation of a secular purpose, it is required that the statement of such purpose be sincere, and not a sham."[33]

As in the state-level court judgments, the Supreme Court justices could find no secular (i.e., scientific) merit in the brand of creation science being defended and so were forced to judge the case on whether the act gave unfair advantage to one religious doctrine over another. They ruled that "the Act's primary purpose was to change the public school science curriculum to provide persuasive advantage to a particular religious doctrine."[34] Thus, a majority of U.S. Supreme Court justices (seven to two) found the act violated the free exercise of religion clause of the U.S. Constitution's First Amendment.

Faulty Science, Closed Door

In the four most important creation-evolution court battles of the past fifty years, the creation side lost every time. Why? Because its defendants could not prove that young-earth creationism had scientific legitimacy.

The Supreme Court justices made their decisions crystal clear. If young-earth creation science were valid as science, its right to be included in the public school curriculum would be assured no matter what its connection to one form of religion or another.[35] Even if young-earth advocates could prove their position had no connection whatsoever with religion, their theory still would be ruled illegitimate due to its lack of scientific integrity. Thus, the appeal to protected access in science coursework was denied.

In all four court judgments, *scientific merit* set the primary standard. The courts acknowledged that this merit does not mean scientific perfection. If it did, no scientific model or interpretation could be taught. However, creation proponents must demonstrate at least some level of scientific value. Without it, access to the public education science curriculum cannot be justified.

These court judgments against young-earth creationism are not the audacious judicial moves many make them out to be. The courts have been consistent. Since the founding of the United States, and in light of the First Amendment's free-exercise clause, American education always has discriminated against religious ideas and doctrines that lack factual support.

The flat-Earth doctrine provides a good example. Until the 1920s, several religious groups believed the Bible taught a flat Earth.[36] Such religious convictions, however, did not sway the nation's educational institutions to allow flat-Earth physics in their science curricula.

Geocentrism—the belief that the Sun, planets, and stars revolve around Earth—serves as a more recent illustration. Several creationist groups assert that the Bible teaches geocentrism and have founded nonprofit organizations to promote this view.[37] Nevertheless, though geocentrism has been part of the American religious landscape throughout the past 250 years, geocentric physics has not been taught as a potentially valid hypothesis in public education textbooks or curricula.

Though each of the courts' decisions has barred the teaching of young-earth creation science, the courts, including the highest U.S. court, have given assurances that the door remains open to scientifically credible creation models.

Good Science, Open Door

At the end of the nineteenth century, the reigning cosmological paradigm was that the universe was infinitely old, infinitely large, and chemically static. Thus, the necessary conditions for life's chemistry presumably remained undisturbed over infinite time. Though this cosmic model endorsed one main ideology—atheistic naturalism—to the exclusion of all others (especially the creation doctrines of Christianity, Islam, and Judaism), it generated no First Amendment legal challenges.

No matter where or how far away they looked, astronomers saw an endless and homogeneous universe. Though scientific evidences seemed compelling, astronomers at the time acknowledged that they had explored only a tiny piece of the observable universe. They also knew that even though Newtonian mechanics was solidly established, it could not explain certain celestial mechanics phenomena in the solar system.

When Einstein's general theory of relativity arrived in 1916 and a 100-inch optical telescope became available in 1917, scientists made the stunning observation that the universe is not static. Later, larger telescopes and new technologies revealed that the universe's properties were radically different billions of years ago and that the universe had a beginning in finite time.

During the last forty years, several mathematical theorems based on general relativity confirmed that space and time had a beginning—coincident with the beginning of the universe.[38] During the past twenty-five years, astronomical measurements have established the Jewish, Christian, and Islamic doctrines of a single beginning universe.[39] (This evidence contradicts the Hindu/Buddhist/New Age doctrine of a universe cycling through an infinite or near infinite succession of beginnings and endings.)

Regardless of the theological/philosophical implications of modern cosmological research and despite how strongly cosmological advances discriminate against the beliefs of certain individuals and major religious bodies, the legislatures and courts of the United States have chosen not to intervene. At least for the hard sciences, legislatures and judges acknowledge that while the First Amendment cannot be used to protect bad science, neither can it be used to banish good science, whatever its theological implications.

Good science involves using testable models that make predictions, whether for creation or evolution. In turn, these predictions can be tested for validity. Exactly how to use predictions to test different creation/evolution models is the subject matter for the next chapter.

16

USING PREDICTIONS
TO TEST MODELS

My first serious read of the Genesis creation accounts took place when I was seventeen years old. I was amazed to see how the creation events matched the scientifically accepted record of nature, all except for Genesis 1:2 and 1:9–10.

These accounts contradicted the geology textbooks I had read, which claimed that continental landmasses had always existed on Earth. Instead, Genesis declared that when Earth began, water covered its whole surface. According to the Bible, continents did not appear until creation day three.

In the months that followed, I read three geophysics books concerning the history of Earth's crust. These texts all treated the continents as historically permanent features of Earth, yet all forthrightly acknowledged that the physics and form of early Earth were still a mystery, not likely to be solved for some time. At that point, for me, the biblical statements about Earth's initial conditions and the timing for development of its continental landmasses became a prediction of future scientific discoveries.

One test for RTB's biblical creation model is to consider what scientific advances reveal about Earth's surface before or at the time of life's origin. Another test focuses on when the greatest continental growth took place.

The Bible's pronouncements about the origin and growth of the continental landmasses provide excellent examples of two tests valued and used by the scientific community. The first examines explanatory power: how well and how completely a model explains what scientists know and understand to be true about the origin and history of the universe, Earth, life, and humanity. The second analyzes predictive success: how well and completely the model predicts future scientific discoveries. Thousands of years before scientists solved the mystery of the origin and history of Earth's continental landmasses, the Bible specifically stated what happened and predicted what would be discovered (see figure 10.1, p. 155).

The cosmos provides even more dramatic examples of the Bible's predictive success (see chapter 7). For thousands of years, Scripture alone asserted that the universe has been continually expanding from the cosmic creation event that brought about the beginning of space and time. That's exactly what astronomers now have found.

Developing Predictions

In addition to fulfilled predictions, Scripture contains predictions that have not yet been fulfilled. The most useful are those that possess a reasonable probability of being affirmed or falsified through scientific advance in the relatively near future.

For each creation/evolution model, several such predictions are easily apparent. Others can be developed by asking questions that test a model's strengths and weaknesses. The effectiveness of these questions depends on:

1. how quickly and extensively the prediction's affirmation or falsification yields further evidence for (or against) the model.
2. if the prediction's affirmation or falsification requires bigger or smaller adjustments to the model.
3. whether the prediction's affirmation or falsification corrects or extends the model.
4. how many disciplines and subdisciplines can supply evidence for or against the prediction's fulfillment.
5. how many independent means of measurement in a particular discipline can produce evidence for or against the prediction.

6. if the independent means of measurement provide increasingly consistent (or inconsistent) results as the measuring accuracy improves over time.
7. whether the prediction's fulfillment enables the model to become more detailed and comprehensive in its explanatory power.
8. if the prediction's affirmation or falsification yields more research questions/problems for researchers to explore.
9. the extent to which the prediction's affirmation or falsification eliminates one or more creation/evolution models and/or compels major alteration of other models into forms more closely resembling the successful model.

Predictions must be detailed, distinctive, and comprehensive to be of any use in evaluating a particular model. When predictions are so vague that the proponent of a particular model runs no risk of being wrong, they are virtually useless.

For example, a prediction that many species of life will continue to adapt to changes in their habitats is not useful. Every model predicts that outcome. An advocate for any particular creation/evolution model must predict the limits of adaptation for a particular species in response to the specific changes taking place in its habitat. Predictions must also estimate how quickly such adaptations will occur, what specific consequences will likely befall the species as it adapts, and most importantly, how and why the proposed change mechanisms will produce these changes.

Designing predictions to show a difference with respect to competing models permits comparisons. Predictions unique to one model and contrary to all other models hold the greatest promise for furthering understanding of specific creation/evolution issues. Such distinctives quickly reveal whether a model should be retained for further development or rejected. The pursuit of distinct features also encourages the necessary creativity to deal with currently unanswered questions.

Finally, a set of predictions must be comprehensive enough to address all (or nearly all) the major relevant issues. While no model can hope to explain everything (human knowledge will always remain finite), a good creation/evolution model needs to provide explanations for already observed relevant phenomena. As such, the model should produce predictions about what researchers will discover as they continue to study the broad array of creation/evolution disciplines.

Contrasting Predictions

Developing predictions of what scientists should discover in the future to differentiate between competing creation/evolution models is an extensive and complicated task. But it must be done to make useful evaluations possible.

Due to space limitations, this book can't possibly contrast predictions for all the creation/evolution models in anything more than a cursory manner. Instead, RTB's creation model is compared with the three most familiar Western models. (For brief descriptions of these models, see chapter 2, pp. 30–33.) They include:

- naturalistic evolution models
- young-earth creationist models
- theistic evolution models

A fourth well-known model, directed panspermia (a hypothesis that extraterrestrial intelligent aliens planted diverse types of life on Earth at various times throughout the past 3.8 billion years), is addressed in other RTB books.[1]

Undoubtedly it would be best for the scientific enterprise if leading advocates for the different creation/evolution positions defined their own predictions in a scientifically valid manner. In most cases, however, only a few predictions have been set forth with enough specificity. Therefore, to facilitate as extensive a comparison as possible, I've taken the liberty to deduce predictions from each of the four models while attempting to remain as neutral and objective as possible. Should any of these predictions be misstated, I have a genuine desire for correction.[2] Where a range of positions is held within a particular camp, unless otherwise qualified, I've attempted to describe the position as held by its most publicly prominent advocates.

These predictions have been limited to future discoveries with a high likelihood of being fulfilled, at least in part, sometime in the next decade. The goal is to provide tools for anyone to analyze emerging scientific discoveries to see how well they either affirm or falsify each of the four models.

Because a list that can be easily updated will do the most to improve scientific understanding, RTB has created an electronic appendix (see

Appendix C, p. 257) that lists the contrasting predictions arising from naturalism, young-earth creationism, theistic evolution, and the RTB creation model (see www.reasons.org/resources/predictions).[3] At the end of 2008, this electronic catalog contained more than a hundred predictions of future discoveries for which the leading advocates of the four creation/evolution models predicted different outcomes. These predictions are organized into three categories: simple sciences, complex sciences, and social sciences. The social sciences category, in addition to sciences like sociology and psychology, also includes philosophy and theology.

As new information for the various positions becomes available, this catalog will be revised and updated.[4] For now, comparing and contrasting just four sets of predictions illustrates how effective this method can be for testing various models. The first two sets, the big bang and humanity's special location, are from the simple sciences. The latter two, fine-tuning of plate tectonics and hominids and humanity, are from the complex sciences.

The Big Bang

RTB's creation model predicts that disputes over the big bang's validity will diminish as astronomers learn more about the universe's origin and structure. The model anticipates that new evidences validating a big bang creation event will emerge.

Astronomers should find additional confirmation that the universe traces back to a single beginning in finite time. Evidence should also validate that the beginning of space and time is coincident with the universe's beginning; the universe began in an infinitely or near infinitely hot, dense state; the universe has continuously expanded since its beginning and has continuously cooled under constant physical laws.

New discoveries increasingly will establish that the physics of the big bang creation event accounts for many, though not all, of the design features of the universe that make life possible. More cosmic design evidence will be found for human life than for life in general.

Nontheistic naturalist models of the universe predict that new astronomical discoveries will increasingly establish that the universe does not have an actual beginning but is eternal and self-caused. Such models also predict that new astronomical discoveries will increasingly disprove the current astronomical consensus that the physics of the big bang event must be exquisitely fine-tuned for life to be possible in the universe.

Young-earth creationist models predict that new astronomical discoveries will prove fatal for all big bang models. Specifically, they predict that evidences for the big bang will be progressively overturned and will lead to more and more astronomers' abandonment of the big bang as a plausible explanation for the origin and structure of the universe. Young-earth models also predict that emerging evidence will show that the physical laws are not constant, that accepted cosmic age indicators are illusory, and that the universe was created by a transcendent Being only thousands rather than billions of years ago.

Theistic evolution models agree with the RTB creation model in predicting that evidences for the big bang creation model will become more numerous, compelling, and consistent. However, these models differ from RTB's in one important respect. These models predict that future astronomical discoveries will increasingly demonstrate how the physics of the big bang creation event explain *all* the universe's design features that make life possible.

Humanity's Special Location

RTB's creation model predicts an increase in astronomical evidence that Earth resides at the ideal location in the cosmos not only for harboring human civilization and technology but also for viewing the totality of cosmic history. This position will increasingly prove rare and ideal for observing the universe's entire history back to the cosmic origin event itself and for discovering and measuring cosmic and galactic design features that make human life uniquely possible on Earth.

In addition, RTB's creation model predicts that astronomers will increasingly confirm that the Milky Way Galaxy, like all galaxies and stars in the universe, resides on the surface of the universe much as cities reside on Earth's surface.

Nontheistic naturalist models for the universe predict that new astronomical discoveries will show how unremarkable Earth's location in the universe is both for habitability and observation. Specifically, naturalistic models predict that astronomers will soon discover other planetary systems in the Milky Way Galaxy where advanced-life-support planets could exist and where observers could view the universe as easily and thoroughly as astronomers do from Earth. Likewise, these models predict astronomers will soon identify many other galaxies where advanced life could exist, and in a position from which the universe would be readily observable.

These cosmic models predict astronomers will increasingly confirm that the Milky Way Galaxy, like all galaxies and stars in the universe, resides on the surface of the universe.

Theistic evolution models agree with RTB's creation model in predicting that astronomers will continue to accumulate evidence of Earth's unique, ideal location for supporting human civilization and for allowing observation of the universe. However, unlike RTB's creation model, they predict that future astronomical discoveries increasingly will establish that the big bang creation event and its physics totally account for Earth's favored position for both habitability and cosmic observation. These models also predict astronomers will increasingly confirm that the Milky Way Galaxy, like all galaxies and stars in the universe, resides on the surface of the universe.

Predominant young-earth creationist models predict that future astronomical discoveries will increasingly establish galactocentrism. That idea places the Milky Way Galaxy at the actual geographical cosmic center.[5] This center is supposedly the unique location for human existence and for humanity's capacity to observe the entirety of the cosmos.

Fine-Tuning of Plate Tectonics

RTB's creation model predicts that as scientists continue to research the causes and effects of plate tectonics, their findings will reveal evidence for the exquisite fine-tuning required for long-lasting, stable plate-tectonic activity on a planet with a thin atmosphere. In addition, evidence will mount for the extreme rarity of such plate tectonics on a planet with a thin atmosphere anywhere else in the universe.

This model also predicts that scientists will find an increasing number of ways in which plate tectonics, at just-right levels, contribute to the support of advanced life and global, high-tech civilization in particular.

The RTB biblical creation model holds that the flood described in Genesis 6–9 destroyed all humankind, except Noah's family, but was local in its extent (because humans were still localized) and that the plate-tectonic activity level has remained relatively constant over the past several million years. RTB's model (like nontheistic and theistic evolutionary models) predicts that with respect to plate tectonics, research will increasingly confirm the fixity of the physical laws and the space-time dimensions.

Nontheistic naturalist models predict that evidence for fine-tuned, long-lasting plate tectonics will weaken as scientists learn more about plate-tectonic phenomena. In contrast to RTB's creation model, these models predict that thin-atmosphered planets (or other bodies) with stable, long-lasting plate-tectonic phenomena will prove relatively common. Naturalist models further predict that these phenomena will prove less and less crucial to the needs of advanced life and human civilization, and their apparent fine-tuning eventually will be seen as vastly overrated.

Theistic evolutionary models anticipate the increasing ability to prove no interventionist miracles (see chapter 6, p. 77) are necessary to explain Earth's plate-tectonic activity or how strategically designed this planet is for the support of a global, intelligent, high-tech civilization.

Young-earth creationist models predict that all plate-tectonic activity occurred during the past ten thousand years. These models claim that the flood described in Genesis 6–9 wiped out all humans and all of Earth's land-dwelling animals except for those on Noah's ark. Young-earth models expect advancing research to show that the bulk of Earth's tectonic activity took place during the thirteen months of a global flood event (roughly 5,000 to 7,000 years ago) and possibly also at the time of Adam's initial rebellion against God (roughly 6,000 to 10,000 years ago).

Models expounding a young-earth view also expect future scientific research to show that many of the physical laws and/or cosmic space-time dimensions were dramatically altered during the Genesis flood and/ or during Adam's initial rebellion against God's authority. Young-earth models claim these alterations account for the dramatic changes in plate-tectonic activity.

Hominids and Humanity

RTB's creation model predicts that future anthropological and genetic research will increasingly confirm that humans are biologically distinct rather than descended from a hominid species. This model predicts stronger evidence for humanity's genetic, anatomical, and behavioral uniqueness—characteristics that could not have evolved by natural process from any hominid or other primate species. Further, the RTB creation model predicts the discovery of additional indications that at least some interventionist miracles were necessary to explain humanity's existence and uniqueness. This biblical model places the earliest hominids at 6.5 million years ago and the first humans at roughly fifty thousand years ago.

Nontheistic naturalist models for humanity's relationship to the hominids predicts exactly the opposite. They anticipate increasing evidence that humanity's apparently unique attributes and behaviors came by natural descent from one or more hominid species. These models further predict that as anthropological and genetic research advances, humanity will prove increasingly less distinct from the most recent hominid species. Likewise, naturalistic models predict that evidence for interventionist miracles to explain humanity's unique characteristics will steadily decline.

Naturalist/evolutionary models place the earliest hominids at 6.5 million years ago and the first "modern humans" at roughly fifty thousand years ago.

Most theistic evolutionary models expect future research to establish that all of humanity's anatomical, genetic, and behavioral characteristics can be explained by divinely directed descent from previously existing species through natural means. Consequently, these models predict that humanity will prove less distinct from recent hominids than predicted by RTB's creation model but more distinct from recent hominids than predicted by nontheistic naturalist or young-earth creationist models.

Theistic evolutionary models place the earliest hominids at 6.5 million years ago with the first "modern humans" at roughly fifty thousand years ago.

Young-earth creationist models predict that advancing research increasingly will prove present-day humans anatomically, genetically, and behaviorally identical to Neanderthals, *Homo sapiens idaltu*, and *Homo erectus*. These models also expect future discoveries to show that humans and all hominid species have come into existence within the past ten thousand years. Young-earth creationist models agree with the RTB creation model that increasing evidence will affirm the necessity for at least some interventionist miracles to explain the origin of humanity and the hominids.

Bringing Out the Best

Advancing research will test most of these predictions (and others out-lined throughout this book, as well as in the electronic catalog) within the next few years. The short range of these forecasts provides substantial appeal. This testing holds potential for objective verification/falsification of creation/evolution models within a relatively short time.

Using specific objective models to test competing ideas can reduce emotion and further scientific dialogue. All sides could simply wait and watch several months or years to see which predictions prove accurate and which do not.

Allowing predictive success and explanatory power to settle creation/evolution differences shifts the emphasis from defending the infallibility and finality of one's interpretation to discovering what's true with deep-ened understanding. The pursuit of truth is a valuable endeavor, worth every bit of struggle and humility it requires.

Ideally the goal should be to improve and extend the models that survive the rigors of predictive testing. Cutting-edge discoveries and measurements, which bring more comprehensive understanding of the natural realm, can improve the breadth and depth of surviving models' explanatory power and capacity to generate even more predictions. This focus remains fixed on learning and on improving and extending the most successful models. That process enhances delight in the scientific enterprise.

More than two years ago, Reasons To Believe formally launched this principle of testing competing creation/evolution models through con-trasting predictions of future discoveries.[6] Within the past two and a half years, numerous predictions made by the different creation/evolution models were fulfilled thanks to advancing research. The next chapter analyzes how these predictions either confirm or falsify the different models.

17

Scoring the Models

Whenever I go for a long hike, I always pack plenty of food. Opting for high-calorie dried food keeps me from carrying unnecessary weight. But once on the trail, I crave fresh fruits and vegetables. Consequently, I keep a sharp eye out for any possible edibles growing alongside the path.

Not being a botanist makes it critical for me to test potential food for what is safe and good. Observing ants and/or fruit flies helps. So does watching the birds. If more than two species of birds consume some part of a plant, I consider it worth trying.

My most frequent hiking partner, my wife, constantly frets that someday I'll poison myself. However, nature's food tasters protect my health and introduce me to many delicious treats.

A model's fulfilled predictions are a lot like those taste testers. They help scientists determine what works. If a model's prediction comes true, then that part of the model on which the prediction rests can be trusted. On the other hand, if the prediction proves false, then that part of the model may need to be revised or abandoned.

Model Adjustments

The need for a model to change in light of a failed prediction depends on the nature of that prediction. Sometimes the failure itself needs to be

242   MORE THAN A THEORY

tested. It is not uncommon in science for subsequent attempts to confirm a result to prove a single discordant measurement invalid instead.

There comes a time, however, when a measurement or observation that exposes a model's failed prediction becomes so well confirmed (through independently performed experiments and/or observations) that no rational basis remains for doubting the outcome. Then the question becomes, to what degree can the model be salvaged?

Falsifications of a model resulting from failed predictions can be classified into three categories: refining, corrosive, and catastrophic. Some discoveries force minor revisions in the details, rather than in the foundations of the model. Typically, these small adjustments clarify the less understood or more speculative parts of a model and increase the model's explanatory scope and power. The explanatory power of the RTB model was enhanced, for instance, through discoveries clarifying the Moon's birth and history. These discoveries forced minor revisions over the past thirty-five years, as revealed in RTB's first booklet on the science of Genesis 1,[1] but the changes consistently made for a more potent biblical creation model.

A corrosive falsification is so damaging to a model that it places the validity of the model in serious doubt and at a minimum forces a major revision. A possible example for RTB's creation model might be discoveries that would prove birds and mammals are no more capable of relating to humans than amphibians, fish, and insects.

A catastrophic falsification disproves the very foundation of the model. For example, the notion that the universe has a beginning and was created by an Agent beyond space and time is so fundamental to RTB's creation model that an undeniable set of proofs showing no beginning would force the model's abandonment.

Test Scores So Far

In 2006 Reasons To Believe published a list of ninety contrasting predictions of future discoveries arising from four different creation/evolution models.[2] This list was deliberately limited to predictions likely to be either confirmed or falsified within a few years. As a result, many new discoveries have since been made that test RTB's model and those of naturalism, theistic evolution, and young-earth creationism.

All four models made predictions about the number of known characteristics of the Local Group of Galaxies, the Milky Way Galaxy, the solar system, and Earth that must be fine-tuned, and to what degree, to make the existence of simple life on one inhabitable body possible for a period of at least three billion years. RTB's model predicted this fine-tuning would dramatically increase as astronomers continue to learn more.[3] Naturalism predicted the fine-tuning evidence would become weaker. The predominant theistic evolutionary models claimed that all fine-tuning became fixed at the cosmic creation event. Young-earth creationism predicted all fine-tuning evidences for the universe being any older than ten thousand years would become much weaker.

A search of the literature published in 2006 uncovered 322 different characteristics for which fine-tuning was needed for simple life to exist on a planet or a moon for at least three billion years.[4] The combined fine-tuning degree revealed that the probability of finding such a planet or moon anywhere within the observable universe (without invoking some kind of miraculous intervention) was one chance in 10^{282}.[5] This probability generously took into account possible dependencies among the different characteristics. It also noted that as many as 10^{22} planets and 10^{24} moons might reside in the observable universe.

A scientific literature search completed thirty months later found 676 different characteristics in which fine-tuning was required to allow simple life to exist for more than three billion years on one body. The combined fine-tuning degree implied that the probability of finding such a body (without invoking divine intervention) is one chance in 10^{556}.

During the time between the two evaluations, astronomers discovered an average of twelve new design characteristics per month necessary to make the existence of simple life possible for at least three billion years. Of the 354 newly found design features, over a third were attributes that could not have been exclusively determined at the cosmic creation event.

Unlike the naturalistic and predominant theistic evolution models, RTB's creation model predicted that astronomers would find much more fine-tuning design evidence for human life than for simple life. At the end of the study search, the list of design traits necessary to make human life possible was 824. The combined fine-tuning degree yielded a probability of only one chance in $10^{1,050}$ for the existence of a body capable of supporting the equivalent of human life anywhere in the observable universe (without invoking any miraculous interventions). In other words, the established probability for the existence of a body that can support human life, as opposed to mere simple life, for three billion years is 10^{494} times more remote.

Table 16.1 shows that many of the twenty-two predictions within the simple sciences (mathematics, physics, astronomy) published by RTB in 2006 have already been fulfilled or falsified and to what extent for each of the four models (naturalism, theistic evolution, young-earth creationism, and RTB's model). Tables 16.2 and 16.3 display the same kind of data for the fifty-two predictions within the complex sciences (geology, chemistry, biology, and anthropology) and the fifteen predictions within the social sciences (sociology, psychology, philosophy, and theology).

Table 16.1: Test Scores for Simple Science Predictions from 2006

	Naturalism	Young-Earth	Theistic Evolution	RTB Creation
Fulfilled	1	3	4	20
Partly fulfilled	1	0	5	1
Not yet fulfilled	1	1	2	1
Partly falsified	3	1	11	0
Falsified	16	17	0	0

Table 16.2: Test Scores for Complex Science Predictions from 2006

	Naturalism	Young-Earth	Theistic Evolution	RTB Creation
Fulfilled	0	10	1	27
Partly fulfilled	0	7	2	16
Not yet fulfilled	9	11	25	9
Partly falsified	19	1	17	0
Falsified	24	23	7	0

Table 16.3: Test Scores for Social Sciences Predictions from 2006

	Naturalism	Young-Earth	Theistic Evolution	RTB Creation
Fulfilled	0	1	0	1
Partly fulfilled	0	1	1	4
Not yet fulfilled	10	10	12	10
Partly falsified	4	3	2	0
Falsified	1	0	0	0

These tabulations deliver significant test results for all four models. Updated predictions in the electronic list (available at www.reasons.org/resources/predictions) promise many more insights as new discoveries continue to be made.

The next and final chapter introduces five additional testing tools for creation/evolution models. These new tools illustrate why the RTB creation model is a viable theory—and more—for the origin and history of the universe and life.

18

EXTRA CREDIT

The first public lecture I ever gave was an intimidating experience. I was only sixteen years old when I walked to the podium and saw two physics professors from the University of British Columbia in the audience. Who was I to speak about the physics of variable stars in front of such distinguished guests?

Recalling something I had once read held me together: public speaking is not about the speaker, it's about the audience. So during my lecture I experimented with different methods of explaining certain physics concepts to see which best helped everyone understand. Those experiments hopefully made my next lecture a little more interesting for my audience and certainly made it a bit less intimidating for me.

Over the years I've never stopped experimenting with communication techniques. In the process I've discovered that one test of a message's validity and integrity is the extent to which it sets people free from their fears. When the information I present corresponds to reality and doesn't contradict itself, people from a wide spectrum of philosophical backgrounds tend to be motivated to ask questions and learn more about the topics.

Eliminating the Fear

This same principle holds true for creation/evolution issues. In addition to explanatory power and predictive success, two measures of a model's soundness are the kind of impact it has on a wide range of audiences and the way it stimulates research progress in science, philosophy, and theology.

Unfortunately, when it comes to issues related to the origins and history of the universe, Earth, and life, fear can generate tension and emotion among certain audiences. These dynamics impede harmony and cooperation and even stymie progress. A major concern, perhaps best illustrated in Richard Dawkins's *The God Delusion*, is how the fear of religion, and Christianity in particular, can impact science.

A Perceived Enemy of Science

Concerns about religious radicalism and the encroachment of church into state affairs have led to public avoidance of anything that might be construed as the unconstitutional "establishment of religion." Religious pluralism is currently in vogue, with one exception—Christianity.

Christophobia[1] appears especially pronounced in academia. Courses and programs on Islam, Hinduism, Buddhism, New Age philosophies, Native American religions, and other religions old and new abound. Alternatives to a Christian perspective are widely encouraged while, subtly or overtly, endorsements of biblical views meet with disdain or outright prohibition.

A Perceived Enemy of Faith

Sciencephobia—the fear of science and avoidance of anything related to the scientific community—has infected many churches, as well as Christian education. Anxiety and distrust frequently lead to barring any teaching of so-called "secular science." In some instances, scientists and science students are even excluded from participation. At the very least, their questions often remain unanswered. At worst, some churches, schools, and Christian institutions teach that secular science is the great enemy of the Christian faith.[2] Consequently, students are strongly exhorted to avoid standard courses in science, especially those leading to science careers, out of fear that their faith might be undermined.

Additional Tests

Neither fear of science nor fear of Christianity should be allowed to get in the way of understanding new discoveries. The goal of research should be to further the scientific, philosophical, and theological endeavors, and fear must not stand in the way. Using five supplemental tests—censorship, stultification, integration, research passion, and destiny implications—can expose biases and assist in determining which models best explain the origins and history of the universe, Earth, and life.

Censorship

Ideologues, who tend toward fear, often censor what they view as serious threats to their paradigms. The prohibition of valid theistic models for the origins and history of the universe, Earth, and life may be an indicator that those scientific models offer a more accurate and comprehensive explanation of nature's record. One measure of RTB's creation model might be the ongoing purposeful attempts to ignore or shut out its claims—not only from naturalists, young-earth creationists, or theistic evolutionists but rather from all three. This censorship differs from the dismissive response sometimes evoked by the young-earth model, which is often subjected to scrutiny as the only Christian position.

Stultification

Within some halls of science, a familiar refrain echoes: Christianity stultifies scientific advance and promotes ignorance, always appealing to the "God of the gaps." This complaint embodies a principle that provides a fourth tier (beyond explanatory power, predictive success, and censorship) for testing creation/evolution models.

The stultification test identifies faulty models by measuring the degree to which a model impedes scientific advance. Likewise, this test identifies successful models by measuring the extent to which a model stimulates scientific progress with the greatest efficiency and economy.

To be sure, some poor interpretations and applications of Scripture today justify the complaint that Christianity stultifies science. However, historically, Christianity gave birth to both the scientific method and the scientific revolution (see chapter 4, pp. 50–52, and Appendix A). A sound biblical interpretation generates a desire to know more about the Creator and his creation. Such motives stimulate increasing research efforts and explorations in the realm of nature.

In much the same way as poor interpretation of Scripture impedes scientific progress, many naturalistic models also fail the stultification test. The assumption that naturalistic evolution governs life's history on Earth, for example, led to the conclusion that genomes for advanced species predominantly contain the accumulation of millions of generations' worth of genetic accidents described as useless junk (see chapter 13, pp. 200–202). This inference led to thirty years of abandoning research into possible functions of nonprotein-coding DNA, the so-called junk DNA.

The delay in studying this DNA is a classic illustration of the pervasive "*no* God of the gaps" (or "naturalism of the gaps") philosophy in science. Recognition by theists of possible purposes for nonprotein-coding DNA unsuccessfully collided with an assumption that no creative intentionality imbued that "junk" with purpose. As a result, valuable time was lost.

Stultification wastes not only research talent but money as well. In astrobiology, for example, the no-Creator assumption combined with awareness that life arose on Earth in a geological instant without benefit of prebiotics compelled the conclusion that life's origin must have been a simple naturalistic event.[3] Therefore, a new science discipline was born. Astrobiology sprang from the conviction that millions of Milky Way Galaxy planets, as well as several solar system bodies, must possess life.

SETI (the Search for Extraterrestrial Intelligence) also combined the no-Creator assumption with the idea that technologically advanced humans apparently arose from bacteria in only a few billion years. The presupposition that bacteria produced humans by a straightforward, strictly natural pathway led to the deduction that technologically advanced civilizations must exist on hundreds, if not thousands, of Milky Way Galaxy planets not yet discovered.

Faith in naturalism, as fervent as any religious zeal, has lured huge amounts of public and private funding, not to mention tremendous chunks of valuable telescope and astronomer time, into efforts to capture signals from distant hypothetical civilizations. For a tiny fraction of those resources, the question of whether life-supportable bodies are common in the universe and whether the molecular building blocks of life (homochiral amino acids and pentose sugars, nitrogenous bases, proteins, DNA, and RNA—see pp. 140–41) are ubiquitous in space could be put to the test.

So far, thirty years of intense research investment has yet to yield any evidence for a single extraterrestrial body capable of supporting life, for the existence of any indigenous extraterrestrial life-building molecules (see pp. 140–41), or for even a star capable of producing the energy spectrum and history advanced life requires (see pp. 123–25). Until NASA can demonstrate that extraterrestrial molecular building blocks exist in significant concentrations and diversity and that mechanisms exist for their safe transport through interstellar space, it seems a waste of valuable space mission resources to look for indigenous life on Mars or inside Europa. Vastly more productive efforts toward understanding life's origin and history might include lunar missions to recover fossilized remains of Earth's first life. Major meteors striking Earth easily could have propelled Earth's soils into outer space, transporting that life to the Moon.[4]

One way to test creation/evolution models can be by examining their efficiency and productivity. If a given model delivers scientific discoveries and understanding at a faster pace and for less research investment than a competing model, then that perspective should be considered a more likely description of reality. Similarly, if one model generates more scientific breakthroughs, better explanations of natural phenomena, and more comprehensive integration of scientific disciplines for less effort and expense than a competing model, then the better model deserves consideration, whatever its philosophical or religious implications.

Integration

Overspecialization in science can also seriously impede the testing of creation/evolution models. Some researchers (e.g., many anthropologists, zoologists, and chemists) have little if any exposure to those eras of cosmic or terrestrial history in which creation proponents claim divine activity occurred. Accordingly, these scientists lack the opportunity—and the impetus—to witness the merits of creation models and put them to the test.

Even for researchers whose studies focus on eras of possible divine activity (e.g., cosmologists, geophysicists, and paleontologists), specialization can pose a problem. One researcher may see evidence that contradicts a particular creation/evolution model in his own subdiscipline and presume such contradictions don't exist in other disciplines and subdisciplines. That "glitch" becomes a single anomaly that future efforts might possibly resolve rather than a contribution to an accumulation of evidence that demands major revisions or outright rejection of a particular model.

In the 1950s and 1960s, origin-of-life research was considered a strictly chemical discipline. While several chemical roadblocks stymied attempts to reconstruct natural pathways to self-assembly of life molecules, confidence remained high that such pathways eventually would be found. Meanwhile, looking at astronomical, geophysical, and atmospheric factors, scientists in other disciplines demonstrated that the hoped-for chemical successes were irrelevant. Naturalistic scenarios had encountered a host of irreconcilable problems across all of these disciplines.[5]

At the same time, Earth's age was thought by many Christians to involve only the discipline of geology. While some serious geological challenges to a young-earth interpretation (thousands of years versus billions of years) were acknowledged, young-earth creationists felt certain that the problems were minor. Through the past half-century, however, that confidence has been seriously undermined by the recognition that every science discipline (and even theology) poses multiple challenges to and falsifications of the young-earth model.[6]

The integration test simply evaluates which creation/evolution models provide the best and most seamless integration of various scientific disciplines. The best model should explain at least some phenomena in *all* disciplines in a manner distinct from and superior to that offered by other models. It should also supply the best integration of the entire history of the universe, Earth, and life. Biblically based creation models must also demonstrate how their particular view produces a superior integration of *all* sixty-six books of the Bible and a superior integration of those explanations with the entire record of nature.

Research Passion

North America today faces a serious science education crisis. That crisis is especially pronounced in the United States. A number of causes largely account for a dramatic drop in the public's zeal for science.

A large percentage, perhaps a majority, of America's science and engineering graduate students now come from other countries.[7] South Korea, with only one-sixth the U.S. population, graduates almost as many engineers.[8] In a 2003 address to the President's Council of Advisors on

Science and Technology, Richard Smalley, Nobel laureate in chemistry (1996), forecast that "by 2010, if current trends continue, over 90 percent of all physical scientists and engineers in the world will be Asians working in Asia."[9]

One possible explanation for this sharply declining science enrollment by Americans and the sharp increase of Asian students comes from scholars in the People's Republic of China. Chinese paleontologists studying the famous Cambrian explosion fossils in the Chengjiang shale in the Yunnan province have commented to their American colleagues, "In China we are not allowed to criticize our government leaders, but we are free to criticize Darwin. In your country you are free to criticize your government leaders, but you are not permitted to criticize Darwin."[10]

Could it be that, to some degree, the American science education crisis stems from the quelling of controversy? Has a dismissive attitude toward any alternative to strict naturalism made science education boring? Is fear of the religious or philosophical implications of amazing new scientific discoveries prompting American science educators to squash discussion of the important and intriguing *why* questions? Do science educators avoid the very issues with the most potential to engage their students? (See "Restoring the Thrill of Scientific Discovery," p. 254.)

The research passion test measures the degree to which a model engenders a zeal for studying science and a joy over what is being discovered, not only for science students but also for the general public. The better the creation/evolution model, the more it ignites enthusiasm for science. The best biblical creation model similarly kindles eagerness for studying the Bible and Christian theology and for anticipating new discoveries.

Destiny Implications

RTB's creation model claims that humans are unique among all lifeforms in that they are spiritual beings (see chapter 12, pp. 182, 190–92). Some physical evidence for that spirituality is that only human brains come equipped with the brain structures and lobes necessary to support spiritual activity. Evidence of that spirituality, according to the Bible, is that God has "set eternity in the hearts of men" (Eccles. 3:11). The awareness

Restoring the Thrill of Scientific Discovery

Fear of controversy and of getting too religious or too philosophical may indeed be making science dull. Consider this story:

Several years ago, I was invited to speak at a large aerospace company in Southern California. My subject: "Creation and Evolution: New Scientific Evidence for God." When I arrived, the four-hundred-seat auditorium was packed to overflowing. After my talk, many stayed more than an hour to ask questions.

Later I was told that for the rest of the day, employees were buzzing about the topic and points raised in the question and answer session. As I was leaving, one of the company's executives, a self-identified atheist, engaged me in a brief conversation. He told me the company had long sponsored science enrichment lectures for employees. Attendance, he said, usually hovered between ten and fifteen, and nobody stayed afterward. Looking me straight in the eye, he added, "I may not like this Jesus Christ stuff, but if that's what it takes to get our employees interested in science, I am all for it." Jesus had been mentioned just once.

This experience is not an anomaly. It has been repeated many times in schools, high-tech firms, professional meetings, university classrooms, and numerous other settings. People everywhere seem to be intensely curious about the interface between science and belief in God.

of something beyond this realm causes human beings to evaluate past actions, contemplate the meaning of life, and consider what lies beyond physical death. It also motivates individuals to find purpose and a sense of destiny for their lives.

This drive to fulfill destiny did not evolve from lower species. No other life-form on Earth manifests it to any degree. Nor did it evolve within the human species. Archaeology shows that the earliest humans displayed the same strong impetus toward eternal destiny as people experience today.

The observation that so many people are so highly motivated to achieve an eternal significance and sometimes even pay the ultimate price for it (see chapter 12, pp. 182, 190–92) implies that the sense of purpose and destiny exists within the human heart for real, achievable reasons.[11] A seventh test for all creation/evolution models, then, is how well does the model explain and satisfy the human drive to seek and achieve an ultimate hope, purpose, and destiny?

Only a Theory

Perhaps the most common exchange on origins issues begins with evolutionists asserting that Darwin's theory is a proven fact. Meanwhile, creationists retort that evolution is only a theory. This rejoinder understandably angers scientists in that it conveys to the public that scientific theories are no more than tentative hypotheses.

In science, a theory is much more. It provides an explanation for natural phenomena that has been tested and confirmed as a general principle through experiments and observations.

Biological evolution (as opposed to Darwinian evolution) is a theory in every sense of the definition in that there exists overwhelming physical evidence that life progressively became more diverse and complex over the past 3.8 billion years and shares common DNA templates, metabolic reaction paths, and common designs in morphology. This is the definition most scientists refer to when they declare biological evolution an established fact. If the reference to 3.8 billion years were removed, every participant in the creation/evolution debates would agree with these conclusions. Leaving in the reference to time excludes only young-earth creationists.

Explanations for precisely *how* life progressed from simple to complex, *how* life became more diverse, and *why* Earth's life-forms display such remarkable relatedness have not yet reached the status of a scientific theory. This book lays out a model for life's origin and history that attempts to provide better and more comprehensive explanations than competing creation/evolution models for these how and why questions. If the model's predictions of future scientific discoveries continue to be fulfilled, then the RTB creation model could indeed be considered a scientific theory. However, it has even greater potential.

More Than a Theory

Hallmarks of a good scientific theory are explanatory power and predictive success. In addition to excelling on these criteria, the RTB creation model performs well in the five additional tests of censorship, stultification, integration, research passion, and destiny implications. These tests make this biblical model, prospectively, far more than a theory.

The RTB creation model has the power to change lives for the better. Frequently people comment on how intensely liberating the model's message is because finally the spiritual heart can rejoice with what the mind knows must be true. With more development, RTB's model has the potential to change more lives in even more dramatic ways.

Building Better Models

Serious comparison and evaluation of creation/evolution models has been hampered by the lack of one or more creation models with sufficient detail, breadth, and testable/verifiable/falsifiable scientific content to be judged on the merits of its explanatory power and predictive success. For that matter, sufficiently developed evolutionary models also are in short supply. Every current evolutionary model can be made much more testable, verifiable/falsifiable, and predictive.

This book places a biblical creation model on the table. In doing so, it invites the development of other models for both creation and evolution, in forms equally open to testing. With such development the comparison, evaluation, and refinement of these models can significantly advance our understanding of the origin and history of the universe, Earth, life, and humanity. When the best models become more than theories, the condition of mankind will be changed for the better.

----------- APPENDIX A -----------

THE SCIENTIFIC METHOD'S BIBLICAL ORIGINS

All creation/evolution proponents seem to agree on the best testing method for their models. Popularly termed the scientific method, this approach could more accurately be called the biblical method.[1]

Among the world's "holy books," the Bible alone exhorts readers to objectively test before they believe. According to the apostle Paul, no teaching should escape testing: "Test everything. Hold on to the good" (1 Thess. 5:21).

Paul explains that to be effective, testing requires objectivity, education, and training: "Do not conform any longer to the pattern of this world, but be transformed by the renewing of your mind. Then you will be able to test and approve what God's will is" (Rom. 12:2).

The idea of testing before believing pervades both the Old and New Testaments. It forms the very heart of the biblical concept of faith. One of the Hebrew words for faith, *ĕmûnâ*, means a strongly held conviction that something or someone is certainly real, firmly established, constant, and dependable.[2] The Greek word for faith, *pistis*, means a strong and welcome conviction of the truth of anything or anyone to the degree that one places deserved trust and confidence in that thing or person.[3]

In every instance, the faith described in the Bible connotes the response to established truth. Just as there is no faith, from a biblical perspective, without an active response (see James 2:18), neither is there faith apart from established truth(s).

Christian scholars throughout church history—from the early church fathers to Renaissance naturalists to Reformation theologians to present-day evangelical scientists, philosophers, and theologians—have noted a pattern in the biblical narratives and descriptions of sequential physical events. Bible authors typically preface such depictions with a statement of the frame of reference (point of view) and the initial conditions. A statement of the final conditions and conclusions about what has transpired follows. That is the scientific method.

Scottish theologian Thomas Torrance has written and edited book-length discussions of how Christian theology (Reformed theology in particular) played a critical role in the scientific method's development and the amazing achievements by Western science because of it.[4] The Bible said it first and best. Others simply applied it to science.

Appendix B

Designed for Life

A catalog of characteristics of the universe and Earth that require fine-tuning for life's existence, including relevant citations to the scientific literature, is available for purchase as an electronic compendium. It may be accessed at www.reasons.org/links/hugh/research-notes.[1] This catalog includes four parts:

Part 1: Fine-Tuning for Life in the Universe—lists 140 features of the cosmos as a whole (including the laws of physics) that must fall within certain narrow ranges to make physical life possible.

Part 2: Fine-Tuning for Intelligent Physical Life—describes 402 quantifiable characteristics of a planetary system and its galaxy that must fall within narrow ranges to make advanced life possible. This list also explains in each case how the slight increase or decrease in the value of the characteristic would destroy the possibility for advanced life's existence.

Part 3: Probability Estimates for the Features Required by Various Life Forms—identifies 922 characteristics of a galaxy and of a planetary system that make physical life possible and gives estimates of the probability that a galaxy and planetary system would manifest such characteristics. This list is broken down into the fine-tuning requirements for various kinds of life.

Part 4: Probability Estimates on Different Size Scales for the Features Required by Advanced Life—presents a breakdown of the 922 characteristics as they arise, separately, from the galaxy cluster, galaxy, planetary system, planet, planet's surface, and planet's other life.

Appendix C

Predictive Tests for Four Creation/Evolution Models

The simplest, cleanest, and least controversial tool for evaluating different creation/evolution models is a list of predictions specific to each model of what researchers will discover as they gather more data and achieve greater understanding of the natural realm. If future research contradicts all or nearly all the predictions arising from a particular model, then that model can be fairly discarded as a failure. However, if the model's predictions prove wholly or largely correct, then that model can be aptly determined as worth refining.

Contrasting predictions of future discoveries arising from four models (naturalism, theistic evolutionism, young-earth creationism, and RTB's creation model) are listed in an electronic addendum to this book. This catalog is available without charge at www.reasons.org/resources/predictions. It will be periodically updated.

NOTES

Chapter 1: Is It Science?

1. Dictionary.com, s.v. "religion," http://dictionary.reference.com/browse/religion, accessed July 9, 2008.

2. Richard Dawkins, *The God Delusion* (Boston: Houghton Mifflin, 2006), 52.

3. Ibid., 348.

4. Ibid., 82.

5. Paul Serrell, "Christian College Fights to Teach Creation," CBN News (June 17, 2002): 1–3 http://www.cbn.com/CBNNews/News/020617a.asp>option=private_Christian_col lege_fights_to_teach_creation (accessed June 24, 2002).

6. Ibid., 1.

7. Ibid., 2.

8. Ibid.

9. Penny Higgins, "Why 'Intelligent Design' (ID) Is Not Science, and Why, Therefore, It Should Not Be Taught in a Science Curriculum," Committee for the Scientific Investigation of Claims of the Paranormal, http://csicop.org/intelligentdesignwatch/not-science.html (accessed January 14, 2008); American Astronomical Society Statement on the Teaching of Evolution, Adopted September 20, 2005, *American Astronomical Society Council Resolutions*, http://www.aas.org/governance/resolutions.php#teach; John Thavis, "Intelligent Design Not Science, Says Vatican Newspaper Article," *Catholic News Service*, January 17, 2006, http://www.catholicnews.com/data/stories/cns/0600273.htm.

10. See Hugh Ross, *A Matter of Days* (Colorado Springs: NavPress, 2004), 59–120, 253–54.

11. Ibid., 139–220.

12. The English Language Institute of America, *The Living Webster Encyclopedic Dictionary of the English Language* (Chicago: English Language Institute of America, 1971), s.v. "science"; William L. Reese, *Dictionary of Philosophy and Religion: Eastern and Western Thought* (Atlantic Highlands, NJ: Humanities Press, 1980), s.v. "science"; Jitse M. van der Meer, ed., *Facets of Faith and Science*, vol. 1, *Historiography and Modes of Interaction*

(Lanham, MD: University Press of America, 1996); *McGraw-Hill Dictionary of Scientific and Technical Terms*, 6th ed. (New York: McGraw-Hill, 2003), s.v. "science."
    13. Eugenie C. Scott, "My Favorite Pseudoscience," *Reports of the National Center for Science Education* 23 (January–February 2003): 11.
    14. Lawrence M. Krauss, "'Creationism' Discussion Belongs in Religion Class," *Reports of the National Center for Science Education* 22 (January–April 2002): 11.
    15. Board of Directors, "Statement on the Teaching of Evolution," American Association for the Advancement of Science, February 16, 2006, http://www.aaas.org/news/releases/2006/pdf/0219boardstatement.pdf.
    16. Eugenie C. Scott, "The Big Tent and the Camel's Nose," *Reports of the National Center for Science Education* 21 (January–April 2001): 39.
    17. Zachary D. Blount, Christina Z. Borland, and Richard E. Lenski, "Historical Contingency and the Evolution of a Key Innovation in an Experimental Population of Escherichia coli," *Proceedings of the National Academy of Sciences, USA* 105 (June 10, 2008): 7899–7906.
    18. Ohio State University, University of California at Davis, University of California at Los Angeles, University of California at Santa Barbara, University of Illinois, and Yale are recent examples.
    19. David Deaner, review of *Origins of Life: Biblical and Evolutionary Models Face Off*, by Fazale Rana and Hugh Ross, *Origins of Life and Evolution of Biospheres* 37 (April 2007): 201–3.
    20. David L. Block and Hugh N. Ross, "Unser Universum: Zufall oder Absicht?" ed. and trans. Gero Rupprecht, *Die Sterne* 68 (June 1992): 325–39; Jacquelyn A. Thomas and F. R. Rana, "The Influence of Environmental Conditions, Lipid Composition, and Phase Behavior on the Origin of Cell Membranes," *Origins of Life and Evolution of Biospheres* 37 (June 2007): 267–85.
    21. Richard E. Smalley won the 1996 Nobel Prize in chemistry for his contribution to the discovery of fullerenes. The RTB books most responsible for Smalley's changed perspective were *The Creator and the Cosmos*, *Origins of Life*, *Who Was Adam*, *Beyond the Cosmos*, *The Genesis Question*, and *A Matter of Days*. For a summary of the story of Smalley's change of perspective see "Dr. Hugh Ross' remarks at the memorial service for Dr. Richard Smalley," Reasons To Believe, November 2, 2005, http://www.reasons.org/about/staff/richard_smalley_memorial_service.shtml.
    22. Guido de Brès, "The Belgic Confession," Article 2, in *Ecumenical Creeds and Reformed Confessions* (Grand Rapids: CRC Publications, 1988), 79.
    23. Earl D. Radmacher and Robert D. Preus, eds., *Hermeneutics, Inerrancy, and the Bible* (Grand Rapids: Academie Books, 1984): 901.
    24. Hugh Ross, *Genesis One: A Scientific Perspective*, 4th ed. (Pasadena, CA: Reasons To Believe, 2006).
    25. Hugh Ross, *The Creator and the Cosmos*, 3rd ed. (Colorado Springs: NavPress, 2001); Fazale Rana and Hugh Ross, *Origins of Life* (Colorado Springs: NavPress, 2004); Fazale Rana with Hugh Ross, *Who Was Adam?* (Colorado Springs: NavPress, 2005); Hugh Ross, *A Matter of Days* (Colorado Springs: NavPress, 2004); Fazale Rana, *The Cell's Design* (Grand Rapids: Baker, 2008); Kenneth Samples, *A World of Difference* (Grand Rapids: Baker, 2007): Hugh Ross, *Why the Universe Is the Way It Is* (Grand Rapids: Baker, 2008); Hugh Ross, Kenneth Samples, and Mark Clark, *Lights in the Sky and Little Green Men* (Colorado Springs: NavPress, 2002).

Chapter 2: Multiple Choice

1. Isaac Asimov, "The 'Threat' of Creationism," in *Science and Creationism*, ed. Ashley Montagu (New York: Oxford University Press, 1984), 190, http://www.stephenjaygould .org/ctrl/azimov_creationism.html.

2. Ibid., 183.

3. Ibid., 193.

4. "Parliamentary Assembly Resolution 1580 (2007): The Dangers of Creationism in Education," Council of Europe, October 4, 2007, http://assembly.coe.int/main.asp?Link=/ documents/adoptedtext/ta07/eres1580.htm.

5. Ibid.

6. Ibid.

7. Henry M. Morris, "Is Creationism Important in Education?" *Creation* 10 (June 1988): 29–31, http://www.answersingenesis.org/creation/v10/i3/education.asp.

8. Henry Morris, "Why ICR—and Why Now?" *Impact*, no. 337, July 2001, ii, http:// www.icr.org/i/pdf/imp/imp-337.pdf.

9. *Expelled*, DVD, directed by Nathan Frankowski (Santa Fe, NM: Premise Media Corporation, 2008).

10. Werner Gitt, "10 Dangers of Theistic Evolution," *Creation Magazine* 17 (September–November 1995): 51, http://www.christiananswers.net/q-aig/aig-c015.html.

11. Ken Ham et al., *War of the Worldviews* (Hebron, KY: Answers in Genesis, 2005), 109.

12. Richard Dawkins, *The God Delusion* (Boston: Houghton Mifflin, 2006), 347.

13. Ibid., 216.

14. Ibid., back cover.

15. Johnjoe McFadden, *Quantum Evolution* (New York: W. W. Norton, 2000).

16. Edward J. Larson and Larry Witham, "Scientists Are Still Keeping the Faith," *Nature* 386 (April 3, 1997): 435–36.

17. William Paley, *Natural Theology*, 12th ed. (1802; Weybridge, Surrey, UK: S. Hamilton, 1809).

18. See Lane Coffee, comp., "Notable Christians Open to an Old-Universe, Old-Earth Interpretation," Reasons To Believe, http://www.reasons.org/resources/apologetics/notable _leaders/index.shtml (accessed October 11, 2005).

Chapter 3: Different Strategies

1. Niles Eldredge, *The Triumph of Evolution: And the Failure of Creationism* (New York: Nevraumont, 2000).

2. James H. Leuba, *The Belief in God and Immortality* (Boston: Sherman, French, 1916).

3. Jennifer Cheeseman Day and Kurt J. Bauman, *Have We Reached the Top? Educational Attainment Projections of the U.S. Population*, Working Paper Series No. 43 (Washington, D.C.: Population Division, U.S. Census Bureau, May 2000): 1–2.

4. U.S. Census Bureau, "S1501. Educational Attainment," American FactFinder, 2006, http://www.factfinder.census.gov/servlet/STTable?_bm=y&-geo_id=01000US&-qr_ name=ACS_2006_EST_G00_S1501&-ds_name=ACS_2006_EST_G00_ (accessed July 28, 2008).

5. "Religious Views and Beliefs Vary Greatly by Country, According to the Latest Financial Times/Harris Poll," HarrisInteractive, http://www.harrisinteractive.com/news/ allnewsbydate.asp?NewsID=1131 (accessed July 28, 2008).

6. "Evolution, Creationism, Intelligent Design," Gallup, http://www.gallup.com/poll/21814/Evolution-Creationism-Intelligent-Design.aspx (accessed July 28, 2008).

7. Edward J. Larson and Larry Witham, "Scientists Are Still Keeping the Faith," *Nature* 386 (April 3, 1997): 435–36.

8. Reprinted from The Harris Poll #52, Tables 1, 3, and 5, "Nearly Two-thirds of U. S. Adults Believe Human Beings Were Created by God," *Harris Interactive*, July 6, 2005, http://harrisinteractive.com/harris_poll/index.asp?PID=581. Other polls have been done more recently, but the questions are not the same as previous polls.

9. Edward O. Wilson, ed., *From So Simple a Beginning: The Four Great Books of Charles Darwin*, by Charles Darwin (New York: Norton, 2006), 1479.

10. James H. Leuba, "Religious Beliefs of American Scientists," *Harper's Magazine* 169 (August 1934): 291–300.

11. Edward J. Larson and Larry Witham, "Leading Scientists Still Reject God," *Nature* 394 (July 23, 1998): 313.

12. The number of professional scientists and science professors who believe (at least publicly) in the foundational young-earth creationist doctrines of a recent global Earth-altering flood and ages for the universe and Earth in the thousands rather than billions of years based on scientific evidence alone (that is, independent of any particular interpretation of the Bible or any other holy book) has been noted by several Christian organizations to measure zero. Even prominent young-earth creationist leaders admit this assessment. For example, talk radio host John Stewart asked John Morris, president of the Institute for Creation Research, in my presence and broadcast on the air (*Bible on the Line*, KKLA, December 6, 1987), if he or any of his associates had ever met or heard of a scientist who became persuaded the Earth or the universe is only thousands of years old based on scientific evidence, without any reference to a particular interpretation of the Bible. Morris answered no. Stewart has since asked the same question of several other prominent young-earth creationist proponents, and the answer has been a consistent no. Likewise, I have continued asking this question of young-earth creationist leaders with the same result.

13. While a few professors teaching at conservative evangelical seminaries do believe in a recent global flood and ages for the Earth and universe less than a few tens of thousands of years, I and others have observed that their numbers represent a rapidly shrinking minority. My conclusion is based on my experience in addressing professors at leading conservative evangelical seminaries over the past twenty-five years where in each instance I asked the professors in attendance to estimate the percentage of their colleagues that would uphold one or both of these two young-earth creationist doctrines.

14. *Edwards v. Aguillard*, 482 U.S. 578 (1987), statement 1(a) under "Held," http://caselaw.lp.findlaw.com/cgi-bin/getcase.pl?court=us&vol=482&invol=578.

15. This point is conceded even by the nontheistic skeptic and anticreationist Michael Shermer in his book *Why People Believe Weird Things* (New York: Henry Holt, 2002), 162.

16. No major Christian denomination, either pre– or post–Christopher Columbus, has ever held to a flat-Earth doctrine. However, several churches and a few small sects did teach that Earth was flat. Perhaps the most famous flat-Earth proponent was the radio preacher Wilbur Glenn Voliva of Zion, Illinois. For a list of flat-Earth advocates see Library of Congress Science Reference Guides, "The Flat Earth and Its Advocates: A List of References," May 1998, http://www.loc.gov/rr/scitech/SciRefGuides/flatearth.html. The Flat Earth Society, for its part, has always claimed that the Bible is a flat-Earth book. I heard this claim myself years ago when I participated in a radio debate on the shape of Earth on KKLA.

17. Prominent Protestant apologists for geocentrism include Gerardus Bouw, Malcolm Bowden, James Hanson, and Tom Willis. Leading Catholic apologists for geo-

centrism are R. G. Elmendorf, Paul Ellwanger, Paula Haigh, and Robert Sungenis. The two largest nonprofit organizations dedicated to promoting geocentrism are Catholic Apologetics International and The Biblical Astronomer. The following websites are devoted to promoting geocentrism: Official Geocentricity Website at http://www.geocentricity.com (accessed August 4, 2008); The Non-Moving Earth and Anti-Evolution Web Page of The Fair Education Foundation, Inc. at http://www.fixedearth.com (accessed August 4, 2008); and Bellamarine Theological Forum at http://www.catholicintl.com (accessed August 4, 2008).

18. Phillip E. Johnson, *Darwin on Trial*, 2nd ed. (Downers Grove, IL: InterVarsity, 1993); Phillip E. Johnson, *Reason in the Balance* (Downers Grove, IL: InterVarsity, 1995); Phillip E. Johnson, *Defeating Darwinism by Opening Minds* (Downers Grove, IL: InterVarsity, 1997); Phillip E. Johnson, *The Wedge of Truth* (Downers Grove, IL: InterVarsity, 2000).

19. Phillip E. Johnson, interview by Tal Brooke, "The Intelligent Design Movement: Asking the Right Questions," *SCP Journal* 27, no. 2–3 (2003): 5.

20. Jerry A. Coyne, "Creationism by Stealth," review of *Icons of Evolution*, by Jonathan Wells, *Nature* 410 (April 12, 2001): 745–46.

21. Mark Perakh, "A Presentation without Arguments: How William Dembski Defeats Skepticism, or Does He?" Mark Perakh, June 27, 2002, http://members.cox.net/perakm/Dem_burbank21jun02.htm.

22. Lawrence M. Krauss, "'Creationism' Discussion Belongs in Religion Class," *Reports of the National Center for Science Education* 22 (January–April 2002): 11.

23. Jennifer Palonus, "Ohio's Saga Approaches an Intermission," *Creation/Evolution: The Eternal Debate*, http://crevo.bestmessageboard.com/vThreadID=227 (accessed November 15, 2001; site now discontinued).

24. The financial support from wealthy young-earth creationist advocates is well-known. An executive at Illustra Media, which produces most of the DVD documentaries for the intelligent design movement, informed me in 2004 that purchases by young-earth creationist organizations exceeded those of all other organizations by a ratio of 19 to 1.

25. Philip Kitcher, "Born-Again Creationism," in *Intelligent Design Creationism and Its Critics*, ed. Robert T. Pennock (Cambridge, MA: MIT Press, 2001), 271.

26. Adrian L. Melott, "Intelligent Design Is Creationism in a Cheap Tuxedo," *Physics Today* 55 (June 2002): 48–50, http://scitation.aip.org/journals/doc/PHTOAD-ft/vol_55/iss_6/48_1.shtml.

27. Carl Wieland, "AiG's Views on the Intelligent Design Movement," Answers in Genesis, August 30, 2002, http://www.answersingenesis.org/docs2002/0830_IDM.asp.

28. Ibid.

29. Ibid.

30. Patricia Princehouse, "Ohio Overthrows Scopes Legacy," *Reports of the National Center for Science Education* 22 (September–October 2002): 4.

31. *Tammy Kitzmiller et al. v. Dover Area School District et al.*, case 4:04-cv-02688-JEJ (M.D. Penn. 2005), page 43, http://www.pamd.uscourts.gov/kitzmiller/kitzmiller_342.pdf.

32. Stephen Jay Gould, "Non-Overlapping Magisteria," in *Leonardo's Mountain of Clams and the Diet of Worms* (New York: Random House, 1998), 269–84.

33. John A. Moore, *From Genesis to Genetics* (Berkeley, CA: University of California Press, 2002), 198.

34. Ibid.

35. National Academy of Sciences, *Teaching about Evolution and the Nature of Science* (Washington, D.C.: National Academies Press, 1998), 58.

36. Norman L. Geisler and J. Kerby Anderson, *Origin Science* (Grand Rapids: Baker, 1987).

37. See Kenneth Richard Samples, *Without a Doubt* (Grand Rapids: Baker, 2004), 24–27, 190–94.

38. Stuart A. Kauffman, *Investigations* (New York: Oxford University Press, 2000), 207–9.

39. I give several examples with documentation in *The Creator and the Cosmos*, 3rd ed. (Colorado Springs: NavPress, 2001), 119–36, 162–74.

Chapter 4: An Objective Testing Method

1. A more detailed account of the historical development of cosmology is given in Hugh Ross, *The Fingerprint of God*, 2nd ed. (Orange, CA: Promise Publishing, 1991), 9–118.

2. Albert Einstein, *Relativity*, trans. Robert W. Lawson (New York: Bonanza, 1961), 126.

3. See Albert A. Michelson and Edward W. Morley, "On the Relative Motion of the Earth and the Luminiferous Ether," *American Journal of Science*, 3rd ser., 134 (November 1887): 333–45.

4. For a review of the development of relativity replete with the relevant equations, anomalies that have been resolved, predictions made, and citations to the discovery papers, see Ross, *Fingerprint of God*, 39–59.

5. Albert Einstein, "Erklärung der Perihelbewegung des Merkur aus der allgemeinen Relativitätstheorie," *Sitzungsberichte der Königlich Preussischen Akademie der Wissenschaften* (November 18, 1915): 831–39; Albert Einstein, "Die Grundlage der allgemeinen Relativitätstheorie," *Annalen der Physik*, ser. 4, 49 (May 11, 1916): 769–822. The English translation is in *The Principle of Relativity* by H. A. Lorentz, A. Einstein, H. Minkowski, and H. Weyl with notes by A. Sommerfeld and translated by W. Perrett and G. B. Jeffrey (London: Methuen, 1923), 109–64.

6. Arthur S. Eddington, "The End of the World: From the Standpoint of Mathematical Physics," *Supplement to Nature* 127 (March 21, 1931): 450.

7. Arthur S. Eddington, "On the Instability of Einstein's Spherical World," *Monthly Notices of the Royal Astronomical Society* 90 (May 9, 1930): 672.

8. See Ross, *Fingerprint of God*, 61–105 for details on these three models.

9. Masataka Fukugita and P. J. E. Peebles, "The Cosmic Energy Inventory," *Astrophysical Journal* 616 (December 1, 2004): 643–68.

10. Ibid.

11. E. Komatsu et al., "Five-year *Wilkinson Microwave Anisotropy Probe (WMAP)* Observations: Cosmological Interpretation" *Astrophysical Journal Supplement Series* (forthcoming).

12. Fang Li Zhi and Lu Shu Xian, *Creation of the Universe*, trans. T. Kiang (Teaneck, NJ: World Scientific, 1989): 173.

Chapter 5: Resources and Standards for RTB's Model

1. "The Heidelberg Catechism," *Ecumenical Creeds and Reformed Confessions* (Grand Rapids: CRC Publications, 1988), 15, 22–23; "The Belgic Confession," *Ecumenical Creeds*, 79, 87–88, 91; "Chapter IV: Of Creation," in "The Westminster Confession of Faith," Center for Reformed Theology and Apologetics, http://www.reformed.org/documents/wcf_with_proofs/ (accessed August 23, 2008); Hugh Ross, *A Matter of Days* (Colorado Springs: NavPress, 2004), 51–57.

2. Hugh Ross, comp., "Scriptures Related to Creation," Reasons To Believe, January 23, 2001, http://www.reasons.org/resources/apologetics/p0014.shtml.

3. Hugh Ross, *Fingerprint of God*, 2nd ed. (Orange, CA: Promise Publishing, 1991), 39–118; Hugh Ross, *Creator and the Cosmos*, 3rd ed. (Colorado Springs: NavPress, 2001),

23–136; Hugh Ross, *Beyond the Cosmos*, 2nd ed. (Colorado Springs: NavPress, 1999), 27–52; Hugh Ross, "A Beginner's—and Expert's—Guide to the Big Bang," *Facts for Faith*, no. 3, third quarter 2000, 14–32.

4. Ross, *Fingerprint of God*, 107–18; Ross, *Creator and the Cosmos*, 99–136; Ross, *Beyond the Cosmos*, 27–46; Hugh Ross, "Cosmic Brane Scans," *Facts for Faith*, no. 10, third quarter 2002, 13; Hugh Ross, "Predictive Power: Confirming Cosmic Creation," *Facts for Faith*, no. 9, second quarter 2002, 32–39.

5. Hugh Ross, "The Physics of Sin," *Facts for Faith*, no. 8, first quarter 2002, 46–51; Ross, *Creator and the Cosmos*, 145–67; Hugh Ross, "Physicalism and Free Will," *Facts for Faith*, no. 7, fourth quarter 2001, 48; Hugh Ross, "Time and the Physics of Sin," in *What God Knows*, ed. Harry Lee Poe and J. Stanley Mattson (Waco: Baylor University Press, 2005), 121–36.

6. Ross, *Matter of Days*, 97–120, 163–214; Ross, "Time and the Physics of Sin," 121–36.

7. Ross, *Fingerprint of God*, 53–118; Ross, *Creator and the Cosmos*, 23–98, 150–57; Ross, "Predictive Power," 32–39; Hugh Ross, "Facing Up to Big Bang Challenges," *Facts for Faith*, no. 5, first quarter 2001, 42–53.

8. Ross, *Creator and the Cosmos*, 50–53, 150–57; Hugh Ross, "The Haste to Conclude Waste," *Facts & Faith*, third quarter 1997, 1–3; Hugh Ross, Kenneth Samples, and Mark Clark, *Lights in the Sky and Little Green Men* (Colorado Springs: NavPress, 2002), 33–41, 161–62.

9. Ross, *Fingerprint of God*, 119–38; Ross, *Creator and the Cosmos*, 45–67, 137–212; Hugh Ross, "Anthropic Principle: A Precise Plan for Humanity," *Facts for Faith*, no. 8, first quarter 2002, 24–31; Ross, "Predictive Power," 32–39; Guillermo Gonzalez and Hugh Ross, "Home Alone in the Universe," *First Things*, no. 103, May 2000, 10–12.

10. Ross, *Matter of Days*, 218–20; Ross, "Time and the Physics of Sin," 121–36; Hugh Ross, "The Faint Sun Paradox," *Facts for Faith*, no. 10, third quarter 2002, 26–33.

11. Ross, *Creator and the Cosmos*, 56, 179, 183; Ross, "Time and the Physics of Sin," 121–36; Guillermo Gonzalez and Jay W. Richards, *The Privileged Planet* (Washington, D.C.: Regnery, 2004); Ross, "Anthropic Principle," 24–31.

12. Ross, *Creator and the Cosmos*, 56, 179, 183; Ross, "Time and the Physics of Sin," 121–36; Gonzalez and Richards, *Privileged Planet*; Ross, "Anthropic Principle," 24–31.

13. Ross, *Creator and the Cosmos*, 176–78; Fazale Rana and Hugh Ross, *Origins of Life* (Colorado Springs: NavPress, 2004), 211–13.

14. Ross, *Creator and the Cosmos*, 184–85; Rana and Ross, *Origins of Life*, 87–88.

15. Rana and Ross, *Origins of Life*, 72–73, 82–85; Hugh Ross, Fazale Rana, and Krista Bontrager, "Magma Ocean," *Creation Update*, May 18, 2004, http://www.reasons.org/resources/multimedia/rtbradio/archives_creation_update/200401-06archives.shtml.

16. Hugh Ross, *Why the Universe Is the Way It Is* (Grand Rapids: Baker, 2008), 57–58.

17. Ross, Samples, and Clark, *Lights in the Sky and Little Green Men*, 33–54.

18. Rana and Ross, *Origins of Life*, 63–92.

19. Ibid.

20. Ibid.

21. Rana and Ross, *Origins of Life*, 93–181; Fazale Rana, "Yet Another Use for 'Junk' DNA," *Facts for Faith*, no. 3, third quarter 2000, 56–57; Fazale R. Rana, "Protein Structures Reveal Even More Evidence for Design," *Facts for Faith*, no. 4, fourth quarter 2000, 4–5.

22. Rana and Ross, *Origins of Life*, 93–181; Fazale R. Rana, "30% Inefficiency by Design," *Facts for Faith*, no. 6, second quarter 2001, 10–11.

23. Rana and Ross, *Origins of Life*, 74–75, 217; Hugh Ross, "Bacteria Help Prepare Earth for Life," *Connections*, first quarter 2001, 4.

24. Rana and Ross, *Origins of Life*, 219; Hugh Ross, "The Case for Creation Grows Stronger," *Facts & Faith*, first quarter 1990, 1–3.

25. Rana and Ross, *Origins of Life*, 218–20.

26. Rana and Ross, *Origins of Life*, 213–22; Ross, "Faint Sun Paradox," 26–33.

27. Fazale Rana, "New Insight into the Ecology of the Cambrian Fauna: Evidence for Creation Mounts," *Facts for Faith*, no. 3, third quarter 2000, 54–55; Fazale Rana and Hugh Ross, "'Exploding' with Life! Interview with Dr. Paul Chien," *Facts for Faith*, no. 2, second quarter 2000, 12–17; Fazale Rana, "The Explosive Appearance of Skeletal Designs," *Facts for Faith*, no. 3, third quarter 2000, 52–53; Hugh Ross, "Biology's Big Bang #2," *Facts & Faith*, fourth quarter 1993, 2–3; Fazale R. Rana, "Cambrian Flash," *Connections*, first quarter 2000, 3.

28. Hugh Ross, *The Genesis Question*, 2nd ed. (Colorado Springs: NavPress, 2001), 50–53; Rana and Ross, *Origins of Life*, 82–84, 215–31; Hugh Ross, "Creation on the 'Firing Line,'" *Facts & Faith*, first quarter 1998, 6–7; Hugh Ross, "Fungus Paints Darker Picture of Permian Catastrophe," *Facts & Faith*, second quarter 1996, 3; Hugh Ross, "Life's Fragility," *Facts & Faith*, third quarter 1994, 4–5; Hugh Ross, "Dinosaurs and Cavemen: The Great Omission?" *Facts & Faith*, third quarter 1992, 6–7; Hugh Ross, "Dinosaurs' Disappearance No Longer a Mystery," *Facts & Faith*, third quarter 1991, 1–3.

29. Ross, *Genesis Question*, 50–53; Rana and Ross, *Origins of Life*, 82–84, 215–31; Ross, "Creation on the Firing Line," 6–7; Hugh Ross, "Rescued from Freeze Up," *Facts & Faith*, second quarter 1997, 3; Ross, "Fungus Paints Darker Picture," 3; Ross, "Life's Fragility," 4–5; Ross, "Dinosaurs and Cavemen," 6–7; Ross, "Dinosaurs' Disappearance No Longer a Mystery," 1.

30. Hugh Ross, "The Raising of Lazarus Taxa," *Facts & Faith*, third quarter 1994, 5.

31. Fazale R. Rana, "Repeatable Evolution or Repeated Creation?" *Facts for Faith*, no. 4, fourth quarter 2000, 12–21; Fazale R. Rana, "Convergence: Evidence for a Single Creator," *Facts for Faith*, no. 4, fourth quarter 2000, 14–20.

32. Fazale R. Rana with Hugh Ross, *Who Was Adam?* (Colorado Springs: NavPress, 2005), 199–225; Ross, *Genesis Question*, 110–15; Fazale Rana, "Humans and Chimps Differ," *Connections*, third quarter 2001, 1, 4–5.

33. Ross, *Genesis Question*, 63–65.

34. Hugh Ross, "Petroleum: God's Well-Timed Gift to Mankind," *Connections*, third quarter 2004, 2–3.

35. Ibid.

36. Hugh Ross, "Symbiosis—More Complex Than We Knew," *Connections*, second quarter 1999, 2–3.

37. Ross, *Why the Universe Is the Way It Is*, 147–81; Kenneth Richard Samples, *Without a Doubt* (Grand Rapids: Baker, 2004), 229–53.

38. Ross, *Matter of Days*, 97–109; Fazale Rana, "Extinct Shell Fish Speaks Today," *Connections*, second quarter 2001, 1–2.

39. Ross, *Genesis Question*, 50–54; Fazale Rana, "'Evolving' Robots Challenge Evolution," *Facts for Faith*, no. 5, first quarter 2001, 10–11; Fazale Rana, "Marine Body Sizes Add Weight to Creation Model," *Facts for Faith*, no. 5, first quarter 2001, 12–13.

40. Rana, "Extinct Shell Fish Speaks Today," 1–2.

41. Ross, *Creator and the Cosmos*, 139–43; Rana, "30% Inefficiency by Design," 10; Rana, "Yet Another Use for 'Junk' DNA," 56–57; Rana, "'Evolving' Robots Challenge Evolution," 10–11.

42. Rana, *Who Was Adam?*, 183–225.

43. Fazale Rana, "New Y Chromosome Studies Continue to Support a Recent Origin and Spread of Humanity," *Facts for Faith*, no. 3, third quarter 2000, 52–53.

44. Fazale R. Rana, Hugh Ross, and Richard Deem, "Long Life Spans: 'Adam Lived 930 Years and Then He Died,'" *Facts for Faith*, no. 5, first quarter 2001, 18–27; Hugh Ross, "Why Shorter Life Spans?" *Facts for Faith*, no. 5, first quarter 2001, 25; Rana with Ross, *Who Was Adam?* 111–21.

45. Rana with Ross, *Who Was Adam?* 77–95; Fazale Rana, "A Fashionable Find," *Connections*, first quarter 2002, 2–3.

46. See Hugh Ross, *Creation as Science*, 159–60.

47. Rana, *Who Was Adam?*, 55–75. The data is not yet sufficiently definitive to distinguish the difference between present-day humans being descended from one or a few men and one or a few women.

48. Ross, "Time and the Physics of Sin," 121–36.

Chapter 6: The Biblical Structure of RTB's Creation Model

1. Fred Hoyle, *The Nature of the Universe* (Oxford: Basil Blackwell, 1952), 109.

2. Guido de Brès, "The Belgic Confession," in *Ecumenical Creeds and Reformed Confessions* (Grand Rapids: CRC Publications, 1988), 79.

3. This particular question has been addressed in my book *Why the Universe Is the Way It Is* (Grand Rapids: Baker, 2008).

4. Hugh Ross, *Why the Universe Is the Way It Is*, 193–206; Hugh Ross, *Beyond the Cosmos*, 2nd ed. (Colorado Springs: NavPress, 1999), 217–28.

5. For a discussion of the biblical content on God's last creation acts on Earth, see Hugh Ross, *The Genesis Question*, 2nd ed. (Colorado Springs: NavPress, 2001), 53–57.

6. For a discussion of the biblical content on God's rest day, see Hugh Ross, *A Matter of Days* (Colorado Springs: NavPress, 2004), 81–84.

7. Ross, *A Matter of Days*, 97–109.

8. For more on the impact of the fall of Adam upon his physical environment, see Ross, *A Matter of Days*, 97–109.

9. This theme is addressed in my book *Why the Universe Is the Way It Is*.

10. See, for example, Victor J. Stenger, *God: The Failed Hypothesis* (Amherst, New York: Prometheus Books, 2007), 156–57.

11. Charles Seife, "Big Bang's New Rival Debuts with a Splash," *Science* 292 (April 13, 2001): 189–90.

12. Ross, *A Matter of Days*, 90–91.

13. Francis Brown, S. R. Driver, and Charles A. Briggs, *The Brown-Driver-Briggs Hebrew and English Lexicon* (1906; repr., Peabody, MA: Hendrickson, 1997), 398–401; William Gesenius, *Gesenius' Hebrew and Chaldee Lexicon to the Old Testament Scriptures*, trans. Samuel Prideaux Tregelles (1847; repr., Grand Rapids: Baker, 1979), 341–42; R. Laird Harris, Gleason L. Archer Jr., and Bruce K. Waltke, eds., *Theological Wordbook of the Old Testament* (Chicago: Moody, 1980), 1:370–71.

14. For a thorough analysis of the biblical, theological, and scientific evidence for long creation days, see my book *A Matter of Days*, 59–250.

15. This implication is explained in Ross, *The Genesis Question*, 27–28.

16. Fazale Rana and Hugh Ross, *Origins of Life* (Colorado Springs: NavPress, 2004), 36–45.

17. Ross, *The Genesis Question*, 27–58.

18. These creatures are identified by the Hebrew noun *nepesh*. Genesis 1 states that God created these species for the first time during the fifth creation day. In Job 38–42, one of the creation accounts paralleling Genesis 1, the strictly physical components of creation are discussed in Job 38 and the *nepesh* creatures in Job 39–41.

19. Kenneth Richard Samples, *A World of Difference* (Grand Rapids: Baker, 2007), 171–88.

20. Only one New Testament passage besides Romans 5:12 pertains to this subject. First Corinthians 15:21–23 states, "For since death came through a man, the resurrection of the dead comes also through a man. For as in Adam all die, so in Christ all will be made alive. But each in his own turn: Christ, the firstfruits; then, when he comes, those who belong to him." This context clearly limits death because of sin to human beings.

21. For more on this topic, see Ross, *A Matter of Days*, 97–109.

22. Ross, *The Genesis Question*, 139–87.

23. Michael J. Denton, *Nature's Destiny* (New York: Free Press, 1998), 127–32, 251–52, 310–13.

24. Harris, Archer, and Waltke, *Theological Wordbook*, 1:199, 213–14.

25. For an in-depth discussion of life beyond the present creation, see Ross, *Beyond the Cosmos*.

26. Ross, *The Creator and the Cosmos*; Ross, *Beyond the Cosmos*; Ross, Samples, and Clark, *Lights in the Sky and Little Green Men*; Rana and Ross, *Origins of Life*; Ross, *A Matter of Days*; Rana with Ross, *Who Was Adam?*; Ross, *The Genesis Question*; Fazale Rana, *The Cell's Design* (Grand Rapids: Baker, 2008); Ross, *Why the Universe Is the Way It Is*.

Chapter 7: Putting RTB's Model for the Cosmos to the Test

1. Though the development of RTB's cosmic creation model remains ongoing, its foundations and scientific assessments are explained more fully in my books *The Creator and the Cosmos*, 3rd ed. (Colorado Springs: NavPress, 2001); *Beyond the Cosmos*, 2nd ed. (Colorado Springs: NavPress, 1999); and *Why the Universe Is the Way It Is* (Grand Rapids: Baker, 2008).

2. Stephen Hawking and Roger Penrose, "The Singularities of Gravitational Collapse and Cosmology," *Proceedings of the Royal Society of London, Series A* 314 (1970): 529–48.

3. For an explanation of these theorems and a description of the observational and theoretical evidence in support of these theorems, along with citations to the original research, see Ross, *Creator and the Cosmos*, 77–108, 169–74.

4. Arvind Borde, Alan H. Guth, and Alexander Vilenkin, "Inflationary Spacetimes Are Incomplete in Past Directions," *Physical Review Letters* 90 (April 18, 2003): doi:10.1103/PhysRevLett.90.151301; Arvind Borde and Alexander Vilenkin, "Violation of the Weak Energy Condition in Inflating Spacetimes," *Physical Review D* 56 (July 15, 1997): 717–23; Arvind Borde and Alexander Vilenkin, "Singularities in Inflationary Cosmology: A Review," *International Journal of Modern Physics D* 5, #6 (December 15, 1996): 813–24; Arvind Borde, "Open and Closed Universes, Initial Singularities, and Inflation," *Physical Review D* 50 (September 15, 1994): 3692–3702; Arvind Borde and Alexander Vilenkin, "Eternal Inflation and the Initial Singularity," *Physical Review Letters* 72 (May 23, 1994): 3305–8.

5. Roger Penrose, *Shadows of the Mind* (New York: Oxford University Press, 1994), 230.

6. Ross, *Beyond the Cosmos*, 33–35.

7. E. Komatsu et al., "Five-Year *Wilkinson Microwave Anisotropy Probe (WMAP)* Observations: Cosmological Interpretation," *Astrophysical Journal Supplement*, forthcoming; Jonathan Coles, "A New Estimate of the Hubble Time with Improved Modeling of Gravitational Lenses," *Astrophysical Journal* 679 (May 20, 2008): 17–24.

8. Ross, *Beyond the Cosmos*, 53–228.

9. For highly readable descriptions and explanations of these evidences, see James S. Trefil, *The Moment of Creation* (New York: Collier Books, 1983), 87–110; John D. Barrow and Joseph Silk, *The Left Hand of Creation* (New York: Basic Books, 1983), 73–101.

10. J. C. Breckenridge et al., "Macroscopic and Microscopic Entropy of Near-Extremal Spinning Black Holes," *Physics Letters* B 381 (July 25, 1996): 423–26; Curtis G. Callan Jr. and Juan M. Maldacena, "D-Brane Approach to Black Hole Quantum Mechanics," *Nuclear Physics* B 472 (July 29, 1996): 591–608; Juan M. Maldacena and Andrew Strominger, "Statistical Entropy of Four-Dimensional Extremal Black Holes," *Physical Review Letters* 77 (July 15, 1996): 428–29; Andrew Strominger and Cumrun Vafa, "Microscopic Origin of the Bekenstein-Hawking Entropy," *Physics Letters* B 379 (June 27, 1996): 99–104; Gary Taubes, "How Black Holes May Get String Theory Out of a Bind," *Science* 268 (June 23, 1995): 1699.

11. Ross, *Beyond the Cosmos*, 40–43.

12. My book *Beyond the Cosmos* recounts in greater detail the discovery of extra dimensions and how that discovery attests to and elucidates various aspects of the Christian faith.

13. For a discussion of exactly what the Bible states about cosmic expansion, see Ross, *Creator and the Cosmos*, 24–26.

14. Ross, *Creator and the Cosmos*, 41–42, and references therein.

15. Richard C. Tolman, *Relativity, Thermodynamics, and Cosmology* (New York: Oxford University Press, 1934): 467.

16. Allan Sandage and Lori M. Lubin, "The Tolman Surface Brightness Test for the Reality of the Expansion. I. Calibration of the Necessary Local Parameters," *Astronomical Journal* 121 (May 2001): 2271–88; Lori M. Lubin and Allan Sandage, "The Tolman Surface Brightness Test for the Reality of the Expansion. II. The Effect of the Point-Spread Function and Galaxy Ellipticity on the Derived Photometric Parameters," *Astronomical Journal* 121 (May 2001): 2289–2300; Lori M. Lubin and Allan Sandage, "The Tolman Surface Brightness Test for the Reality of the Expansion. III. *Hubble Space Telescope* Profile and Surface Brightness Data for Early-Type Galaxies in Three High-Redshift Clusters," *Astronomical Journal* 122 (September 2001): 1071–83; Lori M. Lubin and Allan Sandage, "The Tolman Surface Brightness Test for the Reality of the Expansion. IV. A Measurement of the Tolman Signal and the Luminosity Evolution of Early-Type Galaxies," *Astronomical Journal* 122 (September 2001): 1084–1103.

17. S. Blondin et. al., "Time Dilation in Type Ia Supernova Spectra at High Redshift," *Astrophysical Journal* 682 (August 1, 2008): 724–36; B. Leibundgut et al., "Time Dilation in the Light Curve of the Distant Type Ia Supernova SN 1995K," *Astrophysical Journal Letters* 466 (July 20, 1996): L21–L24; A. G. Riess et al., "Time Dilation from Spectral Feature Age Measurements of Type Ia Supernovae," *Astronomical Journal* 114 (August 1997): 722–29; G. Goldhaber et al., "Observation of Cosmological Time Dilation Using Type Ia Supernovae as Clocks," in *Thermonuclear Supernovae, Proceedings of the NATO Advanced Study Institute, held in Begur, Girona, Spain, June 20–30, 1995*, NATO Advanced Science Institutes, series C, 486, ed. P. Ruiz-LaPuente, R. Canal, and J. Isern (Dordrecht, Netherlands: Kluwer Academic Publishers, 1997): 777–84; G. Goldhaber et al., "Timescale Stretch Parameterization of Type Ia Supernova B-Band Light Curves," *Astrophysical Journal* 558 (September 1, 2001): 359–68; Ming Deng and Bradley E. Schaefer, "Time Dilation in the Peak-to-Peak Timescales of Gamma-Ray Bursts," *Astrophysical Journal Letters* 502 (August 1, 1998): L109–L113.

18. D. Russell Humphreys, *Starlight and Time* (Green Forest, AR: Master Books, 1994); Hugh Ross, *A Matter of Days*, 151, 166–69.

19. Ross, *Creator and the Cosmos*, 151.

20. Ibid., 150–51.

21. Ross, *Why the Universe Is the Way It Is*, 39–41, 209–11.

22. It also exceeds by 10^{97} times the fine-tuning in what probably is humanity's best engineering achievement, a gravity wave telescope that can make length measurements with a precision of one part in 10^{23}.

23. The Laser Interferometer Gravitational-Wave Observatory (LIGO) currently ranks as the most exquisitely designed instrument ever made operational by humanity. It can make length measurements to within one part in 10^{23}. This one part in 10^{23}, however, ranks 10^{97} times inferior to the level of fine-tuning design present in cosmic dark energy. Such fine-tuning implies that the causal Agent that brought into existence the universe must be at least 10^{97} times more knowledgeable and more intelligent than the Caltech and MIT physicists that designed LIGO and 10^{97} times more powerful than the U.S. government that funded LIGO.

24. Lisa Dyson, Matthew Kleban, and Leonard Susskind as quoted by Philip Ball, "Is Physics Watching Over Us?" http://www.nature.com/nsu/020812/020812-2.html (accessed August 14, 2002). The preprint to which Philip Ball refers (arXiv:hep-th/0208013v1 1 Aug 2002) was published in October 2002 by the *Journal of High Energy Physics*: Lisa Dyson, Matthew Kleban, and Leonard Susskind, "Disturbing Implications of a Cosmological Constant," http://ej.iop.org/links/q72/EzjZUjDJyeH0t0iDSa6pPg/jhep102002011.pdf (accessed April 2, 2006). Pertinent quotes are: (1) "Some Unknown agent initially started the inflation high up on its potential," 1; (2) "the world started in a state of exceptionally low entropy. . . . However, there is no universally accepted explanation of how the universe got into such a special state," 2; (3) "The question then is whether the origin of the universe can be a naturally occurring fluctuation, or must it be due to an external agent which starts the system out in a specific low entropy state?" 4; (4) "Perhaps the only reasonable conclusion is that we do not live in a world [universe] with a true cosmological [dark energy] constant," 18.

25. Victor J. Stenger, *God, The Failed Hypothesis* (Amherst, NY: Prometheus Books, 2007): 154.

26. Ibid., 160.

27. Ibid., 161.

28. Bernard E. J. Pagel, *Nucleosynthesis and Chemical Evolution of Galaxies* (New York: Cambridge University Press, 1997), 103–30; Ross, *Creator and the Cosmos*, 57–63.

29. Pagel, *Nucleosynthesis*, 198–320.

30. Joel Baker et al., "Early Planetesimal Melting from an Age of 4.5662 Gyr for Differentiated Meteorites," *Nature* 436 (August 25, 2005): 1127–31; C. J. Allègre, G. Manhès, and C. Göpel, "The Age of the Earth," *Geochimica et Cosmochimica Acta* 59 (April 1995): 1445–56.

31. Robert H. Dicke, "Dirac's Cosmology and Mach's Principle," *Nature* 192 (November 4, 1961): 440–41.

32. See the lists of these characteristics compiled by Hugh Ross, "Fine-Tuning for Life on Earth," "Probabilities for Life on Earth," and "Fine-Tuning for Life in the Universe," *Reasons To Believe*, http://www.designevidences.org (accessed April 24, 2008).

33. Brandon Carter, "Large Number Coincidences and the Anthropic Principle in Cosmology," *Confrontation of Cosmological Theories with Observational Data*, ed. M. S. Longair (Dordrecht, Netherlands: D. Reidel, 1974), 291–98.

34. Brandon Carter, "The Anthropic Principle and Its Implications for Biological Evolution," *Philosophical Transactions of the Royal Society* A 310 (December 20, 1983): 347–63.

35. John D. Barrow and Frank J. Tipler, *The Anthropic Cosmological Principle* (New York: Oxford University Press, 1986), 556–70.

36. Ibid.

37. Ross, *Why the Universe Is the Way It Is*, 43–56; Ross, *Creator and the Cosmos*, 145–99.

38. Fazale Rana with Hugh Ross, *Who Was Adam?* (Colorado Springs: NavPress, 2005), 97–105.

39. Q. R. Ahmad et al., "Measurement of the Rate of $v_e + d \boxtimes p + p + e^-$ Interactions Produced by ^8B Solar Neutrinos at the Sudbury Neutrino Observatory," *Physical Review Letters* 87 (July 25, 2001): 71301–5.

40. Adam Eyre-Walker and Peter D. Keightley, "High Genomic Deleterious Mutation Rates in Hominids," *Nature* 397 (January 28, 1999): 344–47; James F. Crow, "The Odds of Losing at Genetic Roulette," *Nature* 397 (January 28, 1999): 293–94; Hugh Ross, "Aliens from Another World," *Facts for Faith*, no. 6, second quarter 2001, 30–31.

41. See Hugh Ross, *Why the Universe Is the Way It Is*, 113–15.

42. John N. Bahcall, Charles L. Steinhardt, and David Schlegel, "Does the Fine-Structure Constant Vary with Cosmological Epoch?" *Astrophysical Journal* 600 (January 10, 2004): 520–43; P. C. W. Davies, Tamara M. Davis, and Charles H. Lineweaver, "Cosmology: Black Holes Constrain Varying Constants," *Nature* 418 (August 8, 2002): 602–3; Alexander Y. Potekhin et al., "Testing Cosmological Variability of the Proton-to-Electron Mass Ratio Using the Spectrum of PKS 0528–250," *Astrophysical Journal* 505 (October 1, 1998): 523–28; D. B. Guenther, L. M. Krauss, and P. Demarque, "Testing the Constancy of the Gravitational Constant Using Helioseismology," *Astrophysical Journal* 498 (May 10, 1998): 871–76.

43. E. Peik et al., "Limit on the Present Temporal Variation of the Fine Structure Constant," *Physical Review Letters* 93 (October 18, 2004), doi: 10.1103/PhysRevLett.93.170801, http://prola.aps.org/abstract/PRL/v93/i17/e170801.

44. Antoinette Songaila et al., "Measurement of the Microwave Background Temperature at a Redshift of 1.776," *Nature* 371 (September 1, 1994): 43–45; David M. Meyer, "A Distant Space Thermometer," *Nature* 371 (September 1, 1994): 13; K. C. Roth et al., "C I Fine-Structure Excitation by the CMBR at z=1.973," *Bulletin of the American Astronomical Society* 29 (January 1997): 736; R. Srianand, P. Petitjean, and C. Ledoux, "The Cosmic Microwave Background Radiation Temperature at a Redshift of 2.74," *Nature* 408 (December 21, 2000): 931–35; P. Molaro et al., "The Cosmic Microwave Background Radiation Temperature at z_{abs} = 3.025 toward QSO 0347–3819," *Astronomy and Astrophysics* 381 (January 2002): L64–L67; E. S. Battistelli et al., "Cosmic Microwave Background Temperature at Galaxy Clusters," *Astrophysical Journal Letters* 580 (December 1, 2002): L101–L104; D. J. Fixsen and J. C. Mather, "The Spectral Results of the Far-Infrared Absolute Spectrophotometer Instrument on *COBE*," *Astrophysical Journal* 581 (December 20, 2002): 817–22; J. C. Mather et al., "Calibrator Design for the *COBE* Far Infrared Absolute Spectrophotometer (FIRAS)," *Astrophysical Journal* 512 (February 20, 1999): 511–20; J. C. Mather et al., "Measurement of the Cosmic Microwave Background Spectrum by the COBE FIRAS Instrument," *Astrophysical Journal* 420 (1994): 439–44; Katherine C. Roth, David M. Meyer, and Isabel Hawkins, "Interstellar Cyanogen and the Temperature of the Cosmic Microwave Background Radiation," *Astrophysical Journal Letters* 413 (August 20, 1993): L67–L71.

45. I give a description of the discovery and subsequent measurements of dark energy and the implication of dark energy on the design and past and present history of the universe in *Creator and the Cosmos*, 45–56.

46. For details and photo images, see my book *Why the Universe Is the Way It Is*, 79–89.

47. For details and photo images see *Why the Universe Is the Way It Is*, 87–89.

Chapter 8: Putting RTB's Model for Galaxies, Stars, and Planets to the Test

1. These purposes (over twelve of them) are described in some detail in my book *Why the Universe Is the Way It Is* (Grand Rapids: Baker, 2008).

2. Jorge Meléndez and Iván Ramírez, "HIP 56948: A Solar Twin with a Low Lithium Abundance," *Astrophysical Journal Letters* 669 (November 10, 2007): L92.

3. G. F. Porto de Mello and L. da Silva, "HR 6060: The Closest Ever Solar Twin?" *Astrophysical Journal Letters* 482 (June 10, 1997): L89–L92; Jorge Meléndez, Katie Dodds-Eden, and José A. Robles, "HD 98618: A Star Closely Resembling Our Sun," *Astrophysical Journal Letters* 641 (April 20, 2006): L133–L136; Y. Takeda et al., "Behavior of Li Abundances in Solar Analog Stars: Evidence for Line-Width Dependence," *Astronomy & Astrophysics* 468 (June 2007): 663–77.

4. Meléndez and Ramírez, "HIP 56948: A Solar Twin," L89.

5. Ibid., L89–L92.

6. Ibid.

7. T. A. Michtchenko and S. Ferraz-Mello, "Resonant Structure of the Outer Solar System in the Neighborhood of the Planets," *Astronomical Journal* 122 (July 2001): 474–81; E. Pilat-Lohinger et al., "The Influence of Giant Planets Near a Mean Motion Resonance on Earth-Like Planets in the Habitable Zone of Sun-Like Stars," *Astrophysical Journal* 681 (July 10, 2008): 1639–45.

8. E. W. Thommes, M. J. Duncan, and H. F. Levison, "The Formation of Uranus and Neptune Among Jupiter and Saturn," *Astronomical Journal* 123 (May 2002): 2862–83; S. Ida and D. N. C. Lin, "Toward a Deterministic Model of Planetary Formation. I. A Desert in the Mass and Semimajor Axis Distributions of Extrasolar Planets," *Astrophysical Journal* 604 (March 20, 2004): 388–413; K. Tsiganis et al., "Origin of the Orbital Structure of the Giant Planets of the Solar System," *Nature* 435 (May 26, 2005): 459–61.

9. Edward W. Thommes, Soko Matsumura, and Frederic A. Rasio, "Gas Disks to Gas Giants: Simulating the Birth of Planetary Systems," *Science* 321 (August 8, 2008): 814–17.

10. Jean Schneider, "Interactive Extra-solar Planets Catalog," *The Extrasolar Planets Encyclopedia*, http://exoplanet.eu/catalog-all.php (accessed May 31, 2008).

11. Sean N. Raymond, "The Search for Other Earths: Limits on the Giant Planet Orbits That Allow Habitable Terrestrial Planets to Form," *Astrophysical Journal Letters* 643 (June 1, 2006): L131–L134.

12. J. T. Wright et al., "The Jupiter Twin HD154345b," *Astrophysical Journal Letters* 683 (August 10, 2008): L63–L66.

Chapter 9: Putting RTB's Model for Life's Beginning and Extraterrestrial Homes to the Test

1. Previously published RTB books that include detailed portions of RTB's biblical creation model as it pertains to life's origin and exobiology include: Hugh Ross, *The Creator and the Cosmos*, 3rd ed. (Colorado Springs: NavPress, 2001); Fazale Rana and Hugh Ross, *Origins of Life* (NavPress: Colorado Springs, 2004); Hugh Ross, Kenneth Samples, and Mark Clark, *Lights in the Sky and Little Green Men* (Colorado Springs: NavPress, 2002); Hugh Ross, *Why the Universe Is the Way It Is* (Grand Rapids: Baker, 2008); and Fazale Rana, *The Cell's Design* (Grand Rapids: Baker, 2008). Two additional books (scheduled for release by Baker Books in 2010 and 2011, respectively) feature Fazale Rana's research on the challenge of making life in the lab and my insights on the origin and history of physical, soulish, and spiritual animals.

2. Robin M. Canup, "Simulations of a Late Lunar-Forming Impact," *Icarus* 168 (April 2004): 433–56; Herbert Palme, "The Giant Impact Formation of the Moon," *Science* 304 (May 14, 2004): 977–79.

3. Louis A. Codispoti, "The Limits to Growth," *Nature* 387 (May 15, 1997): 237; Kenneth H. Coale et al., "A Massive Phytoplankton Bloom Induced by an Ecosystem-Scale

Iron Fertilization Experiment in the Equatorial Pacific Ocean," *Nature* 383 (October 10, 1996): 495–99.

4. Peter D. Ward and Donald Brownlee, *Rare Earth* (New York: Copernicus/Springer-Verlag, 2000), 191–234.

5. William R. Ward, "Comments on the Long-Term Stability of the Earth's Obliquity," *Icarus* 50 (May–June 1982): 444–48; Carl D. Murray, "Seasoned Travellers," *Nature* 361 (February 18, 1993): 586–87; Jacques Laskar and P. Robutel, "The Chaotic Obliquity of the Planets," *Nature* 361 (February 18, 1993): 608–12; Jacques Laskar, F. Joutel, and P. Robutel, "Stabilization of the Earth's Obliquity by the Moon," *Nature* 361 (February 18, 1993): 615–17.

6. For a partial list, see Neil F. Comins, *What If the Moon Didn't Exist?* (New York: HarperCollins, 1993).

7. Dave Waltham, "Anthropic Selection for the Moon's Mass," *Astrobiology* 4 (Winter 2004): 460–68.

8. Ross, *Creator and the Cosmos*, 180–99.

9. Presented by Marc van Zuilen in his lecture on July 1, 2002, at the International Society for the Study of the Origin of Life Conference in Oaxaca, Mexico, abstract #16.

10. Richard A. Kerr, "Did Jupiter and Saturn Team Up to Pummel the Inner Solar System?" *Science* 306 (December 3, 2004): 1676.

11. Stephen J. Mojzsis, "Lithosphere-Hydrosphere Interactions on the Hadean (>4.0 Ga) Earth," *Astrobiology* 1 (September 2001): 383; Stephen J. Mojzsis and Graham Ryder, "Accretion to Earth and Moon ~3.85 Ga," in *Accretion of Extraterrestrial Matter throughout Earth's History*, ed. Bernhard Peuckner-Ehreinbrink and Birger Schmitz (New York: Kluwer Academic/Plenum Publishers, 2001), 423–26; Stephen J. Mojzsis and T. Mark Harrison, "Establishment of a 3.83-Ga Magmatic Age for the Akilia Tonalite (Southern West Greenland)," *Earth and Planetary Science Letters* 202 (September 2002): 563–76; Ronny Schoenberg et al., "Tungsten Isotope Evidence from ~3.8-Gyr Metamorphased Metamorphosed Sediments for Early Meteorite Bombardment of the Earth," *Nature* 418 (July 25, 2002): 403.

12. Ariel D. Anbar et al., "Extraterrestrial Iridium, Sediment Accumulation and the Habitability of the Early Earth's Surface," *Journal of Geophysical Research* 106 (February 25, 2001): 3219–36; Schoenberg et al., "Tungsten Isotope Evidence," 403–5.

13. David C. Rubie, Christine K. Gessmann, and Daniel J. Frost, "Partitioning of Oxygen During Core Formation on the Earth and Mars," *Nature* 429 (May 6, 2004): 58–61; Carl B. Agee, "Hot Metal," *Nature* 429 (May 6, 2004): 33–35.

14. Manfred Schidlowski, "A 3,800-Million-Year Isotopic Record of Life from Carbon in Sedimentary Rocks," *Nature* 333 (May 26, 1988): 313–18; Manfred Schidlowski, "Carbon Isotopes as Biogeochemical Recorders of Life over 3.8 Ga of Earth History: Evolution of a Concept," *Precambrian Research* 106 (February 1, 2001): 117–34; Yuichiro Ueno et al., "Ion Microprobe Analysis of Graphite from Ca. 3.8 Ga Measurements Metasediments, Isua Supracrustal Belt, West Greenland: Relationship between Metamorphism and Carbon Isotopic Composition," *Geochimica et Cosmochimica Acta* 66 (April 1, 2002): 1257–68; Minik T. Rosing, "^{13}C-Depleted Carbon Microparticles in >3700-Ma Sea-Floor Sedimentary Rocks from West Greenland," *Science* 283 (January 29, 1999): 674–76; Mink T. Rosing and Robert Frei, "U-Rich Archaean Sea-Floor Sediments from Greenland—Indications of >3700 Ma Oxygenic Photosynthesis," *Earth and Planetary Science Letters* 217 (January 15, 2004): 237–44.

15. Rosing, "^{13}C-Depleted Carbon Microparticles," 674–76; Stephen. J. Mojzsis et al., "Evidence for Life on Earth Before 3,800 Million Years Ago," *Nature* 384 (November 7, 1996): 55–59; John M. Hayes, "The Earliest Memories of Life on Earth," *Nature* 384 (November

7, 1996): 21–22; Manfred Schidlowski, "A 3,800-Million-Year Isotopic Record of Life from Carbon in Sedimentary Rocks," *Nature* 333 (May 26, 1988): 313–18; Hubert P. Yockey, "Comments on 'Let There Be Life: Thermodynamic Reflections on Biogenesis and Evolution' by Avshalom C. Elitzur," *Journal of Theoretical Biology* 176 (October 7, 1995): 351; Daniele L. Pinti, Ko Hashizume, and Jun-Ichi Matsuda, "Nitrogen and Argon Signatures in 3.8 to 2.8 Ga Metasediments: Clues on the Chemical State of the Archean Ocean and the Deep Biosphere," *Geochimica et Cosmochimica Acta* 65 (July 1, 2001): 2309.

16. L. E. Snyder et al., "A Rigorous Attempt to Verify Interstellar Glycine," *Astrophysical Journal* 619 (February 1, 2005): 914–30.

17. Yi-Jehng Kuan et al., "A Search for Interstellar Pyrimidine," *Monthly Notices of the Royal Astronomical Society* 345 (October 10, 2003): 650–56.

18. Zita Martins et al., "Extraterrestrial Nucleobases in the Murchison Meteorite," *Earth and Planetary Science Letters* 270 (June 15, 2008): 130–36.

19. Sandra Pizzarello et al., "The Organic Content of the Tagish Lake Meteorite," *Science* 293 (September 21, 2001): 2239, notes 15 and 28; Jeffrey L. Bada, "A Search for Endogenous Amino Acids in Martian Meteorite ALH84001," *Science* 279 (January 16, 1998): 362–65; Keith A. Kvenvolden, "Chirality of Amino Acids in the Murchison Meteorite—A Historical Perspective," in *Book of Abstracts, 12th International Conference on the Origin of Life and the 9th Meeting of the International Society for the Study of the Origin of Life*, July 11–16, 1999, San Diego, California (ISSOL 1999), 41; Daniel P. Glavin et al., "Amino Acids in the Martian Meteorite Nakhla," *Book of Abstracts*, ISSOL 1999, 62; Rana and Ross, *Origins of Life*, 95–96, 130–31, 185–90.

20. Juan Oró, "Early Chemical Stages in the Origin of Life," in *Early Life on Earth: Nobel Symposium #No. 84*, ed. Stefan Bengtson (New York: Columbia University Press, 1994), 49–50.

21. Even if a low concentration of a few simple amino acids and nitrogenous bases were one day discovered in some interstellar cloud, such a discovery would prove no boon for naturalistic models for life's origin. All naturalistic models demand that all the biologically required amino acids and nitrogenous bases be available at one location in high concentration levels.

22. Rana and Ross, *Origins of Life*, 63–92.

23. Jon Cohen, "Getting All Turned Around Over the Origins of Life on Earth," *Science* 267 (March 3, 1995): 1265. In this article Cohen quotes one of the leading origin-of-life researchers, William Bonner. In February 1995, during the "Physical Origin of Homochirality in Life" conference held in Santa Monica, California, Bonner stated to the assembled scientists, "I spent twenty-five years looking for terrestrial mechanisms for homochirality and trying to investigate them and didn't find any supporting evidence. Terrestrial explanations are impotent or nonviable."

24. Robert M. Hazen, "Life's Rocky Start," *Scientific American* 284 (April 2001): 77–85.

25. G. Balavoine, A. Moradpour, and H. B. Kagan, "Preparation of Chiral Compounds with High Optical Purity by Irradiation with Circularly Polarized Light: A Model Reaction for the Prebiotic Generation of Optical Activity," *Journal of the American Chemical Society* 96 (August 7, 1974): 5152–58.

26. Jose J. Flores, William A. Bonner, and Gail A. Massey, "Asymmetric Photolysis of (RS)-Leucine with Circularly Polarized Ultraviolet Light," *Journal of the American Chemical Society* 99 (May 25, 1977): 3622–25.

27. Mark M. McKinnon, "Statistical Modeling of the Circular Polarization in Pulsar Radio Emission and Detection Statistics of Radio Polarimetry," *Astrophysical Journal* 568 (March 20, 2002): 302–11.

28. Yoshinori Takano et al., "Asymmetric Photolysis of (DL)-Isovaline by Synchrotron Radiation," in *Book of Abstracts, 13th International Conference on the Origin of Life and the 10th Meeting of the International Society for the Study of the Origin of Life*, June 30–July 5, 2002, Oaxaca, Mexico (ISSOL 2002), 92–93. The figure, 1.12 percent, was presented in a poster paper.

29. Werner Kuhn, "The Physical Significance of Optical Rotary Power," *Transactions of the Faraday Society* 26 (1930): 293–308; E. U. Condon, "Theories of Optical Rotary Power," *Reviews of Modern Physics* 9 (1937): 432–57.

30. Rana and Ross, *Origins of Life*, 95–101, 123–33, 171–222.

31. F. H. C. Crick and Leslie E. Orgel, "Directed Panspermia," *Icarus* 19 (July 3, 1973): 341–46; Francis Crick, *Life Itself: Its Origin and Nature* (New York: Simon & Schuster, 1981).

32. James H. Cleaves and John H. Chalmers, "Extremophiles May Be Irrelevant to the Origin of Life," *Astrobiology* 4 (March 2004): 1–9; Rana and Ross, *Origins of Life*, 183–204.

33. Ross, Samples, and Clark, *Lights in the Sky and Little Green Men*, 55–64.

34. Stuart Kauffman, *Investigations* (New York: Oxford University Press, 2000), 35, 43, 46, 151; Hubert P. Yockey, *Information Theory and Molecular Biology* (New York: Cambridge University Press, 1992), 289; Niels Bohr, "Light and Life," pt. 1, *Nature* 131 (March 25, 1933): 421–23; Niels Bohr, "Light and Life," pt. 2, *Nature* 131 (April 1, 1933): 457–59.

35. John C. Armstrong, Llyd E. Wells, and Guillermo Gonzalez, "Rummaging through Earth's Attic for Remains of Ancient Life," *Icarus* 160 (November 2002), 183–96.

36. Armstrong, Wells, and Gonzalez, "Rummaging through Earth's Attic," 183–96; S. A. Finney, W. B. Tonks, and H. J. Melosh, "Statistical Evolution of Impact Ejecta from the Earth: Implications for Transfer to Other Solar System Bodies," Contribution #698 in *Proceedings of the Twentieth Lunar and Planetary Science Conference*, March 13–17, 1989, Houston, Texas, 287–88; John Armstrong, "Distribution of Impact Locations and Velocities of Earth Meteorites on the Moon," *Astrobiology* 8 (April 2008): 306.

37. Stephen J. Mojzsis, T. Mark Harrison, and Robert T. Pidgeon, "Oxygen-Isotope Evidence from Ancient Zircons for Liquid Water at the Earth's Surface—4,300 Myr Ago," *Nature* 409 (January 11, 2001): 178–80.

38. Alexander A. Nemchin et al., "A Light Carbon Reservoir Recorded in Zircon-Hosted Diamond from the Jack Hills," *Nature* 454 (July 3, 2008): 92–95.

Chapter 10: Putting RTB's Creation Model for Life's History to the Test

1. Fazale Rana and Hugh Ross, *Origins of Life* (Colorado Springs: NavPress, 2004); Hugh Ross, *Why the Universe Is the Way It Is* (Grand Rapids: Baker, 2008); Hugh Ross, *The Genesis Question*, 2nd ed. (Colorado Springs: NavPress, 2001).

2. Arcady R. Mushegian and Eugene V. Koonin, "A Minimal Gene Set for Cellular Life Derived by Comparison of Complete Bacterial Genomes," *Proceedings of the National Academy of Sciences, USA* 93 (September 17, 1996): 10268–73; Nikos Kyrpides, Ross Overbeek, and Christos Ouzounis, "Universal Protein Families and the Functional Content of the Last Universal Common Ancestor," *Journal of Molecular Evolution* 49 (October 1999): 413–23; Jack Maniloff, "The Minimal Cell Genome: 'On Being the Right Size,'" *Proceedings of the National Academy of Sciences, USA* 93 (September 17, 1996): 10004–6; Mitsuhiro Itaya, "An Estimation of Minimal Genome Size Required for Life," *FEBS Letters* 362 (April 10, 1995): 257–60; Clyde A. Hutchinson III et al., "Global Transposon Mutagenesis and a Minimal Mycoplasma Genome," *Science* 286 (December 10, 1999): 2165–69; Brian J. Akerley et al., "A Genome-Scale Analysis for Identification of Genes Required for Growth or Survival of *Haemophilus influenzae*," *Proceedings of the National Academy of Sciences, USA* 99 (January 22, 2002): 966–71; Rosario Gil et al., "Extreme Genome Reduction in

Buchnera spp.: Toward the Minimal Genome Needed for Symbiotic Life," *Proceedings of the National Academy of Sciences, USA* 99 (April 2, 2002): 4454–58.

3. Minik T. Rosing and Robert Frei, "U-Rich Archaen Sea-Floor Sediments from Greenland—Indications of >3700 Ma Oxygenic Photosynthesis," *Earth and Planetary Science Letters* 217 (January 15, 2004): 237–44.

4. Stephen J. Giovannoni et al., "Genome Streamlining in a Cosmopolitan Oceanic Bacterium," *Science* 309 (August 19, 2005): 1242–45.

5. Alexis Dufresne et al., "Genome Sequence of the Cyanobacterium *Proclorococcus marinus* SS120, A Nearly Minimal Oxyphototrophic Genome," *Proceedings of the National Academy of Sciences, USA* 100 (August 19, 2003): 10020–25; Gabrielle Rocap et al., "Genome Divergence in Two *Prochlorococcus* Ecotypes Reflects Oceanic Niche Differentiation," *Nature* 424 (August 28, 2003): 1042–47; Jonathan A. Eisen et al., "The Complete Genome Sequence of *Chlorobium tepedum* TLS, A Photosynthetic, Anaerobic, Green-Sulfur Bacterium," *Proceedings of the National Academy of Sciences, USA* 99 (July 9, 2002): 9509–14; Yasukasu Nakamura et al., "Complete Genome Structure of the Thermophilic Cyanobacterium *Thermosynechococcus elongatus* BP-1," *DNA Research* 9 (August 31, 2002): 123–30.

6. John Emsley, *The Elements*, 3rd ed. (Oxford: Clarendon Press, 1998), 24, 40, 56, 58, 60, 62, 78, 102, 106, 122, 130, 138, 152, 160, 188, 198, 214, 222, 230.

7. Crisogono Vasconcelos and Judith A. McKenzie, "Sulfate Reducers—Dominant Players in a Low-Oxygen World?" *Science* 290 (December 1, 2000): 1711–12.

8. Matthias Labrenz et al., "Formation of Sphalerite (ZnS) Deposits in Natural Biofilms of Sulfate-Reducing Bacteria," *Science* 290 (December 1, 2000): 1744–47.

9. David W. Schwartzman and Tyler Volk, "Biotic Enhancement of Weathering and the Habitability of Earth," *Nature* 340 (August 10, 1989): 457–60; Richard Monastersky, "Supersoil," *Science News* 136 (December 9, 1989): 376–77.

10. Jihad Touma and Jack Wisdom, "Nonlinear Core-Mantle Coupling," *Astronomical Journal* 122 (August 2001): 1030–50; Gerald Schubert and Keke Zhang, "Effects of an Electrically Conducting Inner Core on Planetary and Stellar Dynamos," *Astrophysical Journal* 557 (August 20, 2001): 930–42; M. H. Acuña et al., "Magnetic Field and Plasma Observations at Mars: Initial Results of the Mars Global Surveyor Mission," *Science* 279 (March 13, 1998): 1676–80; Peter Olson, "Probing Earth's Dynamo," *Nature* 389 (September 25, 1997): 337; Weijia Kuang and Jeremy Bloxham, "An Earth-Like Numerical Dynamo Model," *Nature* 389 (September 25, 1997): 371–74; Xiaodong Song and Paul G. Richards, "Seismological Evidence for Differential Rotation of the Earth's Inner Core," *Nature* 382 (July 18, 1996): 221–24; Wei-jia Su, Adam M. Dziewonski, and Raymond Jeanloz, "Planet Within a Planet: Rotation of the Inner Core of the Earth," *Science* 274 (December 13, 1996): 1883–87.

11. Stephen H. Kirby, "Taking the Temperature of Slabs," *Nature* 403 (January 6, 2000): 31–34.

12. Peter D. Ward and Donald Brownlee, *Rare Earth* (New York: Copernicus/Springer-Verlag, 2000), 191–234.

13. I.-Juliana Sackmann and Arnold I. Boothroyd, "Our Sun. V. A Bright Young Sun Consistent with Helioseismology and Warm Temperatures on Ancient Earth and Mars," *Astrophysical Journal* 583 (February 1, 2003): 1024–39.

14. Ibid.

15. For an explanation see Hugh Ross, *The Creator and the Cosmos*, 3rd ed. (Colorado Springs: NavPress, 2001), 180–81.

16. Donald E. Canfield and Andreas Teske, "Late Proterozoic Rise in Atmospheric Oxygen Concentration Inferred from Phylogenetic and Sulfur-Isotope Studies," *Nature* 382 (July 11, 1996): 127–32; Donald E. Canfield, "A New Model for Proterozoic Ocean

Chemistry," *Nature* 396 (December 3, 1998): 450–53; John M. Hayes, "A Lowdown on Oxygen," *Nature* 417 (May 9, 2002): 127.

17. Paul G. Falkowski et al., "The Rise of Oxygen over the Past 205 Million Years and the Evolution of Large Placental Mammals," *Science* 309 (September 30, 2005): 2202–4.

18. Bing Shen et al., "The Avalon Explosion: Evolution of Ediacara Morphospace," *Science* 319 (January 4, 2008): 81–84.

19. Jeffrey S. Seewald, "Organic-Inorganic Interactions in Petroleum-Producing Sedimentary Basins," *Nature* 426 (November 20, 2003): 327–33.

20. Ian M. Head, D. Martin Jones, and Steve R. Larter, "Biological Activity in the Deep Subsurface and the Origin of Heavy Oil," *Nature* 426 (November 20, 2003): 344–52.

21. Nicky White, Mark Thompson, and Tony Barwise, "Understanding the Thermal Evolution of Deep-Water Continental Margins," *Nature* 426 (November 20, 2003): 334–43.

22. Michael W. Nachman and Susan L. Crowell, "Estimate of the Mutation Rate Per Nucleotide in Humans," *Genetics* 156 (September 2000): 297–304.

23. John C. Sanford, *Genetic Entropy*, 3rd ed. (Waterloo, New York: FMS Publications, 2008).

24. Ecologists Paul and Anne Ehrlich write, "the production of a new animal species in nature has yet to be documented. Biologists have not been able to observe the entire sequence of one species being transformed into two or more. . . . Biologists *have* been able to observe innumerable examples of animal and plant species that appear to be in various stages of splitting. But, in the vast majority of cases, the rate of change is so slow that it has not even been possible to detect an increase in the amount of differentiation over the decades that have been available for observation." Paul and Anne Ehrlich, *Extinction* (New York: Ballantine Books, 1981), 23.

25. Carl Zimmer, *At the Water's Edge* (New York: Free Press, 1998); Michael Behe, David Berlinkski, Phillip Johnson, Barry Lynn, Kenneth Miller, Michael Ruse, and Eugenie Scott, debate hosted by William F. Buckley Jr., "PBS Debate on Creation and Evolution," *Firing Line*, PBS, December 19, 1997.

26. Mandyam V. Srinivasan, "When One Eye Is Better than Two," *Nature* 399 (May 27, 1999): 305–7; J. D. Pettigrew and S. P. Collin, "Terrestrial Optics in an Aquatic Eye: The Sandlance, *Limnichthytes fasciatus* (Creediidae Teleostei)," *Journal of Comparative Physiology* A 177 (October 1995): 397–408; John D. Pettigrew, Shaun P. Collins, and Matthias Ott, "Convergence of Specialised Behaviour, Eye Movements and Visual Optics in the Sandlance (Teleostei) and the Chameleon (Reptilia)," *Current Biology* 9 (April 22, 1999): 421–24.

27. Fazale Rana, *The Cell's Design* (Grand Rapids: Baker, 2008), 205–15.

28. Simon Conway Morris, *Life's Solution* (Cambridge, UK: Cambridge University Press, 2004).

29. Stephen Jay Gould, *Wonderful Life* (New York: W. W. Norton, 1989), 51.

30. Stephen Jay Gould, *The Structure of Evolutionary Theory* (Cambridge, MA: Harvard University Press, 2002), 1224–29.

31. Zachary D. Blount, Christina Z. Borland, and Richard E. Lenski, "Historical Contingency and the Evolution of a Key Innovation in an Experimental Population of Escherichia coli," *Proceedings of the National Academy of Sciences, USA* 105 (June 10, 2008): 7899–7906.

32. Ibid., 7899.

33. Neville J. Woolf, "What Is an Earth-Like Planet?" Abstract #926, Abstracts of the Biennial Meeting of the NASA Astrobiology Institute, April 10–14, 2005, *Astrobiology* 5 (April 2005): 200.

34. Isabelle Basile-Doelsch, Jean Dominique Meunier, and Claude Parron, "Another Continental Pool in the Terrestrial Silicon Cycle," *Nature* 433 (January 27, 2005): 399–402;

Philip W. Boyd et al., "The Decline and Fate of an Iron-Induced Subarctic Phytoplankton Bloom," *Nature* 428 (April 1, 2004): 549–53.

Chapter 11: Putting RTB's Creation Model for Advanced Life to the Test

1. The RTB creation model specific to advanced life is addressed in my book *Why the Universe Is the Way It Is* (Grand Rapids: Baker, 2008), 43–78, 95–106, 165–81. A forthcoming book to be published by Baker with the working title *Answers in Job* will unfold much more.

2. Katherine L. Moulton and Robert A. Berner, "Quantification of the Effect of Plants on Weathering: Studies in Iceland," *Geology* 26 (October 1998): 895–98.

3. Hugh Ross, *The Genesis Question*, 2nd ed. (Colorado Springs: NavPress, 2001), 49–53.

4. Lee Hsiang Liow et al., "Higher Origination and Extinction Rates in Larger Mammals," *Proceedings of the National Academy of Sciences, USA* 105 (April 22, 2008): 6097.

5. Marcel Cardillo et al., "Multiple Causes of High Extinction Risk in Large Mammal Species," *Science* 309 (August 19, 2005): 1239–41.

6. Ibid., 1240.

7. Konstantin Popadin et al., "Accumulation of Slightly Deleterious Mutations in Mitochondrial Protein-Coding Genes of Large Versus Small Mammals," *Proceedings of the National Academy of Sciences, USA* 104 (August 6, 2007): 13390–95.

8. A. P. Martin and S. R. Palumbi, "Body Size, Metabolic-Rate, Generation Time, and the Molecular Clock," *Proceedings of the National Academy of Sciences, USA* 90 (May 1, 1993): 4087–91; James F. Gillooly et al., "The Rate of DNA Evolution: Effects of Body Size and Temperature on the Molecular Clock," *Proceedings of the National Academy of Sciences, USA* 102 (January 4, 2005): 140–45.

9. For an explanation and documentation see my book *A Matter of Days* (Colorado Springs: NavPress, 2004), 121–29.

10. Melinda A. Zeder and Brian Hesse, "The Initial Domestication of Goats (Capra hircus) in the Zagros Mountains 10,000 Years Ago," *Science* 287 (March 24, 2000): 2254–57.

Chapter 12: Putting RTB's Creation Model for the Origin and History of Humanity to the Test

1. While the model's development remains ongoing, its foundation and forecasts are set forth more fully in RTB's book by Fazale Rana with Hugh Ross, *Who Was Adam?* (Colorado Springs: NavPress, 2005).

2. Quoted by Frank J. Tipler in "Intelligent Life in Cosmology," *International Journal of Astrobiology* 2 (2003): 142.

3. Brandon Carter, "The Anthropic Principle and Its Implications for Biological Evolution," *Philosophical Transactions of the Royal Society* A 310 (December 20, 1983): 347–60; John D. Barrow and Frank J. Tipler, *The Anthropic Cosmological Principle* (New York: Oxford University Press, 1986), 510–73.

4. Matthias Krings et al., "Neandertal DNA Sequences and the Origin of Modern Humans," *Cell* 90 (July 11, 1997): 19–30; Ryk Ward and Chris Stringer, "A Molecular Handle on the Neanderthals," *Nature* 388 (July 17, 1997): 225–26; Patricia Kahn and Ann Gibbons, "DNA from an Extinct Human," *Science* 277 (July 11, 1997): 176–78; Matthias Krings et al., "DNA Sequence of the Mitochondrial Hypervariable Region II from the Neandertal Type Specimen," *Proceedings of the National Academy of Sciences, USA* 96 (May 11, 1999): 5581–85; Matthias Höss, "Neanderthal Population Genetics," *Nature* 404 (March 30, 2000): 453–54; Igor V. Ovchinnikov et al., "Molecular Analysis of Neanderthal DNA from the

Northern Caucasus," *Nature* 404 (March 30, 2000): 490–93; Matthias Krings et al., "A View of Neandertal Genetic Diversity," *Nature Genetics* 26 (October 2000): 144–46; Ralf W. Schmitz et al., "The Neandertal Type Site Revisited: Interdisciplinary Investigations of Skeletal Remains from the Neander Valley, Germany," *Proceedings of the National Academy of Sciences, USA* 99 (October 1, 2002): 13342–47; David Serre et al., "No Evidence of Neandertal mtDNA Contribution to Early Modern Humans," *PLoS Biology* 2 (March 15, 2004): e57; Mathias Currat and Laurent Excoffier, "Modern Humans Did Not Admix with Neanderthals during Their Range Expansions into Europe," *PLoS Biology* 2 (November 30, 2004): e421; Cédric Beauval et al., "A Late Neandertal Femur from Les Rochers-de-Villeneuve, France," *Proceedings of the National Academy of Sciences, USA* 102 (May 17, 2005): 7085–90.

5. David Caramelli et al., "Evidence for a Genetic Discontinuity between Neandertals and 24,000-Year-Old Anatomically Modern Europeans," *Proceedings of the National Academy of Sciences, USA* 100 (May 27, 2003): 6593–97; Oliva Handt et al., "Molecular Genetic Analyses of the Tyrolean Ice Man," *Science* 264 (June 17, 1994): 1775–78; Giulietta Di Benedetto et al., "Mitochondrial DNA Sequences in Prehistoric Human Remains from the Alps," *European Journal of Human Genetics* 8 (September 2000): 669–77.

6. H. Coqueugniot et al., "Early Brain Growth in *Homo erectus* and Implications for Cognitive Ability," *Nature* 431 (September 16, 2004): 299–302.

7. Marcia S. Ponce de León and Christoph P. E. Zollikofer, "Neanderthal Cranial Ontogeny and Its Implications for Late Hominid Diversity," *Nature* 412 (August 2, 2001): 534–38; B. Bower, "Neanderthals, Humans May Have Grown Apart," *Science News* 160 (August 4, 2001): 71; Fernando V. Ramirez Rozzi and José Maria Bermudez de Castro, "Surprisingly Rapid Growth in Neanderthals," *Nature* 428 (April 29, 2004): 936–39; Jay Kelley, "Neanderthal Teeth Lined Up," *Nature* 428 (April 29, 2004): 904–5.

8. Linda Vigilant et al., "African Populations and the Evolution of Human Mitochondrial DNA," *Science* 253 (September 27, 1991): 1503–7; Margellen Ruvolo et al., "Mitochondrial COII Sequence and Modern Human Origins," *Molecular Biology and Evolution* 10 (November 1993): 1115–35; Stephen T. Sherry et al., "Mismatch Distributions of mtDNA Reveal Recent Human Population Expansions," *Human Biology* 66 (October 1994): 761–75; Satoshi Horai et al., "Recent African Origin of Modern Humans Revealed by Complete Sequences of Hominoid Mitochondrial DNAs," *Proceedings of the National Academy of Sciences, USA* 92 (January 17, 1995): 532–36; Masami Hasegawa and Satoshi Horai, "Time of the Deepest Root for Polymorphism in Human Mitochondrial DNA," *Journal of Molecular Evolution* 32 (January 1991): 37–42; Mark Stoneking et al., "New Approaches to Dating Suggest a Recent Age for the Human mtDNA Ancestor," *Philosophical Transactions of the Royal Society of London* B 337 (August 29, 1992): 167–75; Max Ingman et al., "Mitochondrial Genome Variation and the Origin of Modern Humans," *Nature* 408 (December 7, 2000): 708–13; S. Blair Hedges, "A Start for Population Genomics," *Nature* 408 (December 7, 2000): 652–53; Ann Gibbons, "Calibrating the Mitochondrial Clock," *Science* 279 (January 2, 1998): 28–29. For a thorough review of the genetic origins of human beings see Rana with Ross, *Who Was Adam?*

9. L. Simon Whitfield, John E. Sulston, and Peter N. Goodfellow, "Sequence Variation of the Human Y Chromosome," *Nature* 378 (November 23, 1995): 379–80; Jonathan K. Pritchard et al., "Population Growth of Human Y Chromosomes: A Study of Y Chromosome Microsatellites," *Molecular Biology and Evolution* 16 (December 1999): 1791–98; Russell Thomson et al., "Recent Common Ancestry of Human Y Chromosomes: Evidence from DNA Sequence Data," *Proceedings of the National Academy of Sciences, USA* 97 (June 20, 2000): 7360–65; Peter A. Underhill et al., "Y Chromosome Sequence Variation and the History of Human Populations," *Nature Genetics* 26 (November 2000): 358–61; Ann

Gibbons, "Y Chromosome Shows That Adam Was an African," *Science* 278 (October 31, 1997): 804–5; Mark Seielstad et al., "A View of Modern Human Origins from Y Chromosome Microsatellite Variation," *Genome Research* 9 (June 1999): 558–67; Ornelia Semino et al., "Ethiopians and Khoisan Share the Deepest Clades of the Human Y Chromosome Phylogeny," *American Journal of Human Genetics* 70 (January 1, 2002): 265–68. For a thorough review of the genetic origins of human beings see Rana with Ross, *Who Was Adam?*

10. Ward E. Sanford, "Thoughts on Eden, the Flood, and the Persian Gulf," *The News! Newsletter for the Affiliation of Christian Geologists* 7, Number 1 (Spring 1999).

11. Vincent Macaulay et al., "Single, Rapid Coastal Settlement of Asia Revealed by Analysis of Complete Mitochondrial Genomes," *Science* 308 (May 15, 2005): 1034–36.

12. Tatsuya Anzai et al., "Comparative Sequencing of Human and Chimpanzee MHC Class I Regions Unveils Insertions/Deletions as the Major Path to Genomic Divergence," *Proceedings of the National Academy of Sciences, USA* 100 (June 24, 2003): 7708–13; J. W. Thomas et al., "Comparative Analyses of Multi-Species Sequences from Targeted Genomic Regions," *Nature* 424 (August 14, 2003): 788–93; Ulfur Arnason, Xiufung Xu, and Anette Gullberg, "Comparison between the Complete Mitochondrial DNA Sequences of Homo and the Common Chimpanzee Based on Nonchimeric Sequences," *Journal of Molecular Evolution* 42 (February 1996): 145–52; The International Chimpanzee Chromosome 22 Consortium, "DNA Sequence and Comparative Analysis of Chimpanzee Chromosome 22," *Nature* 429 (May 27, 2004): 382–88; Jean Weissenbach, "Genome Sequencing: Differences with the Relatives," *Nature* 429 (May 27, 2004): 353–55.

13. Dennis Normile, "Gene Expression Differs in Human and Chimp Brains," *Science* 292 (April 6, 2001): 44–45; Mario Cáceres et al., "Elevated Gene Expression Levels Distinguish Human from Non-Human Primate Brains," *Proceedings of the National Academy of Sciences, USA* 100 (October 28, 2003): 13030–35; Monica Uddin et al., "Sister Grouping of Chimpanzees and Humans as Revealed by Genome-Wide Phylogenetic Analysis of Brain Gene Expression Profiles," *Proceedings of the National Academy of Sciences, USA* 101 (March 2, 2004): 2957–62; Philipp Khaitovich et al., "Regional Patterns of Gene Expression in Human and Chimpanzee Brains," *Genome Research* 14 (August 2004): 1462–73; The International Chimpanzee Chromosome 22 Consortium, "DNA Sequence," 382–88; Weisenbach, "Genome Sequencing," 353–55; Peter A. Jones and Daiya Takai, "The Role of DNA Methylation in Mammalian Epigenetics," *Science* 293 (August 10, 2001): 1068–70; Todd M. Preuss et al., "Human Brain Evolution: Insights from Microarrays," *Nature Reviews Genetics* 5 (November 2004): 850–60.

14. Pritchard et al., "Population Growth," 1791–98; Thomson et al., "Recent Common Ancestry," 7360–65; Underhill et al., "Y Chromosome Sequence Variation," 358–61; Whitfield, Sulston, and Goodfellow, "Sequence Variation," 379–80.

15. Ingman et al., "Mitochondrial Genome Variation," 708–13; Hedges, "Start for Population Genomics," 652–53.

16. Lois A. Tully et al., "A Sensitive Denaturing Gradient-Gel Electrophoresis Assay Reveals a High Frequency of Heteroplasmy in Hypervariable Region 1 of the Human mtDNA Control Region," *American Journal of Human Genetics* 67 (August 2000): 432–43; Gibbons, "Calibrating the Mitochondrial Clock," 28–29.

17. Gibbons, "Calibrating the Mitochondrial Clock," 28–29; Hugh Ross and Sam Conner, "Eve's Secret to Growing Younger," *Facts & Faith*, first quarter 1998, 1–2.

18. Rana with Ross, *Who Was Adam?* 46–47.

19. Gary K. Meffe, C. Ronald Carroll, and contributors, *Principles of Conservation Biology*, 2nd ed. (Sunderland, MA: Sinauer Associates, 1997), 87–156; John Alroy, "A Multispecies Overkill Simulation of the End-Pleistocene Megafaunal Mass Extinction," *Science* 292 (June

8, 2001): 1893–96; Richard G. Roberts et al., "New Ages for the Last Australian Megafauna: Continent-Wide Extinction About 46,000 Years Ago," *Science* 292 (June 8, 2001): 1888–92; Paul R. and Anne H. Ehrlich, *Extinction* (New York: Ballantine Books, 1981), 20–21; Jeffrey K. McKee et al., "Forecasting Global Biodiversity Threats Associated with Human Population Growth," *Biological Conservation* 115 (January 2004): 161–64; Leigh Dayton, "Mass Extinctions Pinned on Ice Age Hunters," *Science* 292 (June 8, 2001): 1819; Gerardo Ceballos and Paul R. Ehrlich, "Mammal Population Losses and the Extinction Crisis," *Science* 296 (May 3, 2002): 904–7; David W. Steadman, "Prehistoric Extinctions of Pacific Island Birds: Biodiversity Meets Zooarchaeology," *Science* 267 (February 24, 1995): 1123–31; "Human Impact on the Earth: Journey into New Worlds," *The Sacred Balance*, http://www.sacredbalance.com/web/drilldown.html?sku=35 (accessed June 29, 2005).

20. Christopher Stringer and Robin McKie, *African Exodus: The Origins of Modern Humanity* (New York: Henry Holt, 1997), 165–66; Paul S. Martin and Richard G. Klein, eds., *Quaternary Extinctions* (Tuscon: Arizona University Press, 1984).

21. Scott A. Elias et al., "Life and Times of the Bering Land Bridge," *Nature* 382 (July 4, 1996): 61–63; Heiner Josenhans et al., "Early Humans and Rapidly Changing Holocene Sea Levels in the Queen Charlotte Islands—Hecate Strait, British Columbia, Canada," *Science* 277 (July 4, 1997): 71.

22. Richard G. Klein with Blake Edgar, *The Dawn of Human Culture* (New York: Wiley, 2002), 230–37. There is some evidence that late Neanderthals may have stolen and used tools manufactured by humans in the same manner that monkeys today frequently steal and use human implements.

23. Richard G. Klein, *The Human Career: Human Biological and Cultural Origins*, 2nd ed. (Chicago: University of Chicago Press, 1999), 520–29; *Encyclopedia of Human Evolution and Prehistory*, 2nd ed., ed. Eric Delson et al. (New York: Garland, 2000), s.vv. "Later Stone Age," "Late Paleolithic."

24. Ralf Kittler, Manfred Kayser, and Mark Stoneking, "Molecular Evolution of *Pediculus humanus* and the Origin of Clothing," *Current Biology* 13 (August 19, 2003): 1414–17.

25. *Encyclopedia of Human Evolution and Prehistory*, s.v. "Late Paleolithic"; Klein with Edgar, *Dawn of Human Culture*, 11–15; Klein, *Human Career*, 512–15; Steven L. Kuhn et al., "Ornaments of the Earliest Upper Paleolithic: New Insights from the Levant," *Proceedings of the National Academy of Sciences, USA* 98 (June 19, 2001): 7641–46.

26. Roger Lewin, *Principles of Human Evolution: A Core Textbook* (Malden, MA: Blackwell Science, 1998), 469–74; Rex Dalton, "Lion Man Takes Pride of Place as Oldest Statue," *Nature News*, http://www.nature.com/news/2003/030901/full/030901-6.html (accessed June 25, 2005); Nicholas J. Conrad, "Paleolithic Ivory Sculptures from Southwestern Germany and the Origins of Figurative Art," *Nature* 426 (December 18, 2003): 830–32; *Encyclopedia of Human Evolution and Prehistory*, s.v. "Late Paleolithic"; Achim Schneider, "Ice-Age Musicians Fashioned Ivory Flute," *Nature News*, http://www.nature.com/news/2004/041217/full/news041213-14.html (accessed June 25, 2005); Tim Appenzeller, "Evolution or Revolution?" *Science* 282 (November 20, 1998): 1451; Klein, *The Human Career*, 550–53.

27. Stephen Jay Gould and Richard C. Lewontin, "The Spandrels of San Marco and the Panglossian Paradigm: A Critique of the Adaptionist Programme," *Proceedings of the Royal Society of London, Series B* 205, No. 1161 (1979): 581–98. (Also available at http://ethomas.web.wesleyan.edu/wescourses/2004s/ces227/01/spandrels.html.)

28. Hugh Ross, *A Matter of Days* (Colorado Springs: NavPress, 2004): 221–26.

29. Available from http://en.wikipedia.org/wiki/Carbon_dioxide_in_the_Earth's_atmosphere (accessed: 6/17/08).

30. Hugh Ross, *Why the Universe Is the Way It Is* (Grand Rapids: Baker, 2008): 147–206.

Chapter 13: Putting RTB's Creation Model to the "Why" Question Test

1. Hugh Ross, *The Creator and the Cosmos*, 3rd ed. (Colorado Springs: NavPress, 2001); Fazale Rana with Hugh Ross, *Who Was Adam?* (Colorado Springs: NavPress, 2006); Fazale Rana and Hugh Ross, *Origins of Life* (Colorado Springs: NavPress, 2004); Hugh Ross, *Beyond the Cosmos*, 2nd ed. (Colorado Springs: NavPress, 1999); Hugh Ross, *Why the Universe Is the Way It Is* (Grand Rapids: Baker, 2008).

2. Greg Dwyer, Jonathan Dushoff, and Susan Harrell Yee, "The Combined Effects of Pathogens and Predators on Insect Outbreaks," *Nature* 430 (July 15, 2004): 341–45; Lewi Stone, "A Three-Player Solution," *Nature* 430 (July 15, 2004): 299–300.

3. Harvey Lodish et al., *Molecular Cell Biology*, 4th ed. (New York: Freeman, 2000), 297–303; Wen-Hsiung Li, *Molecular Evolution* (Sunderland, MA: Sinauer Associates, 1997), 395–99.

4. Edward E. Max, "Plagiarized Errors and Molecular Genetics: Another Argument in the Evolution-Creation Controversy," *The TalkOrigins Archive*, http://www.talkorigins.org/faqs/molgen (accessed May 9, 2005).

5. Ibid.; Lodish et al., *Molecular Cell Biology*, 299–301, 303.

6. R. N. Mantegna et al., "Linguistic Features of Noncoding DNA Sequences," *Physical Review Letters* 73 (December 5, 1994): 3169–72.

7. For an in-depth discussion of these newly discovered designs and functions, see Fazale Rana with Hugh Ross, *Who Was Adam?* (Colorado Springs: NavPress, 2005), 227–45.

8. Sergei A. Korneev, Ji-Ho Park, and Michael O'Shea, "Neuronal Expression of Neural Nitric Oxide Synthase (nNOS) Protein Is Suppressed by an Antisense RNA Transcribed from an NOS Pseudogene," *Journal of Neuroscience* 19 (September 15, 1999): 7711–20; Shinji Hirotsune et al., "An Expressed Pseudogene Regulates the Messenger-RNA Stability of Its Homologous Coding Gene," *Nature* 423 (May 1, 2003): 91–96; Jeannie T. Lee, "Complicity of Gene and Pseudogene," *Nature* 423 (May 1, 2003): 26–28; Evgeniy S. Balakirev and Francisco J. Ayala, "Pseudogenes: Are They 'Junk' or Functional DNA?" *Annual Reviews of Genetics* 37 (December 2003): 123–51.

9. Esther Betrán et al., "Evolution of the *Phosphoglycerate mutase* Processed Gene in Human and Chimpanzee Revealing the Origin of a New Primate Gene," *Molecular Biology and Evolution* 19 (May 2002): 654–63.

10. Christopher B. Marshall, Garth L. Fletcher, and Peter L. Davies, "Hyperactive Antifreeze Protein in a Fish," *Nature* 429 (May 13, 2004): 153.

11. Wen-Man Liu et al., "Cell Stress and Translational Inhibitors Transiently Increase the Abundance of Mammalian SINE Transcripts," *Nucleic Acid Research* 23 (May 25, 1995): 1758–65; Tzu-Huey Li et al., "Physiological Stresses Increase Mouse Short Interspersed Element (SINE) RNA Expression in vivo," *Gene* 239 (November 1, 1999): 367–72; Richard H. Kimura, Prabhakara V. Choudary, and Carl W. Schmid, "Silk Worm Bm1 SINE RNA Increases following Cellular Insults," *Nucleic Acids Research* 27 (August 15, 1999): 3380–87; Wen-Ming Chu et al., "Potential Alu Function: Regulation of the Activity of Double-Stranded RNA-Activated Kinase PKR," *Molecular and Cellular Biology* 18 (January 1998): 58–68.

12. Wen-Man Liu et al., "Alu Transcripts: Cytoplasmic Localisation and Regulation by DNA Methylation," *Nucleic Acid Research* 22 (March 25, 1994): 1087–95; Wen-Man Liu and Carl W. Schmid, "Proposed Roles for DNA Methylation in *Alu* Transcriptional Repression and Mutational Inactivation," *Nucleic Acid Research* 21 (March 25, 1993): 1351–59; Carol M. Rubin et al., "Alu Repeated DNAs Are Differentially Methylated in Primate Germ Cells," *Nucleic Acid Research* 22 (November 25, 1994): 5121–27; Igor N. Chesnokov and Carl W. Schmid, "Specific Alu Binding Protein from Human Sperm Chromatin Prevents DNA Methylation," *Journal of Biological Chemistry* 270 (August 4, 1995): 18539–42; Utha

Hellman-Blumberg et al., "Developmental Differences in Methylation of Human *Alu* Repeats," *Molecular and Cellular Biology* 13 (August 1993): 4523–30.

13. Jeffrey A. Bailey et al., "Molecular Evidence for a Relationship between LINE-1 Elements and X Chromosome Inactivation: The Lyon Repeat Hypothesis," *Proceedings of the National Academy of Sciences, USA* 97 (June 6, 2000): 6634–39; Mary F. Lyon, "LINE-1 Elements and X Chromosome Inactivation: A Function for 'Junk' DNA?" *Proceedings of the National Academy of Sciences, USA* 97 (June 6, 2000): 6248–49.

14. Edith Heard, Philippe Clerc, and Philip Avner, "X-Chromosome Inactivation in Mammals," *Annual Review of Genetics* 31 (December 1997): 571–610; Jack J. Pasternak, *An Introduction to Human Molecular Genetics: Mechanisms of Inherited Diseases* (Bethesda, MD: Fitzgerald Science Press, 1999), 31–32.

15. Elena Allen et al., "High Concentrations of Long Interspersed Nuclear Element Sequence Distinguish Monoallelically Expressed Genes," *Proceedings of the National Academy of Sciences, USA* 100 (August 19, 2003): 9940–45.

16. Alan G. Atherly, Jack R. Girton, and John F. McDonald, *The Science of Genetics* (Fort Worth: Saunders College Publishing, 2000), 597–608; Greg Towers et al., "A Conserved Mechanism of Retrovirus Restriction in Mammals," *Proceedings of the National Academy of Sciences, USA* 97 (October 24, 2000): 12295–99; Jonathan P. Stoye, "An Intracellular Block to Primate Lentivirus Replication," *Proceedings of the National Academy of Sciences, USA* 99 (September 3, 2002): 11549–51; Theodora Hatziioannou et al., "Restriction of Multiple Divergent Retroviruses by Lv1 and Ref1," *European Molecular Biology Organization Journal* 22 (February 3, 2003): 385–94.

17. François Mallet et al., "The Endogenous Retroviral Locus ERVWE1 Is a Bona Fide Gene Involved in Hominoid Placental Physiology," *Proceedings of the National Academy of Sciences, USA* 101 (February 2, 2004): 1731–36.

18. Clare Lynch and Michael Tristem, "A Co-opted Gypsy-Type LTR-Retrotransposon Is Conserved in the Genomes of Humans, Sheep, Mice, and Rats," *Current Biology* 13 (September 2, 2003): 1518–23.

19. Wenhu Pi et al., "The LTR Enhancer of ERV-9 Human Endogenous Retrovirus Is Active in Oocytes and Progenitor Cells in Transgenic Zebrafish and Humans," *Proceedings of the National Academy of Sciences, USA* 101 (January 20, 2004): 805–10; Catherine A. Dunn, Patrik Medstrand, and Dixie L. Mager, "An Endogenous Retroviral Long Terminal Repeat Is the Dominant Promoter for Human β1,3-Galactosyltransferase 5 in the Colon," *Proceedings of the National Academy of Sciences, USA* 100 (October 8, 2003): 12841–46.

20. Stephen Jay Gould, *The Panda's Thumb* (New York: Norton, 1980), 24.

21. Peter Gordon, "The Panda's Thumb Revisited: An Analysis of Two Arguments Against Design," *Origins Research* 7 (Spring/Summer 1984): 12–14.

22. Hideki Endo et al., "Role of the Giant Panda's 'Pseudo-Thumb,'" *Nature* 397 (January 28, 1999): 309.

23. Ibid., 310.

24. Amélie Davis and Xiao-Hai Yan, "Hurricane Forcing on Chlorophyll-a Concentration Off the Northeast Coast of the U.S.," *Geophysical Research Letters* 31 (September 14, 2004): doi:10.1029/2004GL020668.

25. D. M. Murphy et al., "Influence of Sea-Salt on Aerosol Radiative Properties in the Southern Ocean Marine Boundary Layer," *Nature* 392 (March 5, 1998): 62–65.

26. Nicholas R. Bates, Anthony H. Knap, and Anthony F. Michaels, "Contribution of Hurricanes to Local and Global Estimates of Air-Sea Exchange of CO_2," *Nature* 395 (September 3, 1998): 58–61.

27. Peter D. Moore, "Fire Damage Soils Our Forests," *Nature* 384 (November 28, 1996): 312–13.

28. A. U. Mallik, C. H. Gimingham, and A. A. Rahman, "Ecological Effects of Heather Burning: I. Water Infiltration, Moisture Retention and Porosity of Surface Soil," *Journal of Ecology* 72 (November 1984): 767–76.

29. Ross, *Why the Universe Is the Way It Is*, 147–206.

Chapter 14: Putting New Atheist Cosmic Models to the Test

1. Richard Dawkins, *The God Delusion* (Boston: Houghton Mifflin, 2006), 187–89.

2. Ibid., 188.

3. Ibid.

4. Ibid.

5. Ibid., 189.

6. Ibid., 187.

7. For a detailed response to Dawkins's central argument, see my book *Beyond the Cosmos*, 2nd ed. (Colorado Springs: NavPress, 1999), 27–115.

8. Victor J. Stenger, *God: The Failed Hypothesis* (Amherst, NY: Prometheus Books, 2007), 61–67.

9. Ibid., 61.

10. Ilya Prigogine and Isabelle Stengers, *Order Out of Chaos* (New York: Bantam Books, 1984).

11. Stuart Kauffman, *At Home in the Universe* (New York: Oxford University Press, 1995); Stuart Kauffman, *Investigations* (New York: Oxford University Press, 2000).

12. Kauffman, *Investigations*, 3–4, 150–52, 207–9.

13. Paul Davies, *The Cosmic Blueprint* (New York: Touchstone, Simon & Schuster, 1988), 203.

14. Geoff Brumfiel, "Our Universe: Outrageous Fortune," *Nature* 439 (January 5, 2006): 10–12.

15. Freeman Dyson, *Disturbing the Universe* (New York: Harper and Row, 1979), 250.

16. Stephen W. Hawking, *A Brief History of Time* (New York: Bantam, 1988), 127.

Chapter 15: Putting RTB's Creation Model to the U.S. Constitution Test

1. Martin Enserink, "Is Holland Becoming the Kansas of Europe?" *Science* 308 (June 3, 2005): 1394; Editor, "Dealing with Design," *Nature* 434 (April 28, 2005); Geoff Brumfiel, "Intelligent Design: Who Has Designs on Your Students' Minds?" *Nature* 434 (April 28, 2005): 1062–65; Geoff Brumfiel, "Biologists Snub 'Kangaroo Court' for Darwin," *Nature* 434 (March 31, 2005): 550.

2. Robert T. Pennock, "Why Creationism Should Not Be Taught in the Public Schools," in *Intelligent Design Creationism and Its Critics*, ed. Robert T. Pennock (Cambridge, MA: MIT Press, 2001): 764.

3. Americans United for Separation of Church and State, http://www.au.org (accessed March 5, 2004); People for the American Way, http://www.pfaw.org (accessed March 5, 2004).

4. *Epperson v. Arkansas*, 393 U.S. 97 (1968), 1.

5. Ibid., 107–9.

6. Ibid., 107.

7. Thomas Jefferson, "Letter of January 1, 1801," in *Thomas Jefferson: Writings*, ed. Merrill D. Peterson (New York: Library of America, 1984): 510.

8. The four references are (1) to "Nature's God" who is responsible for "the Laws of Nature," (2) "that all Men are created equal, that they are endowed by their Creator with certain unalienable Rights," (3) "appealing to the Supreme Judge of the world," and (4) "a

firm Reliance on the Protection of divine Providence." For the full context see The Declaration of Independence, *U. S. Constitution Online*, http://www.usconstitution.net/declar.html (accessed August 26, 2008).

9. George Washington, "Thanksgiving Proclamation, October 3, 1789," *George Washington Papers at the Library of Congress*, http://lcweb2.loc.gov/ammem/GW/gw004.html (accessed August 26, 2008).

10. "Chaplain's Office," *United States Senate*, http://www.senate.gov/reference/office/chaplain.htm (accessed March 4, 2004).

11. See "Origins of the American Military Chaplaincy," U. S. Army Chaplain Center and School, March 3, 2004, http://www.usachcs.army.mil/history/brief/chapter_1.htm.

12. Examples would be the state's intolerance of geocentrism and the flat-Earth hypothesis. Belief in geocentrism (view that Earth is the center of the solar system and universe) as a fundamental Christian doctrine is still held by a few Christian organizations and churches (see note 36 below). Well into the latter half of the twentieth century, the Flat Earth Society appealed to the Bible for its flat-Earth doctrine (see note 35 below).

13. General Assembly of the State of Arkansas, "The State of Arkansas, Act 590 of 1981," in *Philosophy of Biology*, ed. Michael Ruse (Amherst, NY: Prometheus Books, 1998): 324.

14. *McLean v. Arkansas Board of Education*, 529 F. Supp 1255 (E.D. Ark 1982), section III, http://www.talkorigins.org/faqs/mclean-v-arkansas.html (accessed October 15, 2008).

15. *McLean v. Arkansas Board of Education*, sections IV(A), IV(D).

16. Testimony of Dr. G. Brent Dalrymple, *McLean v. Arkansas* Documentation Project, 410, http://www.antievolution.org/projects/mclean/new_site/pf_trans/mva_tt_p_dalrymple.html (accessed August 26, 2003).

17. Ibid., 411.

18. Eugenie C. Scott, *Evolution vs. Creationism* (Westport, CT: Greenwood Press, 2004), 108; Michael Ruse, ed., *But Is It Science? The Philosophical Question in the Creation/Evolution Controversy* (Amherst, NY: Prometheus Books, 1996), 28; Edward J. Larson, *Trial and Error*, 3rd ed. (New York: Oxford University Press, 2003), 162–63.

19. Chandra Wickramasinghe, "Evidence in the Trial at Arkansas, December 1981," *Cosmic Ancestry*, http://www.panspermia.org/chandra.htm (accessed March 10, 2004).

20. *McLean v. Arkansas Board of Education*, section IV(D).

21. Ibid.

22. Ibid.

23. Ibid., 2.

24. Ibid., 15, 19–20.

25. *Edwards v. Aguillard*, 482 U.S. 578 (1987), section I, http://caselaw.lp.findlaw.com/scripts/getcase.pl?court=US&vol=482&invol=578 (accessed February 23, 2005); Michael Shermer, *Why People Believe Weird Things* (New York: Freeman, 1997): 161–62.

26. *Edwards v. Aguillard*, section Held: 1(a).

27. Ibid.

28. Ibid., section III, A.

29. Ibid., section Held: 1(a).

30. Ibid., section Held: 2.

31. Ibid.

32. Ibid., section Held: 1.

33. Ibid., section III, A.

34. Ibid., section Held: 1(b).

35. This point is conceded even by the nontheistic skeptic and anticreationist Michael Shermer in his book *Why People Believe Weird Things*, 162.

36. No major Christian denomination, either pre–Christopher Columbus or post–Christopher Columbus, ever held to a flat-Earth doctrine. However, a few small sects did teach that Earth is flat. Perhaps the most famous flat-Earth proponent was the radio preacher Wilbur Glenn Voliva of Zion, Illinois. For a list of flat-Earth advocates see http://www.loc.gov/rr/scitech/SciRefGuides/flatearth.html (accessed April 4, 2004). The Flat Earth Society has always claimed that the Bible is a flat-Earth book. I heard this assertion myself in the early 1990s when I participated in a radio debate on the Earth's shape on John Stewart's *Live from LA* program on KKLA, Los Angeles.

37. Prominent Protestant apologists for geocentrism include Gerardus Bouw, Malcolm Bowden, James Hanson, and Tom Willis. Leading Catholic apologists for geocentrism are R. G. Elmendorf, Paul Ellwanger, Paula Haigh, and Robert Sungenis. The two largest nonprofit organizations dedicated to promoting geocentrism are Catholic Apologetics International and The Biblical Astronomer. The following websites are devoted to promoting geocentrism: http://www.geocentricity.com, http://www.fixedearth.com, and http://www.catholicintl.com (accessed April 4, 2004).

38. Hugh Ross, *The Creator and the Cosmos*, 3rd ed. (Colorado Springs: NavPress, 2001): 99–108. This reference includes the original research source citations.

39. Ibid., 87–98, 169–74. This reference includes the original research source citations.

Chapter 16: Using Predictions to Test Models

1. Hugh Ross, *Why the Universe Is the Way It Is* (Grand Rapids: Baker, 2008), 57–78; Hugh Ross, Kenneth Samples, and Mark Clark, *Lights in the Sky and Little Green Men* (Colorado Springs: NavPress, 2002), 33–64; Fazale Rana and Hugh Ross, *Origins of Life* (Colorado Springs: NavPress, 2004), 202–8.

2. Readers are encouraged to send in their corrections to predictions@reasons.org or to Reasons To Believe, Attn. Predictions, P.O. Box 5978, Pasadena, CA 91117.

3. Readers without Web access can obtain a printed copy of the catalog for a nominal fee by contacting the Customer Service Department at Reasons To Believe, 800-482-7836.

4. Readers are encouraged to send in their suggestions to predictions@reasons.org or to Reasons To Believe, Attn. Predictions, P.O. Box 5978, Pasadena, CA 91117.

5. D. Russell Humphreys, "Our Galaxy Is the Center of the Universe, 'Quantized' Red Shifts Show," *Creation Ex Nihilo Technical Journal* 16 (August 2002): 95–104; Robert V. Gentry, *Creation's Tiny Mystery*, 3rd ed. (Knoxville: Earth Science Associates, 1992), 287–90; Jonathan Sarfati, *Refuting Compromise* (Green Forest, AR: Master Books, 2004), 156.

6. Hugh Ross, *Creation as Science* (Colorado Springs: NavPress, 2006).

Chapter 17: Scoring the Models

1. Hugh Ross, *Genesis One: A Scientific Perspective*, 4th ed. (Pasadena, CA: Reasons To Believe, 2006).

2. Hugh Ross, *Creation as Science* (Colorado Springs: NavPress, 2006), 183–90, 227–52.

3. Ibid., 230–32.

4. Ibid., 179–80.

5. Ibid.

Chapter 18: Extra Credit

1. The term "Christophobia" was first used by the Jewish legal scholar Joseph H. H. Weiler in his book *Un'Europa cristiana: Un saggio esplorativo* (Milan: Biblioteca Universale

Rizzoli, 2003), and more broadly popularized by the Catholic theologian George Weigel in his book *The Cube and the Cathedral* (New York: Basic Books, 2005).

2. These Christian leaders include John MacArthur, *The Battle for the Beginning* (Nashville: W Publishing Group, 2001), 11–65; James B. Jordan, *Creation in Six Days* (Moscow, ID: Canon Press, 1999), 113–130; Douglas F. Kelly, *Creation and Change* (Ross-shire, UK: Mentor, 1997), 137–80; Ian T. Taylor, *In the Minds of Men* (Toronto: TFE Publishing, 1984), 340–430.

3. P. C. W. Davies and Charles H. Lineweaver, "Finding a Second Sample of Life on Earth," *Astrobiology* 5 (April 1, 2005): 154–63.

4. Geochemical evidence establishes that life has been abundantly present on Earth as far back as 3.8 billion years (see chapter 9, pages 134–36). Metamorphic processes, though, have destroyed all fossils older than 3.5 billion years. Between 3.8 and 3.5 billion years ago, however, intense meteoritic and asteroidal bombardment of Earth resulted in the transport and deposit of over 10,000 tons of Earth material on every 100 square kilometers of the Moon. See John C. Armstrong, Llyd E. Wells, and Guillermo Gonzalez, "Rummaging through Earth's Attic for Remains of Ancient Life," *Icarus* 160 (November 2002): 183–96. Because the moon has lacked the metamorphic and tectonic forces that were prevalent on Earth, scientists possess an excellent opportunity of recovering on the moon pristine fossils of Earth's first life.

5. A detailed account of this development may be found in Fazale Rana and Hugh Ross, *Origins of Life* (Colorado Springs: NavPress, 2004).

6. A detailed account of this development may be found in Hugh Ross, *A Matter of Days* (Colorado Springs: NavPress, 2004).

7. Ibid.

8. "Appendix Table 2-34, S&E First University Degrees in Selected Western and Asian Countries, by Field: 1975–2001 (revised)," *Science and Engineering Indicators 2004*, vol. 2, National Science Board, March 2005, http://www.nsf.gov/statistics/seind04/append/c2/at02-34.pdf.

9. Richard E. Smalley in a PowerPoint presentation, "Nanotechnology, the S&T Workforce, Energy, and Prosperity," to the President's Council of Advisors on Science and Technology (PCAST), March 3, 2003, slide 7, http://cohesion.rice.edu/NaturalSciences/Smalley/emplibrary/PCAST%20March%203,%202003.ppt (accessed May 16, 2008).

10. Paul Chien, University of San Francisco biologist, in a recorded interview. Dr. Chien has made several visits to the Chengjiang shale and has published collaborative research with China's leading researchers. For an abridged version of the interview, see Paul Chien, interview by Fazale Rana and Hugh Ross, "'Exploding' with Life!" *Facts for Faith*, no. 2, second quarter 2000, 12–17.

11. For a more complete deduction of this point see Hugh Ross, *Why the Universe Is the Way It Is* (Grand Rapids: Baker, 2008), 115–17.

Appendix A: The Scientific Method's Biblical Origins

1. The biblical origin of the scientific method is more fully established in my book *The Genesis Question*, 2nd ed. (Colorado Springs: NavPress, 2001), 195–97.

2. R. Laird Harris, Gleason L. Archer Jr., and Bruce K. Waltke, eds., *Theological Wordbook of the Old Testament* (Chicago: Moody, 1980), 1:51–52.

3. Joseph H. Thayer, *Thayer's Greek-English Lexicon of the New Testament* (Grand Rapids: Baker, 1977), 512–13.

4. Thomas F. Torrance, *Theology in Reconstruction* (Grand Rapids: Eerdmans, 1965); Thomas F. Torrance, *Reality and Scientific Theology* (Edinburgh, UK: Scottish Academic Press, 1985); Thomas F. Torrance, "Ultimate and Penultimate Beliefs in Science," in *Facts of*

Faith & Science, vol. 1, *Historiography and Modes of Interaction*, ed. Jitse M. van der Meer (New York: University Press of America, 1996), 151–76.

Appendix B: Designed for Life

1. This compendium was originally provided as a supplement to *Why the Universe Is the Way It Is* (Grand Rapids: Baker Books, 2008).

INDEX